ASPIRING *to* FULLNESS

*in a* SECULAR AGE

D1592519

# ASPIRING *to* FULLNESS
# *in a* SECULAR AGE

*Essays on Religion and Theology
in the Work of Charles Taylor*

*Edited by*
CARLOS D. COLORADO
*and*
JUSTIN D. KLASSEN

*University of Notre Dame Press*
*Notre Dame, Indiana*

Manufactured in the United States of America

*Library of Congress Cataloging-in-Publication Data*

Aspiring to fullness in a secular age : essays on religion and theology in the work
of Charles Taylor / edited by Carlos D. Colorado and Justin D. Klassen.
pages   cm
Includes bibliographical references and index.
ISBN 978-0-268-02376-8 (pbk. : alk. paper) —
ISBN 0-268-02376-X (pbk. : alk. paper)
1. Taylor, Charles, 1931–   2. Taylor, Charles, 1931– Secular age.
3. Religion.   4. Theology.   I. Colorado, Carlos D., editor of compilation.
B995.T34A87   2014
191—dc23

2013044533

*Dedicated to the memory of*

C A M I L L A   M R Y G L O D
(1960–2010)

*Student, teacher, thinker, friend*

# CONTENTS

# ACKNOWLEDGMENTS

This book has been many years in the making; consequently, the debts of gratitude we owe for its completion are many. We are grateful to Ian Angus for introducing us both to Charles Taylor's work as undergraduate students in the Humanities Department at Simon Fraser University. Later, during Ph.D. studies in the Religious Studies Department at McMaster University, Travis Kroeker encouraged us to engage Taylor's work in its theological implications and thus helped to inspire this project in its early stages. We are grateful to Travis for that, and to our other professors and fellow students at McMaster, who made this undertaking seem important and necessary rather than only daunting. The School of Graduate Studies at Mac has our thanks for building and safeguarding a context in which doctoral students are supported in the pursuit of research projects that stretch and challenge.

Charles Van Hof, our editor at University of Notre Dame Press, has been an invaluable supporter of this project since we first met with him to discuss our proposal at a meeting of the AAR some years ago. We have tried to craft a final product worthy of his confidence. We also thank the anonymous reviewers of the manuscript for their careful attention to the text and for their many helpful suggestions for its improvement.

We are tremendously grateful to all of our contributing authors for the excellence of their submissions, and for trusting the vision (and editorial suggestions) of a couple of green and relatively unknown scholars.

We thank Charles Taylor himself for producing such an enormously engaging body of work, and for being a willing interlocutor over the years. In our experience, Chuck has always made time for conversation at conferences, after public lectures, and by e-mail. We wrote to him with small questions on several occasions and always received expansive, encouraging, and generous responses.

Finally, we thank our families, both spouses and children, for their support, patience, and enthusiasm for a project to which we have devoted many precious hours over the last few years.

*Carlos D. Colorado*

*Justin D. Klassen*

# Introduction

The publication in 2007 of *A Secular Age* reconfirmed Charles Taylor's uniquely comprehensive acumen about the character, promise, and pitfalls of the modern age. As he did in *Sources of the Self*—which surprised both knockers and boosters of modernity with its capacity to give voice to all of their concerns at once, and to disinter their sometimes common root impulses—so again in *A Secular Age* has Taylor cast a new and surprising light on the stage upon which we undertake our most fundamental debates. Diverse interlocutors on the question of the modern experience of secularity will recognize themselves in Taylor's book, but will find themselves situated differently, often with a new and more expansive set of concerns and a view to unexpected paths forward.

The scope of Taylor's insight into modern secularity has been ably recognized by his fellow social theorists and philosophers. The present volume aims to ensure that Taylor's insights do not escape the notice, or indeed the scrutiny, of those thinkers more explicitly concerned with questions of religious experience in the modern era. Thus, *Aspiring to Fullness in a Secular Age* sets out to consider and assess Taylor's broad analysis of the limits and potentialities of the present age in regard to human fullness or fulfillment. The crucial subsets of this consideration include questions about the function and significance of religious accounts of transcendence in Taylor's broader philosophical project, the critical purchase and limitations of Taylor's assessment of the centrality of codes and institutions in modern political ethics, the possibilities inherent in Taylor's brand of post-Nietzschean theism, the significance and meaning of Taylor's ambivalence about the modern destiny (openness or weakness), the possibility of a practical application of his insights among particular contemporary religious communities, and Taylor's reticence to embrace apocalyptic or exilic voices in the contemporary debate about aspirations to fullness. *A Secular Age* contains the most explicitly theistic formulations in Taylor's thought thus far, and while some commentators have therefore taken to speaking of a religious "turn" in Taylor's recent work, the chapters in the present volume examine the ways in which transcendence functions, both explicitly and implicitly, in Taylor's philosophical project as a whole. Special attention is also paid to his recent contributions to the study of secularization.

In *A Secular Age*, Taylor offers a lengthy consideration of processes of secularization that in certain respects have come to determine the character of the "North Atlantic world," meaning they have come to determine how inhabitants of that world experience their proximity to and assuredness of fulfillment. For Taylor, the meaning of *secularity* is most distinguishable when we see it as "coterminous with the rise of a society [such as ours] in which for the first time in history a purely self-sufficient humanism came to be a widely available option." The wide availability of this particular option is therefore a necessary component of what Taylor means by *secularity*. Taylor describes how this novel situation came about, but he does not *only* describe. As he tells us, his expansive genealogy of the advent of this variety of secularity is meant to function also as a polemic against "stories of modernity in general, and secularity in particular, which explain them by human beings having lost, or sloughed off, or liberated themselves from certain earlier, confining horizons, or illusions, or limitations of knowledge." Much is implied in this claim. First, we can venture that the process of secularization and its connection to the appearance of the "exclusive humanist" option is surely contingent upon the collapse of an epistemology that Taylor least of all wants to reinstate. In other words, because we can no longer claim to "know" those *teloi* beyond the "immanent frame" of human flourishing, or at least cannot claim to know them in ways previously available—i.e., naïvely—it makes sense that the possibility of abandoning one's commitment to those ends has arisen. Taylor is then of striking interest because he wants to polemicize not necessarily against "exclusive humanism" as such, but against the notion that such humanism is the destiny of a perfected humanity. Yet he wants to do this without reinvoking within his polemic the possibility of a new epistemological naïveté. In other words, Taylor wants to reinstate or retain the possibility of serious human commitments to "transcendent" ends without resorting to philosophical nostalgia. Taylor believes he can do this by giving a genealogy of our age that counters the proliferating arguments about the secure closure of the immanent frame, as well as those about the total convergence of pure immanence with human fullness.

Because Taylor's entire project, from its very early stages, can be read as a negotiation of the conflict between the declining viability of foundationalist accounts of truth and the lingering problem of justifying human commitments, or at least access to "moral sources," which he believes remain basic to any honest experience of personhood, the direction of his arsenal at the question of secularization is enormously suggestive. For example, if the practice of genealogy, which Taylor has adopted in works previous to *A Secular Age*, is shown in the latter to function in some sense as a defense of religiosity to claims of humanity's "inevitable" immanentization, it may become impossible henceforward to read "religion" out of any of Taylor's genealogical polemical efforts. The present volume takes up, among other things, this hint of a possibly pervasive religious concern in Taylor's thought and works in various ways to show where we might or might not recognize it, as well as questioning and exploring the wider significance of such a concern.

*Aspiring to Fullness in a Secular Age* thus calls upon its contributors to take up in a focused way the role of religion in Taylor's philosophy. The diversity of said contributors is noteworthy in its own right. Crossing disciplinary and geographical boundaries, as well as that between junior and senior scholars, the contributors have been selected in order to ensure a variety of angles of approach to Taylor's work. Unsurprisingly then, *Aspiring to Fullness* contains the fire of its own internal conversation. As the reader will soon discover, this is not a simple compilation of self-contained and static pronouncements on Taylor. We hope the liveliness of the book's trajectory is due at least in part to its deliberate structure, which places thematically related but often argumentatively opposed chapters in conversation with one another under five subheadings. Let us briefly introduce each section and individual chapter in order of appearance in the book.

The first section, "Existential Theism," pairs two chapters that assess, in different ways, the significance of Taylor's apparent theological turn at the end of *A Secular Age* in relation to the existential criteria Taylor applies to the contemporary situation of belief.

Justin D. Klassen's chapter, "The Affirmation of Existential Life in Charles Taylor's *A Secular Age*," begins with the tension in *Sources of the Self* between the ethical fruits of disengaged reason and the "affirmation of ordinary life" accomplished by Romantic expressivism. Klassen argues that Taylor's positive assessment of the modern potential for fullness hinges on the possibility of integrating these two poles of the modern destiny, and notes Taylor's sense that a "certain theistic perspective" is best suited to accomplishing this integration. While this seems a thin rebuttal to the more obvious potential of Nietzschean naturalism to offer a comprehensive affirmation of being, Klassen argues that Taylor moves in the direction of a post-Nietzschean theological materialism in *A Secular Age*. The surprise here, Klassen argues, is that Taylor's constructive proposals in *A Secular Age* register best in the key of Radical Orthodoxy's existentialism, which makes it necessary to reexamine our sense of Taylor's reticence in making normative judgments about modernity. Ultimately, Klassen raises the question of whether Taylor's appeal to modern poetics as a suitable medium of integrated life remains too abstract, too *written*, to be faithful to Taylor's own sense that a comprehensive affirmation of being stands or falls at the level of our capacity for "seeing-good."

Paul D. Janz's chapter, "Transcendence, 'Spin,' and the Jamesian Open Space," highlights Taylor's appeal to the Jamesian open space as the key to understanding the experiential shift that characterizes the secular age. For Taylor, "open space" describes the situation of the modern human being within the immanent frame, in which the persuasive "spins" of two contrasting options in regard to "transcendent" sources of fullness are experienced simultaneously. On Taylor's account, we cannot attribute rational certainty to either of these options, which is what makes the space "open." Decisions for belief or unbelief are taken only on the basis of an anticipatory confidence, and this "leveling of the field" constitutes Taylor's most determinate evaluative position, which Janz calls Taylor's "existential" Jamesianism.

This does not in fact amount to an "apologetic" position in favor of transcendence; it appears as such, according to Janz, only because the ubiquity in the contemporary academy of the spin away from transcendence makes it appear rationally necessary. Janz's main critical argument concerns Taylor's apparent reversion, in the late chapters of *A Secular Age*, to a "believing" spin. The problem, for Janz, is that Taylor discovers the locus of decision in the subject's anticipatory "leap" and then appears to dismiss his own discovery by building a rational bridge to transcendence. It is a move, Janz argues, that directly contradicts Taylor's effective destabilization of the hegemony of unbelief in the contemporary academy.

In the book's second section, "Ontology and Polemic," Carlos D. Colorado and Ruth Abbey negotiate whether and how Taylor's appeal to transcendent moral sources suggests his underlying closure to alternative ontological presuppositions. Colorado addresses this question as it pertains to contemporary pluralism, while Abbey applies her concerns to the ostensible impartiality of Taylor's assessment of modern secularity.

Colorado's chapter, "Transcendent Sources and the Dispossession of the Self," explores in great detail the character and significance of Taylor's appeal to "transcendent" moral sources. Taking as his point of departure Stephen K. White's account of the problems raised by "strong ontologies" for political ethics in light of contemporary pluralism, Colorado explores the points at which Taylor most overtly relies upon a specifically Trinitarian ontology and comes to some surprising conclusions. The first of those conclusions arises from the broader context of Taylor's moral ontology, which stipulates that the relative merits of ontological claims can be measured on the basis of their capacity to evoke and articulate intuited moral impulses, rather than by virtue of their abstract seamlessness. Thus, what Taylor calls "best accounts" cannot function in the literalist fashion of a "strong ontology," for the criterion of their quality pertains to their ability to *move* us. Yet this is not to say that, in favoring the expressivist response to Enlightenment rationalism, Taylor slides fully into subjectivism. For while he avoids foundationalist justifications of our moral sources, Taylor believes nonetheless that we are justified in making strong evaluations on the basis of our intuited moral sense. Moreover, as it turns out, Taylor's own destabilization of monological accounts in virtue of the plurality of expressed intuitions is complemented by, and one might even say founded upon, his Trinitarian ontology. So then, does not Taylor's particular "best account" consign him to the tragically exclusivist history of strong onto-logical claims? Here Colorado does his most constructive work, arguing in manifold ways for the "kenoticism" of Taylor's underlying theology and making the original claim that Taylor deploys his Trinitarianism specifi-cally to counteract "discursive Constantinianism."

Ruth Abbey's chapter, "Theorizing Secularity 3: Authenticity, Ontology, Fragilization," focuses on Taylor's account of the modern situation of re-ligious belief as characterized by the appearance of new "cross pressures," the corollary of the appearance of "exclusive humanism" as a viable option. The presence of such pressures generates a new demand for authenticity in religious (or nonreligious) commitment, according to Taylor. Yet, upon close inspection of Taylor's narration of the shifts that ostensibly come to determine contemporary secularity, Abbey finds the phenomenon of reli-gious authenticity to be neither new nor dependent upon the appearance of exclusive humanism, which casts doubt upon the specifics of Taylor's char-acterization of Secularity 3. The thinness of Taylor's claim that the fragiliza-tion of belief is novel and arises with exclusive humanism is further evi-dent, for Abbey, in Taylor's overemphasis on abstract "cultural" patterns and his reluctance to validate his thesis on the ground. In the end, Abbey wonders whether Taylor's keen interest in exclusive humanism is motivated by his underlying assumption of the ontological necessity of religious com-mitment among human beings. If this is the case, and the cross pressure provided by exclusive humanism is not really a new experiential determi-nant of belief, then exclusive humanism begins to appear not so much a signpost in an impartial description of secularity as the target of a partisan ontological polemic about the possibility of authenticity.

The third section, "Middle Dwellers," offers chapters that examine the possibility of applying Taylor's assessment of the promise and perils of modernity to trajectories Taylor himself either gives short shrift or does not consider. For William Schweiker, this means rehabilitating religious hu-manism in a Protestant key, and for Charles Mathewes and Joshua Yates, it means taking seriously the practical potentialities of contemporary Evan-gelicalism for generating a "loyal opposition" to modernity.

In "Humanism and the Question of Fullness," Schweiker reconstructs Taylor's depiction of the crucial limits to human fullness in our secular age in order to rehabilitate humanism from the malignancy it has acquired among contemporary interpreters of Taylor's work. This sullying of humanistic traditions is partly the result of Taylor's identification of the most suffocating strain of modern secularity as "exclusive humanism." Schweiker thinks this tends to obscure the connection Taylor draws between the dangers of exclusive humanism and the troubling path to purity in modern religion. In other words, it obscures Taylor's own (formal, if not yet substantive) humanistic critique of religion. It is this "religious-humanistic" kernel of Taylor's identification of fruitful avenues to fullness that Schweiker seeks to make more explicit. One of the ways he does so is by making deliberate use of a theological voice, given that one of the basic tasks of theology is the criticism of religion. Ironically, then, for Schweiker, the rehabilitation of humanism via Taylor requires a supplement of theology. More substantively, Schweiker offers from this vantage another take on Protestantism, whose drive to Reform, he argues, was not always in the direction of a kind of destructive "hypertheism," as Taylor often suggests, but more often towards an inhabitable "middle condition" in relation to fullness—deeply realistic about the limits of human transformation, but refusing to despair of the world's fundamental integrity and undertaking painstaking work of fidelity to that integrity. Thus Schweiker makes a convincing case for the symmetry between Taylor's own normative position and the religious humanism of Protestant voices that receive little explicit consideration in Taylor's work.

Charles Mathewes and Joshua Yates, in their chapter, "The 'Drive to Reform' and Its Discontents," focus not so much on secularity as on the residual religiosity inherent in the characteristically modern imperative to take responsibility for the world's improvement, which Mathewes and Yates argue is at the core of Taylor's narrative in *A Secular Age*. The authors aim to assess the fruitfulness of Taylor's genealogical trajectory for "helping religious communities more faithfully inhabit the contemporary world." The drive to Reform, Mathewes and Yates argue, amounts to nothing less than a revolution in the moral order of the West. For these authors, Taylor identifies well the promise of the drive to Reform, in terms of the expanding inclusiveness of modern societies, and the peril of the same in its inherently instrumentalizing immanentism, which produces technological power sheared off from its original telos. Given this sketch of modernity's inner tensions, Mathewes and Yates go on to explore how contemporary Evangelical Protestantism might or perhaps already does take up Taylor's imperative for modern Christians to become modernity's "Loyal Opposition."

Thus, the authors apply Taylor's analysis to functioning religious goals in America, such as the reconciliation of personal fulfillment with spiritual vocation and the imperative to work for cultural renewal for the common good.

In the book's fourth section, "Ethics and Embodiment," Jennifer A. Herdt, along with Eric Gregory and Leah Hunt-Hendrix, takes direct aim at Taylor's obvious indebtedness in *A Secular Age* to Ivan Illich's critique of modernity's "code fetishism." Herdt indicates some problematic ethical outcomes of Illich's analysis and its acceptance by Taylor, while Gregory and Hunt-Hendrix argue for a significant distinction between the two on the question of suffering.

In "The Authentic Individual in the Network of Agape," Herdt begins with Taylor's characteristic wager of complementarity between the modern quest for authentic individuality and the deeply felt human need for community. She notes how Taylor's vision of such a complementarity culminates in *A Secular Age* with the overtly theological proposal of a "communion of disparate itineraries toward God, linked in an ever-expanding network of agape." Herdt takes issue with this latest negotiation of the tension between the individual and the communal, arguing that Taylor's critique of rules and institutions in *A Secular Age* threatens to efface political responsibility entirely, while enshrining a "sphere of immediacy and intimate communion." In the end, Herdt criticizes what she finds to be an overemphasis on this concrete sphere of the face-to-face and argues that Taylor's critique of code fetishization serves better as a corrective than it does as an alternative to codes and institutions.

Eric Gregory and Leah Hunt-Hendrix, in "Enfleshment and the Time of Ethics: Taylor and Illich on the Parable of the Good Samaritan," propose to use Taylor's reading of that parable as a "window" into themes about which Taylor's ambivalence is sometimes just as frustrating as it is fruitful. The authors note Taylor's opposition to the codification of ethics, as expressed in his reading of the parable, and his consequent focus on the spatial and temporal dimensions of ethics. This allows Gregory and Hunt-Hendrix to clarify further Taylor's narration of the modern drive to Reform in terms of the increasing disembodiment of ethical care (a progression of which Taylor is rather too critical, according to Herdt). But here the authors also differentiate Taylor's own imperatives from those of

Ivan Illich, especially concerning the sanctity of suffering, a feature of embodiment embraced by Illich but more or less rejected as a good by Taylor. This distinction helps to clarify the reasons for Taylor's greater openness to modernity in relation to Illich. The key contribution of this chapter thus becomes its distillation of the crucial issues that underlie Taylor's ambivalence toward modernity and its persuasive claim, in light of this clear analysis, that such ambivalence speaks to a hopeful courage more than a lack of theological nerve.

The final section of the book, "Outliers," contains two chapters that offer resistance to Taylor's enduring ambivalence toward modernity—specifically by criticizing, albeit for different reasons, Taylor's ultimate sense of the synthetic power of dialogue. Our final two authors present and side with figures that exceed this Taylorian/Hegelian hope—the figures of the exiled and the apocalyptic.

Ian Angus's chapter, "Recovery of Meaning? A Critique of Charles Taylor's Account of Modernity," sheds light on the philosophical underpinnings of Taylor's genealogy of modernity's advent by focusing on Taylor's indebtedness to Hegel. Angus shows how Taylor's assessment of modernity's aporias and dilemmas hinges upon his critique of technological reason as instrumentalizing and therefore alienating. The objectification accomplished by such reason is for Taylor the key obstacle to the "recovery of meaning" that would pave the way for authenticity. And yet, as Angus ably demonstrates, Taylor is reluctant to reject outright that very medium of modern alienation, for his sense is that such a rejection would be nothing other than a choice for "inner exile." Angus wonders why, if not for an a priori fidelity to the Hegelian diagnosis of modernity, we should not risk such exile, especially since it would amount to exile from our alienation. Taylor rejects all outlying alternatives to modernity, Angus suggests, on the grounds of their ostensible narrowness. Thus, Taylor emerges from Angus's argument as the "philosopher of the middle way," by which he means the way of the Hegelian synthesis reconfigured as a "perpetual balancing act." All Taylor's rejection of the purportedly narrow alternatives does, then, on this account, is guarantee the narrow triumph of the Hegelian starting point. Along these lines, Angus ultimately concludes that the purported ambivalence of Taylor's battle for a recovery of meaning only obfuscates a contestable Hegelian wager that preemptively swears off the *polemos* of exile, the possibility of a genuine ambivalence or a genuinely surprising itinerary.

Bruce K. Ward brings another of Taylor's most enduring yet intractable interlocutors into the foreground in his chapter, "Transcendence and Immanence in a Subtler Language: The Presence of Dostoevsky in Charles Taylor's Account of Secularity." The convergence of Taylor's assessment of our secularity with Dostoevsky's is surprising because they seem to diverge so dramatically in their manners of expression. Ward ably demonstrates first the substantive convergence between Dostoevsky and Taylor on doubt or the fragilization of belief as a key determinant of the modern condition. In the context of the rise of exclusive humanism, both authors also suggest that champions of transcendence must learn to defend their position in a subtler language. With reference to Mikhail Bakhtin's characterization of Dostoevsky's literary vision in terms of his preservation of polyphony, Ward argues that Taylor's polyphonic genealogy in *A Secular Age* recapitulates Dostoevsky's vision in a philosophic mode, a mode whose relentless dialogicality amounts also to the subtlety both Dostoevsky and Taylor advocate. The most significant divergence traced by Ward concerns the authors' respective approaches to exclusive humanism. Specifically, as Ward notes, Dostoevsky deploys a critical apocalypticism where Taylor remains ambivalent to the achievements of modern humanism. Ward suggests that this divergence reveals an unspoken disagreement between Taylor and Dostoevsky on the *limits* of dialogicality, limits that Ward explores to provocative effect. Acknowledging that Taylor would find apocalyptic language incapable of achieving the requisite subtlety, Ward argues convincingly that Dostoevsky himself transfigures that language, from its connotations of monological fundamentalism to an authoritative silence, which in Angus's words might mean something like a willingness to abide the *polemos* of an exile from the violence of dialogue.

PART I

EXISTENTIAL THEISM

# CHAPTER ONE

# The Affirmation of Existential Life in Charles Taylor's *A Secular Age*

JUSTIN D. KLASSEN

In a recent review essay, John Milbank, initiator of the "new theological imperative" known as Radical Orthodoxy and author of *Theology and Social Theory: Beyond Secular Reason*, calls Charles Taylor's *A Secular Age* a "magnificent, epoch-making work" and says that, on its basis, "one could attach the label 'radically orthodox' to Taylor with still more justification" than to Milbank himself.[1] This last claim may come as a surprise to those familiar with Taylor's work, which probably strikes most readers as neither "radical" nor particularly "orthodox." Indeed, Taylor has a well-earned reputation for caution and breadth and for balanced judgments of philosophical and cultural history, in which he is exceedingly well-read. *Sources of the Self,* Taylor's first masterwork, remains unequalled in its poised uncovering of the roots of the modern experience of personhood. With penetrating insight, Taylor addresses the most strident critics of our time, acknowledging the depth of their diverse concerns, and yet ably eliminates the need for a shrill tone in even the most polarizing debates.

Near the end of *Sources*, the debate in question is that between "proponents of disengaged reason" and proponents of what Taylor generally calls "Romantic expressivism," two facets of the essentially modern destiny.[2] The former worry that contemporary expressivists elevate the anthropological significance of the "personal" to irrational and therefore inhuman heights, while the latter question the capacity of disengaged reason to sustain a living connection with nature, in which human beings are to be included. Taylor's book is a wide-ranging effort to complicate the assumed disjunction between these two positions, culminating in an imperative to see *more* of ourselves than what is proffered by ostensibly more certain (because narrower) views. Taylor thus points out the connection between expressivism and the "fulfillment" that no scientific rationalist really wants to deny, as well as that between "instrumental reason and the affirmation of ordinary life" that is so dear to those faithful to various iterations of Romantic expressivism (*SS*, 504). In the end, what is important for Taylor, and what the stridency of critical voices often obscures, is "the search for moral sources *outside* the subject through languages which resonate *within* him or her, the grasping of an order which is inseparably indexed to a personal vision" (*SS*, 510). The uniquely modern constellation of the various "sources" of selfhood makes this kind of search possible, according to Taylor, and it requires a balancing of the objective and the subjective, outer significance and inner resonance.

Taylor's capacity for exposing what we might call the dependent co-arising of such extreme positions on the destiny of the modern subject, and his imperative to use their interrelation to deepen our overall view, can make it hard to pinpoint Taylor's own normative conclusions about modern selfhood and the possibility of fulfillment. This is precisely what makes John Milbank's review surprising, since Taylor's whole method, especially in *Sources*, neither advocates any "radical" position nor moves very far beyond a vague "theistic perspective" (*SS*, 518). Is there something in the trajectory of Taylor's work from *Sources of the Self* to *A Secular Age* that would justify Milbank's boldly sympathetic claim?

It is clear from Milbank's own recent work, and especially from his sustained engagement with self-proclaimed "Christian atheist" Slavoj Žižek, that Radical Orthodoxy seeks to address what it sees as a distinctly modern need for a robust affirmation of material creation.[3] Milbank's perception of the woes of modernity stems from his diagnosis of "secular reason" as an abstracting force that works to separate the locus of truth (words) from the material site of actual human lives. For Milbank, the Christian theological imagination, which begins with a wager that the Word has been made flesh, can overcome the divisive wager of secular reason and thus reconcile truth with life. Indeed, only for such thinking, wherein truth is inseparable from material-temporal performance, is the whole of material creation (not only those parts of it valorized by an abstract philosophy) available to human beings in the mode of fullness.[4] The catch, so to speak, is that the material is not the fullness of life in its objectivity alone, but approaches that fullness when it is deployed in the mode of God's very speaking—i.e., the way of *caritas*. All of creation "exists," then, not to the extent that it resembles God objectively, but to the extent that it participates, analogically, in a God who is not a "thing" but already a movement of Trinitarian love. Milbank will go so far as to say that "just as God is not a 'substance'. . . so also there are no substances in creation, no underlying matter, and no discrete and inviolable 'things.'"[5] For Milbank, such a claim does not imply any denigration of the material, but rather makes possible a fuller affirmation of matter in its true form, which is the form not of discrete thinghood but of a specific temporal deployment. Ultimately, therefore, the "image" that orients the Christian theological imagination, and which by extension overcomes the binaries of secular reason, is a comprehensively affirmative, "existential" image of love's mediation of objective differences.

The existential character of the Radical Orthodox imperative is precisely what Milbank believes connects it with Charles Taylor's thesis in *A Secular Age*, which to Milbank's mind has "consummated [Taylor's] invention of a new intellectual genre—a kind of historicized existentialism."[6] In this chapter I hope, among other things, to substantiate this surprising claim with reference to the most provocative of Taylor's conclusions in *A Secular Age*. In particular, I will argue that we ought to read *A Secular Age* as Taylor's response to the modern need, already subtly indicated in *Sources*, for a more solidly materialist anthropology than the diverse extremes of modern reason can achieve on their own. In order to pursue this thesis, we must first explore the culmination of Taylor's argument in *Sources*, where he suggests that the prospect of fullness for modern selfhood depends on the possibility of a universal "seeing-good," a possibility Taylor says is most fully present to a "certain theistic perspective." Because this conclusion on its own sounds anything but materialist, I will then demonstrate that *A Secular Age* constitutes a fleshing out, literally, of what Taylor means in *Sources* by "theism." I shall argue that what emerges from Taylor's conclusion in *A Secular Age*, especially via his readings of Ivan Illich and Charles Péguy, is nothing less than the radical claim that the dilemmas of modern selfhood and fulfillment, and especially the problem of our lack of "moral sources which might sustain our rather massive professed commitments in benevolence and justice" (*SS*, 518), stem not from bad philosophical definitions, but from what Žižek calls "the fear of four words: he was made man."[7] My ultimate reservation with Taylor's argument to this effect, which we shall entertain briefly at the end, stems from my sense that Taylor may not go far enough with his existential and materialist response to "excarnating" trajectories of secularity, remaining so confident in what he calls the "constitutive power of language" that the subject as an enfleshed, willing agent may be at risk of getting lost in the words. Let us begin by turning to the question of the affirmation of being in *Sources of the Self*.

## COMPETING AFFIRMATIONS

In *Sources of the Self*, Taylor is interested above all in the possibility of re-establishing our connection, as subjects formed by modern conceptions of identity, to "moral sources which might sustain our rather massive professed commitments in benevolence and justice" (*SS*, 518). The possibility of making such commitments—commitments to universal rights and equality, for example—is uniquely modern, the fruit of "disengaged reason." But if these affirmations fail to register materially within the subject who makes them, they risk becoming mere fantasies, whose effect is to distract us from the concreteness of our everyday lives. As I mentioned above, Taylor's book constitutes a concerted effort to ease the tension between the extremes of disengaged reason—which has made the "universality" of our commitments thinkable—and Romantic expressivism—which affirms the significance of every individual's uncategorizable, quotidian experience. Taylor's sense is that, were such a reconciliation of these extremes possible, it would amount to a uniquely comprehensive affirmation of being. His belief that the tension between these extremes can be eased at all amounts to his wager that Kantian ethics, based on principles that hold everywhere and absolutely, must be modified in the direction of Hegelian *Sittlichkeit*, for which ethical action also takes its cues from the push and pull of one's immediate situation.[8] At the end of *Sources*, Taylor hints that the Christian ethic is premised on such an imperative to reconcile the lofty height of a commitment to a universal good with the ostensible lowliness of an enfleshed attunement to the world at every particular moment. As Taylor puts it, in the Bible "there is a divine affirmation of the creature, which is captured in the repeated phrase in Genesis 1 about each stage of creation, 'and God saw that it was good.' *Agape* is inseparable from such a 'seeing-good'" (*SS*, 516). Thus, for Taylor, the Christian ethic may provide a way of reconciling the universal with the singular in virtue of the connection between its universal ethical imperative and its formation of the subject's first-order vision or imagination of the world.

Of course, religion itself has always been implicated in the very tension between rational moral imperatives and the material locus of daily life that characterizes the modern destiny for Taylor. That is, for all its production of effervescent commitments to the good, religion "has been recurrently associated with sacrifice, even mutilation, as though something of us has to be torn away or immolated if we are to please the gods" (*SS*, 519). Thus does Taylor concede that Enlightenment naturalism offers a still-compelling alternative imagination or vision of the world, a "seeing-good" that contests above all the world-denying character of the religious vision, the "calumny implicit in ascetic codes" (*SS*, 516). This concession is made specifically to Nietzsche, whose challenge to the religious vision is important to Taylor "because he is looking precisely for what can release such an affirmation of being" (*SS*, 516). That is to say, Nietzsche is looking for what can release a vision of the world that is wholly affirmative, refusing to divide what is from what is on the basis of calumnious abstraction—a vision that does not, in other words, posit a "really real" existence that is not itself already immediate to life.[9] The possibility of such an affirmation is at stake for Taylor, too, in his negotiation of the divided destiny of modern selfhood. What Taylor finds "unsettling," therefore, is not Nietzsche's goal of affirming life, but his conclusion "that it is the ethic of benevolence which stands in the way" of any genuinely affirmative vision of the world (*SS*, 516). For Nietzsche, "the ethic of benevolence" obstructs such a reconciling affirmation of being because it constitutes a willful blindness and even moral aversion to what "naturally" counts as viable. Benevolence turns life's criterion of material power into a vice; thus it can release no genuine affirmation of being, but only nihilism.

In *Sources*, Taylor more or less concludes this conversation with two seemingly casual yet substantively crucial questions for Nietzsche: "Is the naturalist affirmation conditional on a vision of human nature in the fullness of its health and strength? Does it move us to extend help to the irremediably broken, such as the mentally handicapped, those dying without dignity, fetuses with genetic defects?" (*SS*, 517). Given that Taylor does not pursue these questions extensively, this could amount to a thin critical moment. Yet it should not escape our notice that the questions have surprisingly materialist implications. For if "the naturalist affirmation" is indeed conditional on a particular vision of nature, as Taylor implies, then the problem is not really that Nietzsche is too much a naturalist, but rather that his affirmation is not immediate to material reality at all. Instead, to the extent that Taylor's question is on the mark, we can say that Nietzsche, being unable to affirm what we might call creation's "shadow side," affirms only a metaphysical presupposition that what counts as life is power. The implication here, followed up in Taylor's second question, is that in order to release a genuine and complete affirmation of being, one has to be able *to begin* with the material, to proceed a posteriori, with eyes open to the whole of material reality, in which irremediable brokenness is undeniable. Ironically, then, Nietzschean naturalism, for Taylor, is still too fond of abstract measures of what "counts," still too unable to let go of its metaphysical presuppositions and just *live* a comprehensive "seeing-good."

It may seem strange that instead of working out these implications of his critique of the Nietzschean perspective, Taylor concludes somewhat obscurely that, "great as the power of naturalist sources might be, the potential of a certain theistic perspective is incomparably greater" (*SS*, 518). This is odd precisely because Taylor's implicit critique of a priori suppositions makes a vague appeal to "theism" seem even more likely to guarantee a reversion to a gnostic denial of the material than does Nietzsche's residual metaphysics. Indeed, Žižek seems closer to the mark when he argues that the Christian experience releases a (supra-Nietzschean) affirmation of the material precisely by refuting "theism."[10] For Žižek, the tragedy of modernity is its obstinate refusal to confront the "excess" of life apart from an ideological mitigation of the risk of living. By contrast, he argues, the fundamental Christian affirmation is that "God was made man,"[11] which implies that the properly Christian experience is one of "dereliction."[12] For Žižek, however, this does not mean Christianity is a "failed" experience, but instead that it is an experience of life as such, without possible recourse to any reduction of life's traumatic excess. In this radical version of Christianity, therefore, Christ does not provide "reconciliation" with God in the sense of returning human beings to their transcendent home, but instead reconciles human beings with the real by repeating the Adamic "Fall"—our separation from the "big Other"—but this time in the mode of liberation. Thus, wherever modernity continues to nurture the hope of "theism," it forsakes what Žižek calls the "parallax shift" of its own Christian heritage and ensures that subjects will remain enslaved to an antimaterialist gnosticism—enslaved, in Taylor's terms, to the "calumny implicit in ascetic codes."

And yet it is clear that naturalism's metaphysical presupposition about what should count as life functions for Taylor in a manner that parallels Žižek's analysis of ideology. That is, both forces constitute evasions of living for the sake of "fantasmatic" images of being. This parallel should indicate that Taylor's "certain theistic perspective," his appeal to a "moral source" that "transcends human flourishing," must proceed differently; it must, on Taylor's own terms, constitute a way of beginning with the material, such that it might persuasively address and overcome the "gap" between the universal and the particular, between the measure of goodness and that which is to be measured—the gap Taylor believes is the primary modern obstacle to genuine fullness. My sense is that Taylor does proceed in such a subversive manner, which can be called materialist *and* existential insofar as both of those terms imply eschewals of the objectifying force of a priori definitions of life. If one wants to live via an attunement to life itself, to live out of a truly affirmative "seeing-good," then one must relinquish the desire to measure what is seen against the good that one "already knows." True seeing-good, for Taylor, must find its impetus in an image that is always already on the move, such that it may never be abstracted from the incessant motion of our very temporal lives. Such an image is something like that of the "agapeic" lover, whose task, in the words of Søren Kierkegaard, "is not to find the lovable object but to find the unlovable object lovable."[13] Such an explosion of the conventional understanding of love—of love as the discovery of a particular that "measures up" to our preconceived expectations—captures well Taylor's own intended reconception of the possibility of affirming being as such. Let us now turn to *A Secular Age* in order to pursue my suggestion that Taylor offers there nothing less than an "existentialized" vision of human subjectivity, which also amounts to a destruction of "theism" except via the Incarnation.

### REFORM AS OBJECTIFICATION

*A Secular Age* comprises Taylor's investigation of the rise of "secularity" in the modern West. Instead of the objective facts of recent declines in religious practice and the "liberation" of political institutions from particular religious affiliations, by "secularity" Taylor refers to a shift in the "conditions of belief" for the modern subject. In particular, Taylor is interested in the shift from the premodern experience of a naïve, "axiomatic" belief in a transcendent referent of human fullness to a situation in which no such belief is a given.[14] Indeed, in contrast to previous ages, we now naïvely experience the "non-impinging" of spirits on our selves (*SA*, 30). It is in this sense that Taylor's "secularity" arises in conjunction with the first historical appearance of "exclusive humanism" as a credible human trajectory. Taylor is interested above all in analyzing how this situation arose, how it came about that a self that was once "porous," influenced and affected by a context that was both mysterious and undeniable, became the "buffered" self that characterizes the modern experience of personhood (*SA*, 27).

We are by now quite familiar with what Taylor calls "subtraction theories" about the rise of secularity. Such theories presuppose that the shifts that were crucial to the rise of secularity were moments of liberation, whereby human beings became more immediate to the true human *proprium* and consequently are no longer "impeded by what is now set aside"

(*SA*, 22). Taylor remarks that his book constitutes a sustained polemic against such theories, and in this respect his argument bears a striking similarity to Milbank's in *Theology and Social Theory*, whose first chapter opens with the following statements: "Once, there was no 'secular.' And the secular was not latent, waiting to fill more space with the steam of the 'purely human,' when the pressure of the sacred was relaxed."[15] For Milbank, the reason we are almost unanimously convinced otherwise is that the predominant subtraction theories have their roots in a quasi-religious rhetoric in the first place—the rhetoric of what Milbank calls the "liberal Protestant metanarrative." This story associates salvation with a gospel of freedom from religion itself, a "priesthood of all believers," and relates medieval Catholicism to the enslaving power of religious authority contested by Jesus in the Gospels. Milbank argues that this narrative "has the merit of recognizing the unmistakable uniqueness of both the Jewish presence in history and the Christian ecclesial presence as a new sort of universal society. . . . *But it tries to read this uniqueness as the always implicit presence in the west of a private realm of value.*"[16] For Milbank, therefore, in order to counter subtraction theories of secularity, one must wage a polemic against the commonplace supposition that the shift to Reform in early modern Christianity represents either a necessary shift or an unqualified gain. Both Milbank and Taylor are dedicated to such a polemical retelling of what Taylor broadly labels "the work of Reform," a retelling that highlights the self-alienating results of what is usually cast as a rush toward emancipation.

As Taylor has it, premodern Western societies were characterized by a fundamental tension or strain "between the demands of perfection and those of everyday life," a tension that was "overlaid with an equilibrium based on a complementarity of social functions" (*SA*, 44). In other words, the clergy worked for the perfection of the laity, members of which were busy with the demands of everyday life. Of course, this hierarchical complementarity did not "do away with continuing sources of tension" entirely, which explains the prevalence in such societies of ritual festivities that could provide an outlet for residual strain. Indeed, one gets the sense upon examining premodern Western societies that they harbored a deeply felt need for what Taylor calls "anti-structure" (*SA*, 50). Subtraction theorists would lament any such need, but for Taylor it is an ambivalent sign.

That is to say, even though the particularities of premodern social order were such that they brought subjects periodically to a breaking point, the entirely licit incorporation of anti-structure into social life also indicates that the order itself was not considered to have an *absolute* validity. As Taylor puts it, paraphrasing Victor Turner, it is as if premodern participants in anti-structure were saying, "the order we are mocking is important but not ultimate; what is ultimate is the community it serves. . . . So we periodically renew [the order], rededicate it, return it to its original meaning, by suspending it in the name of the community, which is fundamentally, ultimately of equals" (*SA*, 47). And yet those who favored what we might call the earliest variants of subtraction theories of secularity were more prone to feel that instead of accommodating the imperfection of the present social order via practices of anti-structure, they ought to *do* something about this imperfection. For the first proponents of Reform in Christendom, this primarily meant refusing the assumption "that masses of people were not going to live up to the demands of perfection" (*SA*, 61).

The primary gestures of resistance to a society ordered according to a complementarity of social functions were multivalent in their implications. In the first place, it is not difficult to see the early drive to Reform as a push toward an expanded "seeing-good," as Taylor puts it in *Sources of the Self*. That is, the initial impulse to Reform obviously opposed any rigid identification of the present, hierarchical social order with ultimate, transcendent reality. This delegitimizing impulse thus amounted to a move in the direction of reconciling the universal with the singular, "ultimate" reality with the quotidian experience of the layperson. The Protestant reformers, for example, refused to concede the "rightness" of the prevailing social hierarchy and thus sought to discredit its pretension to mediate divine grace *in virtue of* its abstract structure. One might say that the early Protestant sensibility was that fidelity to such a structure constituted an evasion of a more immediate fidelity to life as such. Thus, it is possible to read the Protestant refusal of the "sacramental" character of the prevailing social order, though it sounds "disenchanting," as stemming from a reverence for every vocation as equally "approximate" to the movement of God in the world. In this way one can argue that the work of Reform functions to reconcile all human vocations with the possibility of transcendent fullness. Its effect is to "release an affirmation of being" that breaks open the "calumny implicit in ascetic codes" that Taylor tells us in, in *Sources,* presents a problem for any religious response to the Nietzschean naturalist. How, then, does Taylor come to associate this very drive to Reform with the problematic and self-alienating tensions that eventually characterize the modern destiny?

To understand this we can begin by considering that Reform's "delegitimizing" impulse vis-à-vis the prevailing social hierarchy, by which it sought to elevate the lowest of human vocations to their due proximity to transcendent fullness, must have felt imperiled from the beginning. In order to justify its resistance to the current social hierarchy and so strengthen its position, the work of Reform sought a way of logically refuting the identification of any social hierarchy with the order of being as such. In other words, it sought to develop a persuasive assertion that one's social status bore no *direct* relation to one's measure of spiritual fullness. But any attempt to *secure* this assertion in a "logic," rather than simply by emphasizing that such relations are *indirect,* opened up the work of Reform to a reversal of its reconciling effect. This reversal occurred when the proper mystery of the relation between immanent vocation and spiritual fullness became a "boundary," according to Taylor, policed with a new, nominalist epistemology (*SA,* 72). For example, one sees this method at work in John Calvin's characteristic certainty that the atonement did *not* mean "that God could have released something of his saving efficacy out there into the world, at the mercy of human action," since the "infinity" of God and the "finitude" of humanity cannot mingle, *by definition* (*SA,* 79). The problem here is that "the sense that this language, above all others, has got a lock on the mysteries, is an invitation to drive its logic through to the most counter-intuitive, not to say horrifying conclusions" (*SA,* 78). That is, the problem is that the work of Reform, while it might have been instigated by a profoundly felt need to reconcile the abstract order of truth with the particularities of quotidian lives excluded by that order, ends up capturing the reality of life as such in a particular *language.* So, for the Reformers, one could "know" the boundary between the transcendent and the immanent simply in virtue of one's epistemological method; lived experience of the intermingling of these realities was entirely beside the point. The new prevailing logic therefore did not allow any experience to count but that of a buffered self.

The sense one gets from Taylor here is that what began as a movement to widen the range of possible affirmations of being ended up narrowing the scope of what counts as real to what can be captured in a relentlessly oversimplified and therefore abstract language (*SA*, 79). Once again, this argument bears a striking resemblance to the diagnosis of the modern destiny found in Radical Orthodoxy. For example, in her book, *After Writing: On the Liturgical Consummation of Philosophy*, Catherine Pickstock makes the argument that the "nihilism" of the modern age consists in its progressive reduction of reality to what can be written and thus secured as a text. This reduction, Pickstock argues, stems from an existential "gesture of security" against the constant becoming and passing away that characterizes our experience of temporal life. Instead of imagining that the truth of life itself might be a word that is only attained in its repeated utterance or performance, anxious modern subjects seek a reality they can transcribe and possess, a reality that "is" even at a remove from the temporal site of life's occurrence. Pickstock elucidates this contrast by comparing Socrates's preference for the oral performance of truth to Phaedrus's confident possession of a polished, timeless *transcription* of a speech in Plato's *Phaedrus*.[17] She then argues that Phaedrus's self-securing, "sophistic" impulse is carried through *ad absurdum* in modernity's reduction of the truth of life to a superlative linguistic simplicity. Reflecting on Peter Ramus's *Logike* (1574), Pickstock notes that its goal is to make reality as such accessible to language by reducing language to its essentially nominative function.[18] Eventually, Ramus believes, if one simplifies one's descriptive terms enough, one will find the whole of reality, though formerly mysterious and outside of one's control, to be essentially algebraic. Pickstock's reading of this modern movement toward simplification closely parallels Taylor's critical assessment of the sense of Calvinist Reform that one language can get a "lock on the mysteries" (*SA*, 78). So at this point our question becomes, why does this characteristically Radical Orthodox diagnosis of the process of secularization as a progressive abstraction of the real in a timeless and rigid order necessitate the recovery of human life as an *existential* possibility, as I am suggesting is the case for Taylor?

The short answer is that while the work of Reform stems from an authentic concern to free "the essentially human" from the clutches of mere structure, its culminating "rage for order" ends up deleting the human being as an enfleshed historical agent. For, eventually, the drive to Reform says that no matter what the material conditions of a human being's lived experience may be, she "is" in virtue of her possession of certain categorical attributes, to which we are therefore quite justified in "reducing" her. But these abstract, categorical properties become convincingly *essential* only when we address the fact that, as temporal creatures, we are always changing, never objectively the same from moment to moment. In other words, time itself has to be mastered, turned into a basically predictable, empty "space" for things to fill up, rather than the reminder of contingency that it more accurately is. To render the subject as an "existential" reality is to oppose both of these objectifications—that of essentializing the abstract, and that of "spatializing" time—by wagering that a human being is not essentially a *thing* at all, but a *way* of being, in time. A person considered in this manner cannot be defined in abstraction from her "guts," nor from her temporal comportment. Taylor makes these constructive points via his readings of Ivan Illich and Charles Péguy, respectively, to which I shall now turn.

## Un-defining the Human Subject

One of the side effects of the work of Reform was the emergence of the distinctly modern notion that what is most "real" is whatever can be defined objectively, or that the "essential" is whatever is not subject to the degenerative tendency of bodies or the vicissitudes of time. Such a shift could not but have enormous implications for ethics, since the identification of the essential origin and object of one's ethical obligations could no longer make reference to one's embodied relation with other human beings in a particular social and historical context, but only to one's possession of the categorical "properties" of human beings. This in turn meant that while the criteria of the Christian ethic were formerly present only by virtue of their mediation in a certain material-temporal arrangement, such criteria now became available as a universal "code" whose implementation could be guaranteed by timeless "institutions" (*SA*, 737). While this is most often seen as "a 'progressive' move in history for which the Church is responsible" (*SA*, 737), Taylor feels it is important to ask where this move stands in relation both to the Christian ethic as such and to the modern potential for a broadened affirmation of being.

In order to illustrate what he takes to be a striking contrast between modern and biblical visions of the neighbor, the proper object of the Christian ethical obligation, Taylor refers us to Ivan Illich's reading of the parable of the Good Samaritan. According to Illich, those of us who have been shaped by the Western shift toward an institutionalized Christian ethic will tend to see the parable as rooting our obligation to the wounded man on the road in a universal category of "neighbor," a category that the narrowness of the priest's and Levite's vision could not imagine. But for Illich, as Taylor notes, this reading indicates our readiness to miss what is crucial at this point (*SA*, 738). That is, we hereby reveal our supposition that substituting a new and now "universal" category for our formerly narrow ones can solve the problem of a tendency to exclude some people as the objects of our ethical obligations. For Illich, however, a truly radical re-envisioning of the ethical life cannot concede any ground whatsoever to the human tendency to categorize. Thus Taylor tells us that, on Illich's reading, what is given in the parable "is not a set of universal rules, applying anywhere and everywhere, but another way of being" (*SA*, 738). The story opens us to truly ethical action by sidestepping our tendency to act only once we can see the other as fitting into the right category, even a "universal" one. This moment of rational objectification, this need to fit the other person into an objective category (as a "human being with inalienable rights," for example) is always a deferral of the more enfleshed immediacy of the call to *live ethically*. It is therefore a deferral of a fully affirmative "seeing-good." So for Illich and for Taylor, the Samaritan's action can only be seen as a "free act of his 'I'" if he is called to respond, "not by some principle of 'ought,' but by this wounded person himself" (*SA*, 738). Only if the Samaritan is attuned to this precise call is his response both truly "human" and fully ethical.

When we unpack this reading further, we discover the implication that the new "community" established by such an ethic also cannot be defined objectively. That is, one can no longer say, on the basis of this parable, "I belong to a universal human community in which all human beings share on the basis of their possession of certain categorical properties." Such a community would exist abstractly, or "by definition," separate from the more immediate call to *commune*, in the flesh, with one's actual neighbors. Here the category of "universal humanity" would perform my ethical work for me. For Illich and Taylor, by contrast, the new manner of association established by Jesus's proposed ethic is a "skein of relations which link particular, unique, enfleshed people to each other, rather than a grouping of people together on the grounds of their sharing some important property" (*SA*, 739). This "network" is opposed to even the most universal grouping because its reality is confirmed only when it is materially enacted. The "fittingness" of people on the basis of agape therefore only holds in the absence of any need to define those to whom we would be obligated as part of our "we," and when we act instead on the basis of our precategorical experience of our enfleshed relations to such people—when we feel the call to pity in our "guts," rather than when our definition of humanity is satisfied by the other. The implication pertinent to Taylor's critique of the modern rage for order is that when we want only rules and institutions that derive from a new category, we have not really overcome the evasiveness of the Levite and the priest and have therefore become "living caricatures of the network life" (*SA*, 739). This life, as Illich describes it, disrupts every abstract "established proportion," insisting instead that we *establish new proportions* wherever we find ourselves called by the manifest need of another to do so. For Taylor's Illich, therefore, we become "ethical" beings, practitioners of a true "seeing-good," precisely when we refuse to allow ourselves or others to be "defined" in abstraction from our actual, enfleshed experience.

This once again indicates the Radical Orthodox character of Taylor's polemic, the sense in which, for him, "corrupted Christianity gives rise to the modern," whose dilemmas may therefore be resolved via a renewed appeal to the essentially Christian (*SA*, 740). Specifically, when Taylor argues that the loss of the Christian ethic as a living possibility relates to modernity's rigid codification of social life, he implies that what is really lost here is our sense of the meaning of the Incarnation, which properly indicates that God places no priority on the rational discovery of ethical categories, but affirms the true form of creation as a "word" that is breathed repeatedly in the practice of giving oneself to others in the flesh. And because the modern "North Atlantic world" has been significantly shaped by the movement toward Reform in Christianity, what has been lost more broadly is the sense that the material world can be a world of really human significance, since the progressive immanentization of our society ironically depends on abstract, categorical definitions of human personhood. Even exclusive humanism, with its overt denial of any refer-ent that transcends the material, paradoxically advances through more and more "excarnating" forms. Consider, for example, the recent "medi-calization of the body," whereby we have been "trained to see ourselves from the outside, as it were, as objects of science" (SA, 740). Through this new normative vision we begin to *experience* ourselves more as mecha-nisms defined in books than as bodies alive to the world. As Taylor puts it, "I become more acutely aware of the things I am trained to see as impor-tant symptoms of life-threatening malfunction" (SA, 740).[19] In this and other senses, then, a world that takes its impetus from a desire to "affirm ordinary life," has increasingly made us into terms in an abstract logic or category of immanent humanity. As Taylor helps to show us, it is because the hope of affirming a distinctly human reality, a "secular sphere," was allied early on with an epistemological protection of this realm from any "transcendent" interference that we are now stuck only *defining* human reality, no longer able to *live* it.

The irony of immanentism's progressive distance from human enflesh-ment is paralleled by its relation to temporality. Ostensibly for the work of Reform, the significance of temporality as such ought to take precedence over a conception of time as significant only insofar as it participates in what Taylor calls "higher times" (SA, 54). But because the exclusively im-manent human being is essentialized in an abstract definition, it should not be surprising that with the work of Reform, temporality as we actually experience it—in our situatedness before an always-uncertain future—drops out of the picture. When reality is supposedly validated by its un-changing objective definition, it becomes problematic to think of tempo-rality as mysterious flux. Thus it comes to be seen as a homogeneous and predictable "space," "indifferent to what fills it" (SA, 746). But just as Taylor uses Illich to disturb our categorical identifications for the sake of elevat-ing the material, so too he would have us think about time in ways that ac-cord better with our actual experience of temporal dynamism.

Taylor derives his preferred alternative to homogeneous, empty time from the work of Charles Péguy, who builds on Bergson's notion that "instead of thinking of time as analogous to space, where moments lie along-side each other, we have to take account of the *lived time* of durée, in which we bridge different moments, and connect them in a single stream, as we experience in action, or in hearing a melody" (*SA*, 746; emphasis added). Péguy illuminates this contrast by distinguishing between *history*, which for him denotes a relation to time as a container for the objective reality of human life, and *memory*, which is a relation to the past that "consists essentially above all not in going outside of [the event], but in remaining there and reliving it from within."[20] This conception of time allows for an affirmative relation to one's actual lived experience, which is the experi-ence not of unchanging categorical properties, but rather of a past to which one can relate in various ways, and of the future's mysterious arrival. For Péguy there is consequently a crucial distinction to be made "between a life dominated by fixed habits, and one in which one could creatively renew oneself, even against the force of acquired and rigidified forms" (*SA*, 747). Only in the latter situation, where temporal action is understood to be in productive tension with a mysteriously present fullness, where it can be-come an "analogy" of that fullness when the subject "bridges" moments via memory and *fidelité* rather than objective history and habituation, is the human being really *alive*, in time. Otherwise, action is not the imme-diate reality that immanentism seeks, but instead the abstract "engineer-ing" of reality, "be it to the new blueprints of 'reason,' or the ancient model of 'tradition'" (*SA*, 748). Ultimately then, for Péguy, we are authentically temporal beings not because our categorical definition fills up time as a ho-mogeneous container, but only when we take up the task of making a genu-inely subjective response to our lived experience—in other words, when we are related to time as *possibility*, rather than as inevitable "habituation."

Thus, in the first case, Illich's analysis of the historical codification of Christianity helps to illuminate Taylor's claim that our "secular age," which is characterized by the possibility and increasing popularity of "exclusive humanism," is determined by such a rigid "knowledge" of the immanent order that it may be said to "fetishize" the abstract categories upon which it is premised. As such, all of the ways in which we experience and live reality as embodied beings, along with all ethical imperatives, are short-circuited by the need to see ourselves and others as things that fit stable definitions. In the second place, Péguy helps Taylor show how the tendency toward objectification in modern knowing has, in the name of safeguarding "our" immanent sphere, made us paradoxically incapable of living genuinely temporal lives. The possibility of such authentic living requires a renewed, precategorical attunement to what in our past can "move" us toward action that will constitute "a creative re-application of the spirit of the tradition" (*SA*, 747). In both cases, then, Taylor's intended sense is that the elimination of any relation between transcendent sources of fullness and the immanent social order paradoxically deletes the human being as a real, enfleshed, and historical agent. The appropriate response, therefore, is not to come up with a new "definition" of the human being, but rather to show how all categorical pronouncements can become dehumanizing, and to appeal instead to our lost but not eradicated sense of ourselves as "ways" of being, shaped by mysterious possibilities rather than by unchanging objective properties. This, I suggest, is the nature of Taylor's existentialism, which depends on a radically critical assessment of objective self-definitions as necessarily self-alienating. Finally, we must ask how exactly Taylor believes a subjective shift of "retrieval" can occur in the face of the alienation wrought by nominalism.

### Overcoming Nominalism

After discussing Péguy's argument for a retrieval of fullness through the engagement of "new itineraries" in our temporal living, Taylor moves on to consider itineraries offered by modern poetics in general and the work of Gerard Manley Hopkins in particular. Taylor's assessment of the capacity of modern poetry to offer us itineraries of selfhood that are fuller than those provided by our objective self-definitions derives from his sense of the function of language as such. On this score, Taylor essentially argues that, since Hamann and Herder, poetry constitutes for us the existential boon of the "linguistic turn." This is to say that modern poetry (Hopkins being Taylor's paradigmatic example) is where the insight that "words don't just acquire meaning through designating things we already experience" (*SA*, 756) becomes a *practice* that can usher us toward a fuller mode of living. Put another way, poetry for Taylor is where the nominalism that predominates in our secular age is actively subverted. Let us back up for a moment to see how this claim is generated and what it can imply normatively for a recovery of fullness.

The assertion fundamental to the linguistic turn is that language has not only a "representative" function, but also a "constitutive power" (*SA*, 758). That is to say, words and speech do not convey "reality" to us with transparency and indifference, but in some measure *construct* the reality we experience, making "things exist for us in a new mode" (*SA*, 756). Such a claim presents a clear challenge to modern, objectifying modes of thought, speech, and action, which are only persuasive—even when they seem to have become "axiomatic"—in virtue of the subject's *belief* that the language of our knowledge, the language of our categories and self-definitions, is "adequate" to its object. The basic wager of the linguistic turn is that we can look at language in another way, just as Illich and Péguy suggest we can look at our bodies and our temporal lives, respectively, in ways that are not objectifying. So what Taylor calls the "Hamann–Herder understanding" of language argues that language does not give us access to pristine versions of ourselves, as if we were essentially texts. Instead, it functions both to constitute and to reveal how it is that we are comported to reality. And in this regard, Taylor suggests, an objectifying language such as ours, determined by centuries of a nominalist epistemological method, constitutes our lives in a poor and self-deceptive way, a way that occludes creative, "existential" possibilities. For Taylor, as for Pickstock, the appeal of the reductive tendency of modern language, its disdain for rhetorical flourish, derives from the notion that simple linguistic definitions of things can mitigate the mysterious flux of our temporal experience. Thus, a reductive language addresses our anxiety about our actual lives, and yet it can do this only by alienating us from those very lives, as we saw above. For Taylor, the question is, therefore, what kind of language can lead us to the greater existential "fullness" signaled by Illich and Péguy?

The short answer here is that modern language must regain the "performative power" that would enable subjects to be "constituted" by their linguistic contexts without at the same time removing them from the material-temporal site of their actual lives. Language must be restored in its capacity to offer the human being an *inscription* in a navigable text without giving it the power to reduce persons to abstract definitions. More specifically, this means that we need a language that can constitute subjects in relation to their past in ways that nonetheless allow them to move forward in the hope of new creative possibilities. For Taylor, such a language is best exemplified in modern poetry, which seeks to resonate with our past experience but "doesn't rely on already recognized structures." Instead, "it opens new paths, 'sets free' new realities" (SA, 758). To put this claim in Péguy's terms, modern poetics designates for Taylor a language of memory and action rather than history and habituation.

The claim that underlies such a distinction between a language such as that of Hopkins's poetry, which seeks to resonate with the subject in ways that will surprise rather than stifle, and the language of the immanent, buffered self, which secures the subject in static simplicity, is that the character of words as such can determine the narrowness or breadth of our perspective on the world. This is, on the one hand, obviously true; more expansive language can always help one to imagine and so experience the world more expansively. But, on the other hand, such a claim is also tricky, especially considering that Taylor's goal is to loosen the lock-tight grip that one particular language (the nominalist one) has exerted on the modern subject. Taylor, like Illich and Péguy, is interested in releasing "an affirmation of being" with its eyes open to "persons" before written "definitions" of what counts as real. Above all, such a goal demands an exercise of caution to avoid locating the problem of our "loss" of fullness only at the abstract level, the level of ostensibly impoverished languages. For if the point crucial to any expansion of the scope of fullness is that, as human beings, we are more than what can be written about us, that we are not only how we can be categorized abstractly, then the critic must consequently refrain from directly identifying spiritual malaise with *any* particular language, even the most apparently "limiting" ones. In this regard, it seems at least potentially problematic when Taylor claims that "in the light of this new understanding of language, this deadness, routine, which used to be seen as a lack in the worshipper, can now be situated in our language" (SA, 759).

Allow me to retrace our most recent steps in order to flesh out this possible difficulty more fully. In the first place, we saw how the modern tendency to read possibilities of fullness in terms that can be "categorically" rendered is revealed by the linguistic turn to be unnecessary rather than axiomatic, and possibly damaging to human beings as existing persons.

Thus can we say that the linguistic turn shows us that we do not *need* to understand ourselves as objects and that knowing or understanding ourselves and reality as such can occur in another, more creative mode. But the trick here is not to suggest, as Pickstock does, that modern language itself is the deadening factor in our lives, which would also imply that an inscription in a more inventive, expansive script would constitute freedom from our despair. The problem with these related suggestions is that predicating the subjective shift toward broader possibilities of fullness on a change in the script risks turning the human being into an object all over again—an object, granted, not of categorical thought, but of a "properly constitutive" modern poetics. Perhaps Taylor would guard against this "rage for poetic order" (as we might call it) by suggesting that the human being's "translation" into the antinominalist language of modern poetics is really the whole point, because unlike nominalism, it *does not have objects*. To be "in" this language is not to be defined, but to be alive to fullness, he might say. But here we could still counter that the linguistic turn also shows us that former, "excarnating" languages did not really have "objects" either; the crucial problem is that human subjects *wanted* them to. Therefore the shift we have to be concerned with in terms of recovering human life in a broadened sense of fullness is not a shift in language as such, but in human disposition. In other words, if words do not "represent" reality, then the problem with our limited affirmation of being cannot be that our language is too nominalist, but precisely that out of a desire for security, we *want* to be alienated, via written language, from our material-temporal lives. This desire for security must be the focus of any discussion of a shift toward broader possibilities of fullness, since such desire is able to turn *any* script into an occasion of the subject's numbing alienation from enfleshed experience.

In Radical Orthodoxy, the trickiness we are discussing here either goes unnoticed or is essentially denied. For example, though Pickstock argues that an existence that truly reconciles words with life is not "written" but must be *lived*, she nonetheless finds the possibility or impossibility of a "liturgical attitude towards reality" to be legible in the "syntax" of a particular script. This means she ironically finds the modern nominalist script to be utterly deficient, religiously speaking, because it seems to offer the subject no character whose role is adequately "written." Her slip in logic here can perhaps be aligned with Taylor's unfortunate claim that the cause of the spiritual deadness brought about by the work of Reform "can now be situated in our language." Such suggestions seem to contradict both Taylor's and Pickstock's best insights about the differences between an enfleshed and a "categorical" existence. Moreover, they confound what appears to be the thrust of St. Paul's "*hos mē*" imperative in 1 Corinthians 7, which suggests that however it is you are "written" (and Paul grants that there are many ways: married, single, worldly or not, etc.), no matter how apparently spiritually deficient is the text, or indeed, how spiritually excellent, you can and must *live as if your inscription does not define you.* In Pickstock's case specifically, I would argue that both her identification of modern language with subjective despair and her nostalgia for the inscription offered by the "syntax" of early medieval Christendom ultimately threaten any fidelity to extratextual life.

Ultimately, however, what is a criticism in the case of Pickstock and Radical Orthodoxy generally is more of a reminder in the case of Taylor. Taylor's entire argument tends toward the claim that elements of the work of Reform constitute losses because they despairingly inscribe the subject in a rigid linguistic schema, which elides the subject's authentic material and temporal personhood. Taylor's reference to the alternate script of modern poetics ought to make us wary only in the sense that we must remember it is possible for human beings to relate to *any* script as if it has a "lock on the mysteries." However, we should also notice that Taylor's longstanding refusal to dogmatically assert the unique authority of a specific theological discourse or of a particular liturgical script, a refusal Radical Orthodoxy does not countenance, becomes interesting in a new way here. The apparent vagueness of Taylor's relationship to theology has dogged him from both sides throughout his career; but in light of Radical Orthodoxy's overreach in diagnosing and supposedly overcoming the nominalism of modernity, Taylor's reticence on this score begins to look both purposeful and astute.

A final specific reference to Pickstock may be helpful here. Pickstock argues that the modern prioritization of the noun is the linguistic equivalent of the development of the art of photography in the nineteenth century, an art that "seemed to actualize a summoning of reality distilled from the flux of time, as a spatial given."[21] Just as photography makes "being" present to a gaze that seeks an atemporally static and epistemologically certain reality, so modern language renders reality as a series of nouns devoid of persons as temporal actors. The key aspect of nominalization is therefore that it "elides grammatical voice."[22] Our nominal language thus removes "the personal *from itself*," preventing language from becoming the medium of a fuller life.[23] It is important to remember, however, that photography itself cannot accomplish the objectification of reality, which ultimately depends on a specific comportment of the photographer or the viewer to the "objects" of this art. That is to say, the objectification of reality that occurs in conjunction with the art of photography is not really a possibility of the "thing" called the photograph, but instead of the subject who is related to photography and to photographs in a despairing way. Many diverse ways of being related to the photograph are possible, such that "salvation" from the spatialization of reality that photography seems to produce does not require the elimination of cameras so much as a turn in the subject—a turn that makes a genuinely hopeful "seeing" possible, beyond the merely autoerotic gaze of objective possession. My point here is that surely the same thing might be said about modern language—that the objectification of reality it seems to indicate is pertinent only in reference to the individual subject's comportment to that reality, which language alone, as a "thing," cannot determine. But this, strangely, is what Pickstock and Radical Orthodoxy will not allow. Their fidelity to the central tenets of post–linguistic turn philosophy leads them to suggest that the range of possibility for subjective fullness is inextricable from the determinations of the particular linguistic "construal" of reality in which the subject finds herself.

Thus, in the end, I think one can agree with Taylor that the only viable solution to the despair of excarnation is for particular human beings to begin to *live* their "enfleshed" relation to the future in hope rather than by clinging fearfully to objectivity; but one should add that this point complicates our ability to discern such despair *directly*, in any language.[24] In the end, the important alternatives are not John Calvin or Gerard Manley Hopkins, but despair or hope. And yet, this complication itself is not to be despaired over, since on Taylor's own logic, the human possibility of fullness, of an affirmation of being that is unreserved, is not a *written* possibility anyway, but a *living* one.

## CONCLUSION

In this essay I have tried to show, first of all, that Charles Taylor's reputation for moderation in his judgments and reserve in his normative conclusions is somewhat misleading, at least insofar as it obscures his aim of "releasing an affirmation of being" that goes beyond even Nietzsche's yea-saying. I have also tried to demonstrate that Taylor's "certain theistic perspective" consists, in *A Secular Age*, of a theology that begins not with abstract measures but with the particularities of enfleshment—the only sort of theology, on Taylor's account, that can engender a truly comprehensive "seeing-good." Recall that the crucial tension of the modern destiny consists for Taylor in our division between the extremes of our "massive professed commitments" in universal justice and benevolence and our particularizing regard for the significance of the quotidian and the singular. The universal scope of our "seeing-good" is thus potentially (and usually) dislocated from the irreducibly personal site of our most resonant experiences of fullness. The ostensibly "naturalist" solution of Nietzsche is to affirm the goodness of reality by refusing commitments that do not resonate with our feelings of pleasure in our own power. What is really interesting about Taylor's response, in the end, is that he does not argue that Nietzsche ought to temper his affirmation of the natural with a more "abstract" ideal. Instead Taylor shows how the naturalist's sense that what counts is whatever increases strength is already an evasion of the material as such, for the sake of a metaphysically presupposed measure or count. The overcoming of this deficient affirmation of being is accomplished through a contrasting wager that ethics *begins from the material,* that a genuine "seeing-good" hinges not primarily on a need to "know" what is good, but on a more immediate imperative just to *see* the world as it is. Such is the basic premise of a sociality that is on the one hand personally resonant, because it begins with the "guts," yet simultaneously universal, since it relies upon no *categories* (even the most encompassing) against which to measure and possibly exclude an object from the scope of its "seeing-good." Ultimately we may say that, for Taylor, the Christian wager of an Incarnate Word does not have the proper effect of bringing a too-earthbound humanity into contact, finally, with spiritual truth, but of bringing a world-denying and too-abstract subject into contact with the spiritual fullness of its own material-temporal nature. Thus, the Incarnation means that if you want the word of truth, the ultimate "order" of life as such, then you must stop pretending it cannot be present in the one suffering right in front of you. If you want to know the truth about the possibility of a universal community, then there is nothing to do except to become willing, at the very next moment, to *commune* with others.

While making these relatively strong claims about Taylor's development of an existential and Incarnational theology, I have also tried to indicate where his argument approaches the limits of his own most crucial insights. For, if the reconciliation of transcendent word and material life, of eternal truth and temporal existence, depends on a willingness to be comported to created reality in the mode of "seeing-good," then the challenge to the human being is to allow his "linguistic inscription," whatever its objective character, to "hang loosely" on him. And thus the crucial imperative must not be to construct a new language, or to identify particularly bad ones, but to remain *alive* in our diverse linguistic contexts without being defined by them. As Stanislas Breton says about theological language in particular, we must inevitably give voice to our experience, but we must at the same time put the linguistic determinations of those articulations "at a distance," lest we become static and inscribed, rather than hopeful and enfleshed persons.[25] At its best, Taylor's suggestion that we turn to the language of modern poetics for solace is the recommendation of precisely such a posture, rather than of any mere script.

## NOTES

1. John Milbank, "A Closer Walk on the Wild Side: Some Comments on Charles Taylor's *A Secular Age*," *Studies in Christian Ethics* 22, no. 1 (2009): 89–104. See also John Milbank, *Theology and Social Theory: Beyond Secular Reason* (Oxford: Blackwell, 1990); and John Milbank, Catherine Pickstock, and Graham Ward, eds., *Radical Orthodoxy: A New Theology* (London: Routledge, 1999).

2. See, for example, Charles Taylor, *Sources of the Self: The Making of the Modern Identity* (Cambridge, MA: Harvard University Press, 1989), 503–4. Hereafter abbreviated as *SS*.

3. See John Milbank's book, coauthored with Slavoj Žižek, *The Monstrosity of Christ: Paradox or Dialectic?* (London: MIT Press, 2009).

4. See Milbank, *Theology and Social Theory*, esp. 362–76; and Milbank and Žižek, *Monstrosity of Christ*, 215–18.

5. Milbank, *Theology and Social Theory*, 424.

6. Milbank, "A Closer Walk on the Wild Side," 102.

7. Milbank and Žižek, *Monstrosity of Christ*, 24–109.

8. This is John Milbank's term of preference for the requisite fleshing out of Kant's more abstractly "universal" ethics. See *Theology and Social Theory*, 160–173.

9. See, for example, *The Antichrist*, section 11, where Nietzsche's critique of Kantian ethics relates specifically to the separation of Kant's affirmation of being from any natural criterion of good. In *The Portable Nietzsche*, ed. Walter Kaufmann (New York: Viking Press, 1968), 577–78.

10. See Slavoj Žižek, *The Puppet and the Dwarf: The Perverse Core of Christianity* (London: MIT Press, 2003), 127.

11. See Žižek's essay in *The Monstrosity of Christ*, "The Fear of Four Words."

12. See Žižek, *The Puppet and the Dwarf*, 91.

13. Søren Kierkegaard, *Works of Love*, ed. and trans. Howard V. Hong and Edna H. Hong (Princeton: Princeton University Press, 1995), 374.

14. Charles Taylor, *A Secular Age* (Cambridge, MA. Belknap Press, 2007), 3. Hereafter abbreviated as *SA*.

15. Milbank, *Theology and Social Theory*, 9.

16. Ibid., 96. Emphasis added.

17. Catherine Pickstock, *After Writing: On the Liturgical Consummation of Philosophy* (Oxford: Blackwell, 1998), 3–46.

18. Ibid., 51.

19. The resonance of Taylor's analysis here with Michel Foucault's argument in *The Birth of the Clinic* is pronounced.

20. Charles Péguy, quoted in Taylor, *Secular Age*, 746.

21. Pickstock, *After Writing*, 89.

22. Ibid., 93.

23. Ibid., 95.

24. See Kierkegaard, *The Sickness unto Death*, ed. and trans. Howard V. Hong and Edna H. Hong (Princeton: Princeton University Press, 1980), where Kierkegaard writes, "The common view has a very poor understanding of despair. Among other things, it completely overlooks . . . that not being in despair, not being conscious of being in despair, is precisely a form of despair" (23). It seems to me that a direct appeal to the virtues of modern poetics tends to overlook this, and in doing so, it overlooks how the real existential concern lies elsewhere.

25. Stanislas Breton, *The Word and the Cross*, trans. Jacquelyn Porter (New York: Fordham University Press, 2002), 76.

# CHAPTER TWO

# Transcendence, "Spin," and the Jamesian Open Space

## PAUL D. JANZ

One could doubtless find more inviting or compelling ways to begin an essay than to announce in the opening sentence that it is going to be concerned mainly with questions of "method," a term likely to give the impression of something dry, pedantic, and uninspiring, or concerned primarily with technicalities. While I beg the reader's indulgence for a certain amount of pedantry in the next paragraphs, I hope the balance of the essay will, despite the underlying methodological focus, show itself to be addressing matters of both pertinent interest and importance.

At any rate, it is not merely a characteristic of our own intellectual milieu that, as readers or researchers, we find our interests inclining more naturally to "substantive" questions, concerned with the illumination of content in inquiry, than to the drier questions of method, which are concerned merely with ensuring that the procedures by which such illumination is claimed are themselves sound and correct. As Kant remarks in the opening sentences of the Transcendental Doctrine of Method (the second

of the two major divisions of the first *Critique,* largely ignored in favor of
the first, much larger Doctrine of the Elements), the basic propensity of
the human mind, or specifically of human inquiry, is toward the expansion of knowledge, to push positively into new territories of interpretation,
discovery, and innovation. Attention to method in inquiry, by contrast,
runs counter to this natural inclination or drive, inasmuch as judgments
about method are entirely negative and as such offer no satisfaction whatsoever to "humanity's general lust for knowledge," which is why they "do
not stand in high regard."[1] Kant himself pushes this even further. With his
archenemy, dogmatism, clearly the target, Kant deliberately overplays the
case in a rare flourish of hyperbole to make his point, saying, "One regards
[the negative judgments proper to method] as jealous enemies of our un-
remitting drive straining for the expansion of our cognition, and it takes almost an apology to earn toleration for them, let alone favor and esteem."[2]

But the point having been taken, and Kant's hyperbole notwithstanding, it is nevertheless also accurate to say that, with the notable exception
of contemporary analytic philosophy, questions of method in intellectual
discourse are today often not given the same priority of attention that they
have received in the past.[3] Perhaps an important part of the reason for this
is that a prioritization of method can tend to be associated with its prominent place in the prolegomena of the great foundationalist works of early
modern or Enlightenment philosophy, especially from seventeenth-century
rationalism onward, where methodological structures are integral to setting the basic parameters of grand narratives that want to pronounce generally on "the nature of things" and are seen as indispensable for defining
and justifying the "starting point" of such narratives.

Of course, a prioritization of attention to method need not be seen as
leading automatically to the totalizing excesses of Enlightenment foundationalism. Indeed, for Kant himself, who stands at that ambivalent point of
being viewed as both the quintessential philosopher of the Enlightenment
and, at the same time, the inaugurator of its decline or demise, the question of method does not appear as a feature in a general prolegomenon, at
the starting point of the first *Critique,* but rather at the end, where it is dealt
with "critically" simply as an integral feature of any sort of organized discourse or inquiry at all. And what makes methodological questioning integral to any inquiry, as Kant goes on to specify more exactly, is that it is
concerned first and foremost with the "discipline of reason," by which is

meant more exactly the disciplin*ing* of the use of reason according to principles, for the sole purpose of "guarding against error" in judgment with respect to any particular field of inquiry.

From this emerges something important. For, when one analyzes more carefully what is at issue here, it quickly becomes evident that all of what are often called the intellectual virtues, in the epistemological sense—e.g., inferential rigor, consistency, coherence, circumspect attentiveness to subject matter or modesty, clarity, transparent accountability in demonstration, and so on—are fundamentally characteristics of *method* or of principled *procedure* and not features of any ampliative knowledge gained about the content per se (although of course the particular content or subject matter in question will in part determine which methods are appropriate to it and which are not; it is important also to distinguish these epistemic virtues from moral virtue, which is different). But the decisive issue here is that intellectual inquiry is, after all, indispensably a human *endeavor,* and it is with respect to the "how" of such endeavor that the presence or absence of the above-mentioned virtues are expressed or become evident, as practices and as acquired dispositions of practice.

Let me now bring all of this to bear on the focus and designated themes of the present volume, *Aspiring to Fullness in a Secular Age.* I want to raise the important question of method in Taylor, and I wish to explore this specifically with respect to *A Secular Age,* especially given that this book can be found to provide indicative opportunities to uncover certain basic underlying methodological commitments in Taylor's work more broadly. I broach this with three goals or agendas in mind. I do it firstly because questions of method are never explicitly addressed here by Taylor, and such a focus is needed both to clarify the exact positions taken or being advocated and to establish their basic soundness. Secondly, and more importantly, I am interested in this question because even though the lineaments of a method are not easy to tease out, I believe that an important and quite rigorously principled methodological orientation can be discerned in Taylor's project, an orientation that is attuned (at least predominantly) in exemplary ways to the exacting intellectual virtues discussed above. As such, *A Secular Age* offers a methodological orientation with potentially important ramifications for many other studies today that seek, as Taylor does, to hold indispensably to a commitment to pluralism while also recognizing the indispensability of somehow grounding this in something more

generally or universally principled (in order for pluralism not to degener-
ate into mere relativism).

It should quickly be added, however, that in what follows, the whole
exercise will be critical as much as constructive. Indeed, it will among other
things be suggested that Taylor too in the end oversteps the very principles
or procedural limitations of his own discernible "method," or attends to
them with insufficient vigilance by seeking to achieve the cognitive secu-
rities or comforts of a Neoplatonic kind of "closure" in a way that directly
undercuts the discerned method's central principle (the "Jamesian open
space"), with the result that the real constructive edge of what Taylor as-
pires to loses some of its force.

But there is also a third and more specific motivation here that has to
do with my own interests in philosophical theology. It has often been re-
marked (by theologians themselves) that theology cannot provide its own
method, which is to say it cannot derive its method from its transcendent
source of concern or "subject matter," and from the foregoing brief considerations we can see why. There are of course those who might disagree
with this. Karl Barth, for example, separates out procedure in theological
thinking from the rational procedures appropriate to all the other sciences
or intellectual disciplines by making divine activity itself integral to theological "method." It is in part this presupposition of direct divine intervention into human rational processes that leads to charges of voluntarism or
fideism in Barth. But historically, the more prominent strains in theology
have been concerned with upholding the integrity of reason as a *human*
faculty of judgment, even and precisely with respect to a "subject matter"
said to transcend human capacities of reason and sense. And since the
"method" we hope to discern in Taylor also derives its grounding importantly through an orientation to "transcendent sources" (albeit nontheological ones), it is hoped that Taylor may also have certain contributions to
make here.

## "Positions"

A persisting peculiarity in much of Taylor's religiously focused work, especially as it comes to expression in *A Secular Age*—but also in *Sources of*

*the Self*—is that although the project is laid out programmatically around a single defining question and according to a clearly expressed motivating agenda, it is nevertheless often quite difficult to ascertain with any precision and assurance exactly what "positions" Taylor himself wants to commit to normatively or non-neutrally in a generally principled way. This is not to say that there are no clearly inferable orientational preferences or alignments visible (e.g., toward "belief" rather than "unbelief," or toward "openness to transcendence" rather than "closed world structures," and so on). But it is much harder to make out with any clarity the lineaments of well-defined positions or stances that are openly committed to by constructive argumentation in support of these orientations.

Now, as even Jacques Derrida acknowledges, "the imperative of taking a position in philosophy" cannot be avoided. No philosophical enterprise, even the most thoroughly antifoundationalist outlooks, such as his own form of deconstruction, can ever be content simply to "leave things the way they are . . . without a 'show of force' somewhere," for philosophy by definition "is not *neutral*. It *intervenes*."[4] Taylor's reticence to commit to clearly demarcated "positions" or to "intervene" non-neutrally on what *A Secular Age* narrates leads, as I will argue, to a prevailing ambivalence that characterizes much of the narrative's development. This ambivalence is visible not only on its broader structural fronts, as we will demonstrate in due course, but also in Taylor's engagement with particular philosophical sources.

Max Weber, for example, stands as one of the most important resources in Taylor's narrative of the "disenchantment" of the world in modernity. Yet while Taylor strongly concurs with Weber's fundamental assessments on the factors underlying the emergence of modernity, Weber's account is also the main target of the "subtraction stories" (to be discussed below), which bear the brunt of what Taylor calls his own "continuing polemic" as he builds his case.[5] Again, in both *Sources* and *A Secular Age*, Taylor's strong polemic against utilitarianism as one of the main factors in the emergence in the twentieth century of a "bad meta-ethic" that leads to a moral skepticism might seem to align him more naturally to a Kantian moral philosophy. But while Taylor does indeed give indications of a stronger deontological leaning, he also finds the Kantian moral enterprise to be inherently flawed in certain basic ways. The reader thus awaits some kind of structured response, or a commitment to a clearly articulated position that replaces what is rejected in both, but nothing of the sort is offered. In a different context, Marxian historical materialism and Hegelian historical idealism are played against each other as each missing something important that the other recognizes, but no clearly constructive alternative is offered in response to the lack in each. Indeed, even with regard to philosophical sources to which Taylor does seem inclined to commit more wholeheartedly—for example the "expressivist turn," especially as exemplified in Herder—even here, the ultimate concluding judgment on expressivism is one of a characteristic ambivalence: namely, that it "both greatly complicates and enriches the modern moral predicament."[6] One could continue on at length with other similar examples (e.g., with respect to Augustine, Calvin, Hume, Nietzsche, or Heidegger), but lest all of this give the impression of opening on too critical a note, let me quickly add an important caveat in Taylor's defense.

The point is that there are good reasons for the cautionary or non-committal approach taken here, reasons that show the reticence to take "positions" to be not necessarily a shortcoming of the project, but rather an aspect of its implicit methodological integrity or a by-product of certain deeper methodological priorities. One of these is that Taylor's own main concern, as we shall discuss more fully below, is not so much with the stated "positions" of his philosophical interlocutors as it is with uncovering what he calls the "background pictures" or "background frameworks" underlying these positions, with the goal of exposing certain implicit commitments that remain unacknowledged and unstated within them.[7] A second reason for the general characteristic of apparent ambivalence is tied to a certain intellectual virtue that pervades all of Taylor's work in the most exemplary way. I speak of the respectfully attentive and cautious character that informs what we shall see is a pervasively polemical undercurrent of his religiously oriented writings—one that precisely in its polemical criticism is constantly informed by an exemplary intellectual humility, a gracious attentiveness and charitable openness that Taylor brings to the consideration of any of his interlocuting sources, even those with whom he might seem most naturally inclined to disagree. One might say as such that Taylor manages even in his negatively critical readings to be both polemical and irenic at the same time, finding redeemable elements even in those sources that would seem to push most strongly against his own basic orientations. But the gracious magnanimity of the polemic in Taylor also again contributes precisely to the general character of ambivalence we are exploring.

In any case, we are left with a vast and richly textured mosaic, the overall structural lineaments of which remain indistinct and vague, at least in respect to any argumentatively grounded affirmative commitments, such that it is often easier to pick out definitively what Taylor stands against than what he stands for in any clearly committed and defined way. One might say that, insofar as the general contours of an overall picture or "position" emerge at all, they do so primarily through the common factors of what Taylor is seeking to "expose" via a polemic in the "articulation" of the hidden and unacknowledged assumptions among the elements within this mosaic.

But the foregoing considerations are secondary, and the most important reason for the characteristic ambivalence is the fundamentally descriptive or historically narrational, rather than philosophically analytical or critical, mode within which Taylor chooses to operate. More fully— and as much in *Sources* as in *A Secular Age*—it is Taylor's explicitly stated view that the only way for each book to accomplish what it sets out to do (especially in the articulation of the hidden assumptions it seeks to expose) is by making its case "illustratively," that is, through historical narration and description, rather than "demonstratively," through logical or normatively anthropological or sociological argumentation.[8] "The path to articulacy has to be historical," as Taylor says, and the work of the historian is distinguished from that of the philosopher precisely in that it seeks to approach its subject matter in as "neutral" a way as possible, without the influence of any intervening philosophical agenda that could skew the historical narrative to serve other purposes or ends.[9] Indeed, the "Jamesian open space," toward which much of this essay will be building as a center point of normativity, is precisely a place absent of all such agendas, or, in Taylor's term, absent of all "spin."

At any rate, as Taylor repeatedly emphasizes, the primary intention in *A Secular Age* is simply to "tell a story" about changes in the development of the modern human cultural and self-understanding in the societies of the "North Atlantic West." More exactly, it is a story that seeks to trace certain conditions underlying a fundamental transformation, or shift, through which it has become possible to move from a premodern theistic age, in which it was virtually impossible not to believe in God or in transcendent sources, to the present secular age in which—even for religious believers—belief in God is seen as "one option among others," and in which, moreover, "unbelief" has come to have the status of a virtual hegemony in an increasing number and variety of milieux, especially in academic life.[10]

But here we come again to a particular point of methodological tension and ambiguity. For, while the text is indeed mainly historically narrational, it is also, to a lesser but in the end no less important degree, philosophically critical or analytical. Or, as Taylor himself puts this, "Telling the story can't be elided; but it isn't sufficient of itself. In fact, the whole discussion has to tack back and forth between the analytical and the historical."[11] The method charted here, then, is a hybrid, seeking on the one hand to remain true to the noninterventionist character of historical description, and yet on the other to offer, at least implicitly, intervening valuative philosophical judgments on what is described.

For example, it will be obvious to the reader that Taylor's goal is not solely the historical one of tracing the conditions under which the aforementioned shift from belief to unbelief has become possible, but also, against the hegemony of unbelief in the Academy, and as Taylor elsewhere attributes this goal to William James, the philosophical one of supporting the rational "admissibility of belief," or "to rebut the idea that reason forces [us] into the agnostic stance of unbelief."[12] Moreover, while this goal is nowhere directly declared or defended, the indirectly but unmistakably conveyed message is nevertheless that belief in God, or "openness to transcendent sources," is by some distance the better or rationally more sound option for explaining the fundamental questions of human life that press upon us inexorably and with urgency: questions of moral sources, of human aspirations to "fullness," and of responsible human relationality in the world more generally.

My objective in what follows, then, is to make more explicit these basic philosophical commitments and normative positions that remain largely tacit. I also argue that the same ambivalence we encounter on the nonintervening historical fronts is often present in Taylor's basic philosophical commitments as well. The eventual goal will be to bring certain questions to bear on Taylor's understanding of "transcendence," especially as Taylor means this term to provide a normative or principled grounding for the question of human fullness. I will pursue this by tracing what might be called a method of strategic ambivalence or strategic ambiguity, which becomes visible as the project works toward its normative goals. This method of ambiguity will be found to reach its most definitive and pivotal expression in what Taylor calls the "Jamesian open space," which is a "position" of quintessential ambivalence. But before we come to recount and analyze certain key aspects of the main story that Taylor wants to tell, it will be necessary for contextualizing purposes to turn first to a few basic preliminary observations on the term *transcendence* as it comes to expression in Taylor.

## TRANSCENDENCE

With the collapse of essentialist or foundationalist metaphysics after Kant, and with the ensuing metacritiques or polemics in the nineteenth and twentieth centuries against even Kant's more "modest" metaphysics (whether romanticist, existentialist, structuralist, poststructuralist, postphenomenological, or neo-pragmatic metacritiques), it has become increasingly common to appeal to "human flourishing" as a nonfoundationalist, yet truly general, normative point of reference for philosophy (e.g., in Rawls, Dummett, Putnam, Habermas, Murdoch, or MacIntyre). This is also Taylor's starting point in *A Secular Age*, which begins from a series of statements with which virtually no one would want to disagree. For example: "Every person, and every society, lives with or by some conception(s) of what human flourishing is: What constitutes a fulfilled life? What makes life really worth living? What would we most admire people for? We can't help asking these and related questions in our lives."[13] Beginning from this quite common question, Taylor uses it as a backdrop against which to formulate the question of "transcendence" and its relation to "immanence." In other words, the question of transcendence is here defined not first with respect to "God" or "the sacred" or "the supernatural" or any other specifically religious point of orientation, but rather more broadly and formally, simply with respect to a question about "human flourishing."

The question is this: Is "the highest, the best life" to be sought and found ultimately *within* the goals of human flourishing? Or does the highest and best life "involve our seeking, or acknowledging or serving a good which is *beyond* [or transcendent], in the sense of independent of human flourishing? In which case the highest, most real, authentic or adequate human flourishing could include our aiming (also) in our range of final goals at something *other* than human flourishing." It is in this sense that "defining religion in terms of the distinction immanent/transcendent is a move tailor-made for our culture."[14] The question of transcendence can thus also be phrased with regard to fullness: "What does it mean to say that for me fullness comes from a power that is beyond me, that I have to receive it . . . ?"[15] This way of addressing the question of transcendence is of course not without precedent. It bears a strong resemblance, for example, to Augustine's discussions on happiness as an ultimate goal of human striving, where likewise the source of full or true happiness is found not in what humans can give to themselves, but in what only God can give.

Now, prima facie, this way of defining transcendence seems promisingly concrete. In building from the desire for fullness or happiness that we all know or experience as humans, it appears to offer a genuine kind of tangibility for the orientation to transcendence. However, there is a subliminal or hidden assumption involved here, an assumption by which a certain gain can be claimed for the authoritative meaningfulness of transcendent sources that, on closer observation, will be found to be only illusory.

The crux of the problem, as already countenanced in the foregoing quotations, stems from Taylor's continuous treatment of transcendence merely according to its linguistically or conceptually analytical definition as that which is "beyond" the immanent (which effectively turns out to be the merely negative definition of transcendence as "not the immanent"). Now, to claim that we can orient ourselves intelligibly or meaningfully to transcendence, understood merely logically in its analytical definition as that which is "beyond" or "higher than" the immanent, is of course to claim something true and meaningful. But the truth and meaning encountered here, as a truth and meaning that can be affirmed through the logical analysis of the definition of the term alone, has no more to do with the truthfulness and meaningfulness of what is affirmed by those who profess "belief" in a transcendent God or in transcendent "sources" than it does with what is denied by those who profess "unbelief" in God or reject the independent authority of transcendent sources. Indeed, the affirmation of the truth and meaning of the term "transcendence"—understood merely in its negative conceptual definition as that which is "beyond" the immanent and making no claims as to the ontological reality of what is affirmed—is an affirmation that unbelievers will agree to as readily as believers. The truth agreed to here is merely the linguistically necessary or "trivial" truth of a truism or tautology, derived definitionally from the conceptual analysis of the meanings of terms.

But here we come to what will prove to be a crucial oversight. For in this merely truistic sense of its conceptual definition, the term "transcendence" is not yet an independent or "ontological" *source* of anything; it is rather solely a *product* of logical thinking, and an entirely abstract and negative one at that. By treating what is merely a logically and negatively defined notion of transcendence as an independent *source*, Taylor buys into what is essentially an ontological illusion, or inadvertently conjures an ontological trick. What occurs in this illusion is similar to what since Kant has come to be acknowledged as the philosophical error of dogmatism: that is, the rationally unsustainable reification or hypostatization (into a putatively objectively authoritative or ontological source) of a "transcendent" point of reference that is, in truth, only a linguistic (and negative) notion of the intellect.

What really needs to be offered here, in other words, is some sort of critical or rationally demonstrative account, however indirect it might have to be, of what the meaningfully authoritative "content" of the transcendent might be for human life. What is rightly expected here is an account of *how* that which is transcendent announces itself uniquely and genuinely as a life-meaningful authority for questions of moral sources or human fullness. But no such authoritatively ampliative or nontruistic account of transcendence is offered.

It is true that Taylor does attempt to bring a kind of authoritative and nontruistic "content" to transcendence through certain claims about "agape" and "seeing-good," which he attributes to transcendent or theistic sources. But these claims are not demonstrated, in any critically constructive way, to be attributable *uniquely* to transcendent or theistic sources. As a result, it is difficult to distinguish what is truly theistic or "transcendent" about Taylor's account of love as agape from other works that are not the-istically based, such as Harry Frankfurt's *The Reasons of Love* or Thomas Nagel's *The Possibility of Altruism*, the latter of which makes a highly con-vincing case from an expressly atheistic standpoint. Admittedly, the one difference is in Taylor's portrayal of this as something occurring at the "gut level" or "in the bowels." But again, there is no reasoned indication given for why this "gut-level" response corresponds to a uniquely transcendent source, other than perhaps the tying of it to the Gospel account of Christ being moved "in the bowels" by compassion.[16]

## SUBTRACTION

We will return to the question of transcendence below, but on the basis of these preliminaries, let us turn to a closer examination of the main story that Taylor seeks to tell. As a philosophically historical narrative, *A Secular Age* can for one especially crucial reason make a legitimate claim to a kind of uniqueness among other such narratives, and in this uniqueness is found also what many have deemed to be its special importance and value. This is not to say that the basic story it tells per se seems unfamiliar; indeed it seems eminently familiar. It is a story whose marker dates Taylor gives as 1500 and 2000, between which, especially in the North Atlantic societies of the West, a fundamental shift has occurred through the onset of "moder-nity." More specifically, it is a shift from a premodern time (in 1500) when "so many features of [the] world told in favor of belief" (in God), thus mak-ing "the presence of God seemingly undeniable," to a time (in 2000) where "these features have vanished." Among the main features of the premodern understanding that have vanished are (a) the view that the natural order it-self "testifies to divine purpose and action"; (b) the view that God is "impli-cated in the very existence of society"; and (c) the view that "people lived in an 'enchanted' world" of "spirits, demons and moral forces."[17]

   Before coming to what I have suggested is the importantly unique way that Taylor tells this story, let me set a backdrop for it by condensing from Taylor a rough summary of how the story is more commonly told. In fact, the story of the emergence of modernity, and with it secularity, has for Taylor usually been told in one of two basic ways. It is either told as a "subtraction" story—that is, the story of a *loss*, or of something left behind in the abandonment of the premodern view—or it is told conversely as a "coming of age" story—that is, the story of a kind of gain in coming to a new intellectual maturity. More fully, subtraction stories, as stories of a loss, are "stories of modernity in general and secularity in particular, which explain them by human beings having lost or sloughed off, or liberated themselves from certain earlier, confining horizons, or illusions, or limitations of knowledge."[18] "Coming of age" narratives tell their stories in the other direction, as stories of a natural growth toward the "adulthood" of the intellect, especially as an effect of scientific discoveries and the resulting changes in philosophy, through which humans' understanding of themselves and the world has attained to greater levels of clarity and critical accuracy.

Now, one can easily see that subtraction stories as stories of a loss and coming-of-age stories as stories of a gain are really different ways of narrating the same thing. In Taylor's own words, "'Coming of age,' subtraction, these are two faces of this powerful contemporary story."[19] Taylor, however, rejects fundamental aspects of these kinds of narratives, describing his own project as a "continuing polemic against . . . 'subtraction stories'"[20] and, by extension, also against coming-of-age stories. Before coming to what is different and unique about Taylor's own story, however, it is important to recognize that there is another, essentially inverted form of subtraction: a sense of subtraction or loss that implicitly but indispensably underlies the whole development of *A Secular Age* itself, such that Taylor's narrative too turns out at bottom to be also a kind of subtraction story. In this other direction, the subtraction is not that of a "sloughing off" of what is *illusory* and superstitious in the premodern, but rather, inversely, the story of a fundamental loss of something *vital* and indispensable for humans' understanding of themselves and the world they inhabit (i.e., the loss of the natural and nearly universal belief in God), something still present in the premodern self-understanding of 1500 but having virtually vanished by 2000 in many modern milieux.

In fact, this form of subtraction is just as visible in *Sources*, where it comes to expression under the polemic against a "massive blindness" in modernity, a blindness to an element of "higher worth" or "spiritual" worth, or also as a "suppression" of this element, which was present in past (premodern) "visions of the good."[21] This suppression or blindness, moreover, is said to involve a kind of fallacy, insofar as the "modern naturalist views," which suppress the previous theistic vision of the good, can for Taylor be shown nonetheless still to be "living from the spiritual insights of this predecessor which [they] claim to have utterly repudiated."[22] This is why Taylor calls *Sources* both "an essay in retrieval" and an essay in "liberation," inasmuch as it seeks to retrieve for the modern understanding these "spiritual" elements which have been lost; or, conversely, inasmuch as it seeks to liberate the modern understanding from its suppression of these elements.[23]

In *A Secular Age*, the language of retrieval and liberation has disappeared, and the polemical terms used are subtler, but they are no less subtractionist or sweeping. The language here is no longer quite as thematically about a modern "blindness" to transcendent sources, but rather of certain "illusionary" propensities in modernity, illusionary orientations that lead, in Taylor's words, to a "misrecognizing" of "transcendent reality" as something immanent, or again of the "refusal" in many modern milieux "to envisage transcendence as the meaning of fullness." This misrecognizing or refusal is in turn sometimes overtly acknowledged as a kind of "loss."[24]

It is true that this inverted version of subtraction or loss is more explicitly associated with what Taylor calls "Intellectual Deviation" (ID) narratives. As the name itself implies, Intellectual Deviation stories portray the movement into modern paradigms of social and self-understanding as embodying a massively misbegotten "wrong turn" in the intellectual history of the North Atlantic West, especially in the movement of the intellectual disciplines toward autonomy and away from dependence on God. But the point is, even though Taylor's own narrative (what he calls the "Reform Master Narrative," or RMN) differs in one very crucial way from the ID narratives, as we shall see, insofar as Taylor explicitly declares his own RMN to be indispensably "complementary" to the ID narratives for "explain[ing] religion today," his project is nevertheless by this association shown to be itself a story of subtraction or loss.[25]

Taylor himself cites Radical Orthodoxy as a primary exemplar of the tellers of Intellectual Deviation and therefore of subtraction narratives. But one could also add many others, especially from contemporary theology, among whom this type of story is indeed commonly told today. Among these one could include even Joseph Ratzinger himself, who, for example, in a much-discussed 2006 paper, rejects various aspects of modern philosophy, lamenting especially the "modern limitation" of reason in Kant. In its place he advocates a retrieval of the full "breadth and grandeur" of the reason of the premodern past, through what he calls a re-Hellenization or re-Platonization of philosophy, in which reason again can take its rightful place as a "universe of reason" that includes the Logos of God as its apogee.[26]

## NARRATIVITY AND SENSE

But this digresses, and we need to return to explain the decisively unique feature of Taylor's story by which it distinguishes itself from the usual stories of the emergence of modernity and secularity. In order to locate this feature exactly, it is important to identify one further basic characteristic of the way the story is usually told (whether along subtractionist or coming-of-age lines). The point is that the usual narrative is invariably about developments occurring most fundamentally in *intellectual* milieux or domains, most notably in science and philosophy. It is thus a story of the historical development of human *conceptions* and *beliefs* about themselves and the world: conceptions that have changed dramatically as the effects of scientific discoveries, and the revolutions in philosophy that followed, have filtered down to the social life of the common people.

Taylor, however, departs from these top-down narratives and wants to tell the story in the other direction, from the bottom up, as it were. His own story is not primarily about changes in *epistemic* conceptions and beliefs about the world under the influence of science and philosophy (although of course he by no means wishes to dispute this as an important influence), but rather about equally massive changes that have occurred in what he calls the *pre*-epistemic or pre-theoretical "background pictures" or "background frameworks," by which is meant a pre-theoretical "sense" of the world out of which all our beliefs and conceptions are formed.

To emphasize the distinction: the background picture is comprised not of our conceptual *beliefs* about things, but rather of "our *sense* of things,"[27] which precedes the formation of conceptual beliefs as "the sensed context in which we develop our beliefs."[28] The background picture is meant here roughly in the way that Wittgenstein, Heidegger, or Polanyi proposed it: namely that "all beliefs are held within a context or framework of the taken-for-granted, which usually remains tacit, and may even as yet remain unacknowledged by the agent, because never formulated."[29] What is intended here is further amplified by the description of the background picture variously as "our feel of the world"; as "the way the universe is spontaneously imagined and therefore experienced"; and as "our cosmic imaginary."[30] It is also described as our "overall take" on "human life and its cosmic and (if any) spiritual surroundings"; as our "overall sense of things," which manifests itself as "something in the nature of a hunch"—or, to use Taylor's more broadly preferred terms, something in the nature of a "gut instinct," "gut feeling," or "intuition."[31]

At the very heart of the story of the shifts in sensed background frameworks are shifts or transformations in what Taylor calls the "social imaginary." What is meant by this is that the changes in our sense or feel of the world do not simply occur in isolated "subjects" or individuals, for every subject or person ineluctably comes to awareness even of his or her own subjectivity or selfhood already from within a preconceptual "social imaginary." We cannot discuss this term at any length here except to point out two basic ways that the *sensed* "social imaginary," as a fundamental aspect of how human life is received and lived, is for Taylor distinguished from an already *conceptualized* "social theory." First, an "imaginary" speaks "of the way that ordinary people 'imagine' their social surroundings, and this is often not expressed in theoretical terms," but rather in "images, stories, legends, etc." Second, "theory is often the possession of a small minority, whereas what is interesting in the social imaginary is that it is shared by large groups of people, if not the whole society."[32]

At any rate, it is the story of changes at this preconceptual level of the "sensed context" of the world and our place in it that Taylor wishes to tell. It will not be a top-down story of either subtraction or coming-of-age, but rather a bottom-up story to which Taylor gives the name "Reform" or, more fully, the Reform Master Narrative. *Reform* refers to certain drives and changes occurring not in the intellectual domains of science and philosophy, but *in the religious life itself,* which in premodern times was at the heart of the social imaginary.[33] Specifically, Reform in its nascence expressed itself, among other ways, in "a profound dissatisfaction with the hierarchical equilibrium between lay life and the renunciative vocations."[34] Reform here is not meant to be identified only with the defining aspects of the Protestant Reformation; it includes many of these aspects but also goes well beyond them and is rather something "peculiar to Latin Christendom" as a whole. It involves "a drive to make over the whole society to higher standards," with *higher* here meaning standards that apply to all humans and all sectors of society, which is to say, specific to the present context, standards that do not allow exemptions for a religiously privileged, renunciative few.[35] It thus involves a "rage for order" in accordance with these higher or more inclusively applicable standards, which, for Taylor, gives Reform one of its most defining characteristics: homogenization. This also creates the basis in Reform for a tendency toward "excarnational" views of religion, that is, "the transfer of our religious life out of bodily forms of ritual, worship, practice, so that it comes more and more to reside 'in the head.' "[36] In this way, the rage for order that came to dominate the social imaginary became "crucial to the destruction of the old enchanted cosmos and to the creation of a viable alternative in exclusive humanism."[37]

In sum, the narrative seeks to explore the movement from the conditions of premodern "belief" to the conditions of modern "unbelief" by tracing the transformations that have occurred in the preconceptual sensed context of the world, especially as this is rooted in the social imaginary. In turn, these transformations at the sensed "background" level are traced along several constantly interweaving pathways: the path from enchantment to disenchantment, the path from "openness to transcendence" to what Taylor calls "the immanent frame," the path from "embeddedness" to "disembeddedness," and, importantly underlying all of these, the path from the "porous self" to the "buffered self."

Moreover, as we explore any of these interweaving pathways, we encounter again the same characteristic disposition of ambivalence as we saw above, with regard to the question of what exactly the narration of them is meant to achieve, or with regard to any valuative or intervening "position" that Taylor wishes to take in respect of them. Let us look briefly at the last of these—the movement from the premodern "porous self" to the modern "buffered self" (which will in any case involve many of the others)—in order to illustrate this continuing ambivalence.

## AMBIVALENT TRANSITIONS

The premodern porous self lives in an enchanted world of subterranean or supraterrestrial spirits, forces, essences, demons, and powers, and it is for Taylor naturally "open" and susceptible to the activity of these forces and powers.[38] At the heart of what makes this self porous, and by extension its world enchanted, is an understanding of *meanings* different from the way we understand this term predominantly today. Meanings in the premodern sense are not only in minds or given by language in the relation of signifiers and signifieds, as linguistic creatures bring a semantic significance to bear on the sensibly perceived world. Meanings here come to us also from outside: perceived objects are themselves seen as "charged" with their own subterranean, suprasensible or supraphysical meaning.[39] There is therefore a porosity to the boundary between the perceiving self and the world it perceives, one across which meaning-saturated objects— in virtue of their suprasensible and thus invisible "essence"—exert a metaphysical influence upon the meaning-perceiving mind. This porosity of the boundary between self and world in turn implies a natural and inextricable "embeddedness" of the premodern, meaning-perceiving self in the meaning-drenched world.

This view of the world as "charged" with suprasensible meanings of things is essential to what is meant by its enchantment, for it presupposes an objectively real metaphysical realm of invisible essences and spirits underlying the physical realm in which we live corporeally. And because this world is itself seen as infused or enchanted by essences, spirits, powers, and forces not of the visible physical order, but rather of an invisible, subterranean, suprasensible, or metaphysical order, there is therefore also a natural openness to what is perceived as a realm transcending the natural physical or corporeal world in which we find ourselves alive. This is what makes it impossible for the premodern porous self living in an enchanted world not to believe in transcendent sources and ultimately in God. What is vital here again, however, is that this porosity "has to be seen as a fact of [sensed or felt] *experience* not merely of 'theory,' or 'belief.' "[40]

Through the disenchantment of the world in the emergence of modernity, however, the hitherto porous boundary between the self and the world it inhabits becomes gradually less porous or "buffered." In other words, objects are no longer seen as charged with meaning emanating from subterranean or suprasensible essences, forces, and spirits and absorbed by the mind. It is now the determining human mind or self that provides meaning to its world, as through the semantics and grammar of language it brings its own "significance" to bear on the world in relating signifiers to signifieds. Together with the loss of the porosity of the boundary comes not only a corresponding "disembedding" from the world, but also a loss of the natural "openness" to transcendent sources that defines the porous self, such that the buffered self now inhabits what Taylor calls the "immanent frame."

We cannot go into this any further here, and I want to return to what is in any case our more central concern: namely, that of the prevailing ambivalence in *A Secular Age*—an ambivalence with respect to any particular valuative stance that Taylor himself wants to take vis-à-vis the porous and buffered self. The point is that Taylor's objective in narrating the movement from the porous to the buffered self is quite clearly not *only* to tell a story; it is also to make certain intervening judgments on what is told or described. This is where the ambivalence again emerges.

On the one hand, the prima facie dominant impression conveyed is that the porous self is decidedly preferred over the buffered self, both because the former is said to have an inherent openness to transcendence and because the latter is one of the main targets of the book's ongoing polemic. On the other hand, Taylor is also quite clearly not advocating a simple return to the premodern porous self either (as several influential Intellectual Deviation voices in theology do today in calling for a "re-enchantment" of the world). For, as Taylor clearly acknowledges, despite its natural or built-in putative openness to "transcendence," the porous self is equally open to many false superstitions that the modern buffered self dispels.

Furthermore, it is clear throughout the book that despite the implicit polemic against the modern buffered self, this buffered self per se is not seen as *intrinsically* "bad" or as pernicious of itself. The buffered self is simply the self of the "immanent frame," and Taylor makes clear that the buffered immanent frame is the background framework that we *all* inhabit today in the North Atlantic West—"believers" and "unbelievers" alike. It is only in its propensities for leading in directions of "exclusive humanism" or "closed world structures"—i.e., when it follows certain built-in tendencies to close itself to transcendence—that, for Taylor, the buffered self becomes wholly objectionable. In other words, the immanent frame of modernity need not be abandoned—indeed, it is for us today impossible to abandon it, as it constitutes our "social imaginary"—for belief to be possible. Nevertheless, a thoroughgoing ambivalence persists even here as to whether the modern buffered self is only grudgingly accepted by Taylor as an unavoidable *fact* that all of us in the North Atlantic West have to live with, or whether he is willing to view the emergence of the buffered self in some sense also positively, as in certain ways a genuine progression into adulthood or coming-of-age through the banishing of false superstitions.

The same kind of ambiguity also runs throughout Taylor's treatments of related terms such as "disenchantment" or even "modernity" itself. The prima facie dominant impression conveyed is that of a mainly unfavorable or polemical stance against modernity, as the condition in which the "closed world structures" of "exclusive humanism" become possible. Yet Taylor's treatments do not allow themselves to be read as outrightly antimodern either, in the way that some forms of poststructuralism do or as Rortian ultrapragmatism does. Modernity does not, for Taylor, *necessarily* lead to the homogenizing and totalizing destinations that Foucault or Lyotard or Rorty think it does. Nor must it necessarily lead to the kind of closedness to transcendence that the more unreservedly antimodern ID narratives suppose it does. Thus the ambivalence persists.

## The Jamesian Open Space

But here at last we come to what I argue is a kind of methodological center for Taylor, a center in light of which his reticence to commit to any clearly defined "positions" need not be interpreted as a failing or a weakness. It can also be seen as reflective of what is for Taylor the place or position of "fullest lucidity" *within* the immanent frame of modernity—a place he calls "the Jamesian open space"—and is by extension also an expression of the project's own methodological integrity.[41] The point is that the immanent frame is experienced most fundamentally as a place of "cross pressures" or "dilemmas," of "unquiet frontiers" or "malaises." At the very heart of this essential conflictedness, or underlying it, stand "two great polar positions": those "who see immanence as admitting of no beyond," or inversely as demanding "closure," and those who see the immanent frame as still open to a "beyond," or inversely "as something which permits closure without demanding it." Stated more viscerally, "we can either see the transcendent as a threat, a dangerous temptation, a distraction or an obstacle to our greatest good," or "we can read it as answering our deepest craving, need, fulfillment of the good." In short, "the question is whether [the transcendent] is only a threat, or doesn't also offer a promise."[42]

Each of these two polar positions constitutes what Taylor calls a possible "spin" on the immanent frame, one toward openness and belief, and the other toward closure and unbelief, with the spin toward the latter being virtually "hegemonic in the Academy." The point is that to inhabit the Jamesian open space is to stand between these two polar positions, between these two "spins" on the immanent frame. But it is to do so in a very specific way. In fact, as Taylor says, the feat of actually standing in this space is "relatively rare." Few of us who go one way or the other—even few who make "some kind of crucial turning in life in one direction or the other"—have really faced what is at issue here "in the clearest and starkest way."[43]

To understand what is being claimed here, we must remember that "the immanent frame is not usually or even mainly a set of beliefs." It is, rather, the pre-epistemic background framework, which is deemed to be pre-theoretical or pre-epistemic because, as "an overall sense of things," it "leap[s] ahead of the reasons we can muster for it."[44] It is also vital to recognize as such that the immanent frame that we all inhabit is already virtually always experienced and known *as* "spun" in the one direction or the other—excepting the "rare" instances of those who come to inhabit the Jamesian open space. In other words, "spin" in Taylor's sense is not merely the manipulation of data toward a preferred interpretation—in the way that a criminal defense lawyer will spin the facts of a case to the benefit of her client. Taylorian spin is already always *there* in the background—one might say that "spin" is already always "spun"—as the sensed context and social imaginary from which we live and formulate beliefs. It is for this reason that the best that most of us can muster when we seek to understand *other* such background pictures—i.e., pictures that are "spun" and "lived-from" differently than ours—is to be "capable of seeing that there is another way of construing things, but still having great difficulty in making sense of it." This is "the standard predicament in ethnology," that is, the problem that the most we are capable of doing is recognizing from a distance or from the outside the difference that ethnicity, race, or gender might make in viewing the world, without ever being able actually to *inhabit* this difference and to sense or experience it "from the inside," as it were.[45]

Yet the point made here, specifically with respect to the question of belief and unbelief, is that to stand in the Jamesian open space is precisely to inhabit a space in which the sensed context of *both* spins is *felt* and *experienced.* It is to stand "in that open space where you can feel the winds pulling you, now to belief, now to unbelief." In other words, "standing in the Jamesian open space requires that you have gone farther than [merely] ... seeing that there is another way of construing things ... and can actually feel some of the force of each opposing position" without succumbing to either.[46] This is what makes it what Taylor calls a place of "full lucidity," that is, a place absent of all bias, prejudice, or partiality.

There is something potentially profound being proposed here, and it is important to understand it properly. For it is not as if to stand in the Jamesian open space were simply, from a standpoint already committed to belief in God, to consider the *reasonabilities* for unbelief with the greatest honesty, attentiveness, and openness, or likewise in the other direction, from unbelief the reasonabilities of belief. Nor is it simply to be equally convinced or unconvinced about the rationally persuasive pull of the plausibilities, now of the one side and now of the other. It is not like another version of the "undecidability" we encounter in deconstructionist discussions, for example. This is precisely still an undecidability with respect to the reasons that can be mustered for and against the one side or the other. To stand in the Jamesian open space, by contrast, is to stand at what might be called the quintessential point of *experiential* scission between two different pre-theoretical "senses" of the world—the space in which Taylor's recurring references to cross pressures, dilemmas, unquiet frontiers, malaises, and so on are not so much rationally adduced as pre-intentionally *felt.* As such, the better qualifier for describing the full lucidity of the Jamesian open position between the "two great polar positions" might be that of a supreme *vulnerability* rather than that of a supreme undecidability, which in turn would make this one of the most committedly "existential" moments in Taylor. The "relative rarity" of the "lucidity" encountered here, therefore, might perhaps pertain not so much to the small number of human beings who manage to stand in this space as to the rarity of such moments as possible experiences of supreme vulnerability in each of our lives.

If this can be granted, then other possible comparisons also come to mind. For example, the Jamesian open space might be read as having a certain affinity with Schleiermacher's "feeling of absolute dependence," which, at least in its original inception, or in the original experience of it, is nothing like a breakthrough to any kind of cognitive certainty or resolution, but rather, as a place of absolute *dependence*, precisely a place of supreme vulnerability. Or yet again there is a possible resonance with what Kierkegaard means by the "first consciousness of sin," by which he means nothing like a more intense consciousness of wrongdoing, but rather, in his words, the first consciousness of being "before God" (or "before transcendence"). This again, as in Schleiermacher, is not in the first instance a place of sudden, grand illumination, but precisely a place of radical vulnerability—of "despair," in fact—a state especially well captured by the German word for despair, *Verzweiflung*: that is, to be divided in oneself, to be of two orientations in oneself. This again corresponds to Taylor's stance on the Jamesian open space as involving an "understanding of the immanent frame ... that, properly understood ... allows of both readings, *without compelling us to either.*"[47] Or, more fully, to stand in this open space is to admit—or better, to experience—that *neither* option presents itself as rationally conclusive or airtight; in Taylor's words, that neither side presents itself as "obvious, compelling, allowing of no cavil or demurral."[48] To suppose so would be to buy into an "illusion"—the illusion that either spin can be upheld as rationally conclusive—and precisely as such to have abandoned the Jamesian open space.

But, for Taylor, all of this now also means something important for what any eventual decision in favor of either belief or unbelief ultimately involves. It means that because neither side can present itself as rationally conclusive, whichever way the inhabitant of the open space finally decides to go, the decision cannot be based on the deliverances of reason per se. It must rather be based on what Taylor calls an "anticipatory confidence" or also a "leap of faith," such that the decision for *either* side—for the unbelieving as much as for the believing—is taken on the basis of such a "leap." In other words, any such decision, if it is undertaken with "full lucidity," would have to admit that the decision per se is not fully supported by any confidence that could be considered conclusive through rational argumentation. It would rather "involve recognizing that one's confidence is at least partly anticipatory, and hence being aware of the Jamesian open space."[49]

There is thus a quasi-apologetical effect created by the Jamesian open space for Taylor's goals as a whole. For while the Jamesian open space, as a "position" or "stance" to which Taylor commits normatively, is expressly *not* apologetical, inasmuch as it is not about "the reasons we can muster" for either side, it achieves something quasi-apologetical nonetheless. It serves at least to level the playing field—which in the Academy today is hegemonically tilted toward unbelief—by claiming to show that the decision for unbelief is taken as much on the basis of an anticipatory confidence or a "leap of faith" as is the decision for belief.

To summarize this stage of our discussion, the foregoing paragraphs have sought to expand on a certain judgment made earlier regarding *A Secular Age* itself, especially with regard to the ambivalence or ambiguity that pervades it on so many levels. This judgment, as already intimated, is that far from manifesting a shortcoming or weakness of the book, the ongoing ambivalence can be viewed as a mark of its own implicit internal rigor and integrity, especially now as it orients itself methodologically around the most intensified expression of this ambivalence in the Jamesian open space. To put it differently, it is testimony to the integrity of Taylor's project as a whole that almost all of the methodological procedures of *A Secular Age* can in one way or another be seen to reflect this more "existential" Jamesian open stance.

It is therefore all the more puzzling and somewhat disappointing to witness the subsequent abandonment of the rigorously difficult and exacting way of the Jamesian open space—as the place of "full lucidity" within the "immanent frame" that has been worked toward with such diligence—in favor of the safer and broader path of a self-securing form of religious idealism. The signs of slippage away from the double-sided critical rigors of the Jamesian open space are evident in several ways, but most decisively so in the reversion to a "believing" spin (or conversely to a polemic against "unbelieving" spins) in telling the stories of the cross pressure, dilemmas, and unquiet frontiers as experienced in the immanent frame, instead of remaining resolutely within the Jamesian open space and allowing this to cut both ways or against both spins. In thus ultimately reverting back to the believing spin, Taylor misses a vital self-critical opportunity provided by the Jamesian open space, an oversight that will have important ramifications, especially for questions about appropriate orientations to transcendence.

In fact, one of the clearest signs that the Jamesian open space has been abandoned is the explicit and, for Taylor, indispensable alignment in the epilogue of his own Reform Master Narrative with the Intellectual Deviation narratives, despite the differences in the content of what the two are narrating, as explained above.[50] If there is any one point at which Taylor's own Jamesian open commitments must declare a definitive and decisive *departure* from the ID narratives, it is that these latter by definition know utterly nothing of the double-edged rigors and cross pressures of the Jamesian open space. They operate exclusively from within one "spin"—that of "belief"—and treat this presuppositionally precisely as "conclusive" or as "obvious, compelling, allowing for no caveat or demurral."[51] This becomes especially clear in Taylor's own primary example of ID theory in the "radical orthodoxy" of John Milbank. According to Milbank, the "unbelieving" exercise of reason—that is, any disciplined exercise of reason that is removed from what he sees as its necessary theological moorings—unavoidably reaches "nihilistic conclusions" and thus "brings itself . . . to its own end." For Milbank, it is only the believing exercise of reason as grounded in "theology [that] saves reason" and thereby also "fulfills and preserves philosophy."[52] Intellectual Deviation narratives, in other words, are full-blown polemical "subtraction stories" (in the opposite direction from Weber), as the name itself rightly suggests, in that they see everything that departs from the (often premodern-oriented) "open" or "believing" way as a deviation from this true way, or as a loss of the true way—that is, as subtraction.

What is the reason for this "slippage," or for the ultimate abandonment of the fully self-critical opportunity afforded by the Jamesian open space? More than anything, it is arguably once again the fear of losing the conceptually or analytically defined orientation to transcendence as an idealized "beyond," or, to use Taylor's term, a "Plato-type" beyond.[53] Indeed, a fundamental aspect of Taylor's polemic against Reform is precisely that, in his own words, it "narrows the gap" or "reduces the distance" between immanence and transcendence, or more exactly, between the immanence of human life and sources that transcend this life, in the sense of standing "beyond" it.[54] Taylor explicitly rejects any such "narrowing of the gap" as constituting a "loss" for a proper orientation to transcendence, or a forfeiture of the integrity of transcendence.[55]

But, as suggested above, there is a basic logical illusion at work in such a view of transcendence defined in terms of distance and gaps, an illusion that might have been avoided through a more consistent and rigorous application of the double-edged thrust of Taylor's own Jamesian open space. This illusion has long been recognized in theology, which, especially in any of its most rigorous apophatic exercises, has taken care not to be deceived by it. The point is that any attempt to preserve the integrity or "independence" of transcendence through the language of distance and gaps— that is, through the language of extensive magnitudes, whether quantitative or qualitative—is to define and measure the surpassingness of the transcendent precisely in terms of the immanent or "created" extensive magnitudes that it transcends. Genuine transcendence—when the demands of this are attended to with full rational rigor—"transcends" any of the magnitudinal elements that are by definition contained in any human or immanent consideration of distance, gaps, or beyondness.

## TRANSCENDENCE REVISITED

Let me expand somewhat on what is at issue here by borrowing from a discussion I have treated more fully elsewhere, drawing on Augustine's view on divine transcendence as expressed in *De Trinitate*.[56] In its most rigorous "fundamental" exercises, theology has always held that when it uses terms such as "unspeakability," "unthinkability," and "invisibility" to address God's transcendence, those terms do not mean exactly the same thing as what they denote in their normal usage. For God's invisibility is not merely an invisibility and unspeakability predicated on the *limitations* of human perceptual and conceptual capacities (i.e., as a transcendence and invisibility that merely exceeds or is "beyond" these as they reach their creaturely limits). To the contrary, as Augustine says, even if these capacities were able to be magnified to infinity, they would still be entirely unable to afford any glimpse of God in his transcendence.[57] In other words, that God in his transcendence *is* invisible and unthinkable does not mean that God is perceptually "too distant" to see by eyesight or indeed conceptually "too difficult" to comprehend by thinking, such that if these representationally cognitive capacities were infinitely greater, God might indeed become perceptually visible or conceptually apprehensible. It means rather that God is not an objectively apprehensible or objectively representable source *of any kind*—however "indeterminate" or however perfectly idealized—for cognition.

Again, this is something that the most rationally rigorous and consistent forms of apophatic theology have long recognized, as expressed aptly for our own context in Denys Turner's statement that, for a Christian understanding, God's transcendence may not be construed at all in "metaphors of 'gaps,' even infinitely 'big' ones." Drawing specifically again on Augustine's discussions on these matters, Turner speaks further of God's transcendence as being "*closer* to my creaturehood than it is possible for creatures to be to each other. For creatures are more distinct from each other than God [precisely in his transcendence of their creaturehood, and thus also his transcendence of their creaturely distance] can possibly be from any of them."[58]

But the disagreement here with Taylor's "Plato-type" or "Greek" distance-construal of transcendence (as opposed to that of the "Hebraic" and Christian understanding) is not only a logically grounded disagreement. It is also scripturally and (for Christianity) doctrinally grounded, inasmuch as Taylor's account stands quite fundamentally at odds with the Jewish and Christian teaching of "revelation," which is for both traditions the indispensable locus or site for any contentful or authoritatively meaningful consideration of divine transcendence. The point is that the transcendence made manifest in revelation is precisely not spoken of as a transcendence of distance, gaps, and remoteness, but as a transcendence of nearness. The revealed "Word" of the transcendent God is for Christianity expressed as Immanuel—God *with* us: "The Word became flesh, and dwelt among us, and we saw His glory, glory as of the only begotten from the

Father, full of grace and truth" (John 1:14). Likewise, for Judaism, the revealed transcendent Word of God is in Deuteronomy (and as echoed also in
Paul's letter to the Romans) described as follows: "It is not up in heaven, so
that you have to ask, 'Who will ascend into heaven to get it and proclaim it
to us so that we may obey it?' Nor is it beyond the sea, so that you have to
ask, 'Who will cross the sea to get it and proclaim it to us, so that we may
obey it?' No, the word is very near you; it is in your heart and in your mouth
that so that you may obey it" (Deut. 30:11–14; Rom. 10:6–7).

In this last passage we are presented with a new factor in the human encounter with transcendent sources, one that is surprisingly never broached
in *A Secular Age*—surprising especially because of Taylor's concern elsewhere with reinvigorating a proper understanding of practical reason in
current academic discussions, which he sees as often seriously flawed.[59]
The new factor here concerns a certain feature of the authority of the
"transcendent source" as presented in the foregoing passage. The transcendent source in this case (i.e., the word of God disclosed in the form of a
command or a summons to obedient action) addresses itself to humans
not as anything that evokes an "anticipatory *confidence*," which tips the
balance for the inhabitant of the Jamesian open space toward a greater
gut-level sense of a future-oriented plausibility of cognitive "belief," but
rather more simply, through the summons, as evoking the felt presence of
an *obligation* to enacted decision in the present. Or, more fully, the response of "faith" here, in the human "reception" of the revealed transcendent source, is not made manifest in the experience of a future-oriented or
anticipatory confidence that brings a kind of gut-level decrease in what
C. S. Peirce calls the "irritation of doubt," so as to make the "leap of faith"
something cognitively more secure or less precarious. Here, the belief of
faith is rather made manifest or experienced in the lived obedience of an
action that is demanded in the present, an action taken in the face of the
open unpredictability of what, cognitively speaking, looks like a risk.

Such a response of faith, as Dietrich Bonhoeffer, for example, also
sees it (in both his *Discipleship* and his *Ethics*), is also central to the Gospel
account of the revelation of Christ, especially as "belief" in Christ as a
"transcendent source" is here tied inalienably to the action of obedience
in response to Christ's command "follow me": "If anyone wishes to come
after Me, he must deny himself, and take up his cross daily and follow
Me" (Luke 9:23)

To amplify further what is at issue here, we can also refer to another volume that, like *A Secular Age*, grew out of the Gifford Lectures forty-two years prior, in 1957. I speak of the intrepid and rigorously reasoned writings of the important analytical philosopher and Anglican clergyman Austin Farrer, specifically of his book *The Freedom of the Will*, in which he states the following:

> As God himself [in his transcendence] is unimaginable, so also must be the dependence of his creatures on his power. And if this relation [ever] *appears* imaginable, we have reason to fear that we are viewing it unrealistically, and, as it were, from a great distance. The nearer we come to it, and the more we are [actually] involved in it, the less imaginable, the more paradoxical we shall find it to be. But what we lose in imaginative clarity is made up to us in actuality: just where we cease to *conceive* our dependence on God [or on "transcendent sources"], *we begin to live it.*

This is then summarized in the decisive statement, "Will, action, the creative moment in man, is the only object of consideration which ... promises to let through a single ray of uncreated light."[60]

Now, to speak of God's uncreated transcendence in this way, as not admitting of any qualification in terms of created "great distance," but rather as a nearness that is lived in action, does not of course mean that the revealed transcendence of God is *of* the natural created world. But neither can transcendence in this case be oriented to as anything "beyond" the natural world. It must rather, for Christian belief, be found only and nowhere else than *in* the natural world, since this is the indispensable "site" at which divine revelation discloses itself as a transcendent source.

What is called for in all of this, in other words, on both logical and religious grounds, is a fundamental realignment in how "transcendence" must be understood: that is, not as a possible cognitive point of reference for thinking (which would precisely make it something immanent). This is the view that *A Secular Age*, for all the important value of what it accomplishes otherwise, in the end still embraces: whether in its characterization of transcendence as a "Plato-like" beyond or in its almost matter-of-fact identification of the belief of faith with "theism."[61] For theism, by definition, brings God into a cognitive frame of reference, and therefore into immanence, by treating God as an idealized and thus objectified entity residing remotely in the abstract yet still immanent "heights" of a speculative "beyond," or at the highest of these heights. If we find we have no choice but to use the term *beyond*, then we should qualify it as Bonhoeffer did, by saying that "the beyond is not what is infinitely remote but what is nearest at hand."[62]

But more than this, if Farrer, along with Schleiermacher, Bonhoeffer, and others, is right that the human relation to transcendent sources and ultimately to God is a relation of dependence (which of course Taylor would also agree to); and if this dependence is itself not known or encountered as something conceived in thinking, but instead as something experienced and lived in bodily action, then this leads to a further important result. It means that to view the discoveries of modern science as contributing to a kind of coming-of-age through the removal of old superstitions need not be seen as a threat to the admissibility of belief in transcendent sources, but can rather work in the opposite direction.

Among recent theologians, Bonhoeffer has expressed this view most forcefully. Bonhoeffer not only sees advances in science and the consequent changes in philosophy as a natural outcome of the pursuit of their "integrity" as autonomous disciplines, and thus as contributing naturally to a "coming of age." He also actually welcomes the exclusion of "God" they entail, since the "God" they exclude is precisely the false god of speculative human ideals at the margins of human thinking, or beyond these margins. The banishment of this "God" is to be welcomed because it impels Christian thinking to refocus its attention in new and generative ways to where God's transcendence truly declares itself in revelation: at the center of life.

Whether or not we are able follow Bonhoeffer on his particular "coming of age" views, the basic underlying commitment to encountering God in his transcendence at the center of human life is not new; it goes back at least as far as Augustine's view that God in his transcendence is closer to creatures than creatures can possibly be to each other. It is easier to state this, however, than it is to expound it meaningfully, especially in our own age. Farrer is one Gifford Lecturer who has done this powerfully in the focus through action. Taylor's Jamesian open space likewise offers potentially important methodological opportunities for doing so, although not without a robust engagement with the subject of revelation. Contemporary theology would surely benefit, were Taylor to take up this subject.

Notes

1. Immanuel Kant, *Critique of Pure Reason*, trans. Paul Guyer and Allen W. Wood (Cambridge: Cambridge University Press, 1998), A709/B737.

2. Ibid.

3. Analytic philosophy, as A. C. Grayling rightly contends, is not really a "school," but rather a style or a method, specifically a method of meticulous rigor in conceptual analysis and inference. While it is true that this method led to certain well-known excesses in the logical positivism of the mid-twentieth century, the exacting methodological rigor it aimed for continues to be a hallmark and a great strength of analytic philosophy today.

4. Jacques Derrida, *Positions* (London: Continuum, 2004), 76, original emphasis.

5. Charles Taylor, *A Secular Age* (Cambridge, MA: Belknap Press, 2007), 22.

6. Charles Taylor, *Sources of the Self: The Making of the Modern Identity* (Cambridge, MA: Harvard University Press, 1989), 390.

7. See, e.g., Taylor, *Secular Age*, 13.

8. See, e.g., Taylor, *Sources of the Self*, 505; *Secular Age*, 768.

9. Taylor, *Sources of the Self*, 104.

10. Taylor, *Secular Age*, 3, 13.

11. Ibid., 29.

12. Charles Taylor, *Varieties of Religion Today* (Cambridge, MA: Harvard University Press, 2002), 43, 58.

13. Taylor, *Secular Age*, 16.

14. Ibid., 16, emphasis added.

15. Ibid., 10.

16. Ibid., 115.

17. Ibid., 25–26.

18. Ibid., 22.

19. Ibid., 575.

20. Ibid., 22.

21. Taylor, *Sources of the Self*, 104, 504.

22. Ibid., 104.

23. Ibid., 10, 520.

24. Taylor, *Secular Age*, 769, 737.

25. Ibid., 774–76.

26. Joseph Ratzinger, "Faith, Reason and the University, Memories and Reflections," Address at the University of Regensburg, 12 September 2006.

27. Taylor, *Secular Age*, 325.

28. Ibid., 549.

29. Ibid., 13.

30. Ibid., 325.

31. Ibid., 550.

32. Ibid., 171–72.

33. Ibid., 63.

34. Ibid., 61.

35. Ibid., 63.

36. Ibid., 613.

37. Ibid., 63.

38. Ibid., 27.

39. Ibid., 33, 35.

40. Ibid., 39, original emphasis.

41. Ibid., 551.

42. Ibid., 548–49, 544, 550.

43. Ibid., 549.

44. Ibid., 550.

45. Ibid., 549.

46. Ibid., 549.

47. Ibid., 550; emphasis added.

48. Ibid., 551.

49. Ibid., 551.

50. Despite the acknowledgment of these differences, Taylor concludes the book openly with the statement that the two are "complementary" and that "both ID and RMN [are needed] to explain religion today" (*Secular Age*, 773–76).

51. Taylor, *Secular Age*, 551.

52. John Milbank, "The Theological Critique of Philosophy in Hamann and Jacobi," in *Radical Orthodoxy*, John Milbank, Catherine Pickstock, and Graham Ward, eds. (London: Routledge, 1999), 37.

53. In a telling statement, which locates more exactly what he means by the orientation to "the highest" and "the best" in his original definition of transcendence in relation to aspirations to "fullness," Taylor asserts that "The Radical Orthodox are right that we need some sort of Plato-type understanding of what we are made for." Taylor, *Secular Age*, 775.

54. See, e.g., Taylor, *Secular Age*, 735–37.

55. Ibid., 737.

56. For the more extensive discussion of this, see my recent book, *The Command of Grace* (London : T&T Clark, 2009), 73–75.

57. Augustine, *On the Trinity*, vol. 3, book 8, chapter 2 (Cambridge: Cambridge University Press, 2002), 6.

58. Denys Turner, *Faith, Reason and the Existence of God* (Cambridge: Cambridge University Press, 2004), 214.

59. Charles Taylor, "Explanation and Practical Reason," in *Philosophical Arguments* (Cambridge, MA: Harvard University Press, 1995), 34–60.

60. Austin Farrer, *The Freedom of the Will* (London: Adam and Charles Black, 1958), 315, emphasis added.

61. See, e.g., Taylor, *Secular Age*, 550–51.

62. Dietrich Bonhoeffer, *Letters and Papers from Prison*, trans. Reginald Fuller (New York: Macmillan, 1972), 376.

## PART II

ONTOLOGY AND POLEMIC

# CHAPTER THREE

# Transcendent Sources and
# the Dispossession of the Self

CARLOS D. COLORADO

While there is little doubt that the publication of *A Secular Age* has positioned Charles Taylor at the center of many recent important discussions in religion, ethics, and politics, those familiar with his body of work are well aware that his contribution to the study of religion does not begin with this most recent book, and that *A Secular Age* is not Taylor's first project to emphasize religion. Indeed, *A Secular Age* represents the *culmination* of at least a decade's worth of research exploring a wide range of religious themes, including Trinitarianism and Catholicity as possible foundations for a pluralist politics; agape as the grounds for ethics as benevolence; and transcendence as the underpinnings for an entire corner of the "modern moral order." My focus here is largely on the last of these—the concept of transcendence as a moral source—but I will also gesture toward a relationship between transcendence, ethics, and politics in Taylor's body of work. I begin with the uncontroversial claim that transcendence is a constitutive element of Taylor's religious program. My approach here is to consider the role that transcendence plays in his wider moral philosophy as it is fleshed out across numerous works, beginning with his work on Hegel and culminating finally in *A Secular Age*. One of my central claims is that Taylor's conception of transcendence is dispossessive or "kenotic"—a term derived from the Greek *kénōsis*, or "emptying," which is employed most famously in Philippians 2:7.[1] My argument is that such a kenotic conception of transcendence—which as an "emptying" and dispossession resists the pursuit of power—animates Taylor's normative political vision and epistemology in ways that are attentive to the contemporary demands of pluralism.

As a point of departure, it is helpful to consider Stephen K. White's discussion of the basic shape of Taylor's moral ontology. In his important book *Sustaining Affirmation*, White argues that Taylor's philosophical program is best understood in terms of "weak ontology," which is to say that it recognizes its own *contestability* and its own *limits*. White suggests that though weak ontologists recognize that their formulations about the self, the other, and the world must always be tentative, they also "sense that such conceptualizations are nevertheless necessary or unavoidable for an adequate reflective ethical and political life." White contrasts these contestable weak ontologies with strong ontologies "that claim to show us 'the way the world is,' or how God's being stands to human being, or what human nature is." According to the strong ontologist, "It is by reference to this external ground that ethical and political life gain their sense of what is right; moreover, this foundation's validity is unchanging and of universal reach."[2] The ontological turn to weak articulations of both the kinds of realities that underwrite and the demands that animate our moral judgments and our conceptions of the good is significant on White's account for at least two fundamental reasons. First, ontologically weak conceptions of the self, the other, and the world escape the serious foundationalist problems that can plague strong ontology. And second, unlike modern accounts of the subject that conceptualize it as disengaged from any background—thus leading White to describe it as the "Teflon subject"—the weak ontological turn acknowledges the inescapability of ontological claims, insofar as they are necessary for a deep, rich, textured account of selfhood, otherness, and the good.[3] Unlike the Teflon subject, which strives for unimpeded "frictionless motion," weak ontology offers an account of subjectivity that is ultimately "stickier," wherein the self is inexorably shaped by a number of existential realities, including "language, mortality or finitude, natality or the capacity for radical novelty, and the articulation of some ultimate background source."[4] One could also include embodiment here as an inescapable feature of subjectivity, which as we will see below is significant for Taylor's discussion of enfleshment in *A Secular Age*.

White posits that what is critical for the weak ontological turn is a shift in the "how" rather than the "where" of ontological commitments. More fully, against the standard secularist line that establishes a spatial distinction of private and public spheres, White instead emphasizes the *manner* in which ontological commitments are articulated and enacted. And on this point, White asserts that the manner in which Taylor draws on his theism is ontologically weak—or, in Ruth Abbey's words, the classification of Taylor's theism as weak ontology "means that theism shapes and prefigures, but neither determines nor dictates, [Taylor's] political and ethical values."[5]

White acknowledges that there is something to the suspicion that the strong/weak distinction is but another iteration of familiar dualist distinctions such as metaphysical/antimetaphysical or foundational/antifoundational, but he argues that there is a subtle yet important difference between the two. The purpose of White's new terminological distinction of weak ontology is "to call greater attention to the kind of interpretive-existential terrain that anyone who places herself in the 'anti' position must explore at some point."[6] White sets out "to shift the intellectual burden here from a preoccupation with what is opposed and deconstructed, to an engagement with what must be articulated, cultivated, and affirmed in its wake."[7] Moreover, in addition to providing us with new terminology, he also presents a new set of methodological demands. Weak ontology must circumnavigate the philosophical pitfalls of metaphysics and foundationalism and thus offer only "figurations of [anthropological] universals, whose persuasiveness can never be fully disentangled from an interpretation of present historical circumstances."[8] Weak ontology does indeed provide modern agents with the means to discuss the good life and fullness, and to give an account of right behavior, political responsibility, and dignity—themes that are at the very center of Taylor's moral philosophy—but weak ontology does not proceed foundationally, seeking instead to remain fully

attentive to the place of individual judgment and historical embeddedness and the nonlinear (and not always easily discernible) relationship between ontological claims and political and ethical ones.

Interestingly, Abbey applauds White's analysis of Taylor's moral ontology, but states that she is not fully convinced that Taylor's theism, especially insofar as it constitutes a "foundation" for his pluralism, is not in fact
better understood as strong ontology.[9] Because Abbey is generally a careful reader of Taylor's work and an influential contributor to scholarship on
Taylor, her uncertainty about White's conclusions on this point warrants
further investigation. Thus, I will consider whether Taylor's pluralism in
fact emerges from a strong ontology. And, given the depiction of strong
ontology sketched out by White, according to which strong ontologists either ignore or deny the contestability or uncertainty involved in the passage "from ontological truths to moral-political ones," I would suggest that
a strong ontological source for Taylor's pluralism is potentially problematic.[10] Obviously, a strong foundationalist or overly programmatic ontology could indeed make Taylor's theism vulnerable to the charge that it
has deeply ideological and dogmatic components, thus raising questions
about the suitability of such a moral ontology as a point of departure for a
deeply pluralistic politics.[11] In order to explore whether the problematic
possibilities that issue from strong ontology in fact plague Taylor's religious
thought, I take up Abbey's insight about the relationship between Taylor's
theism—especially if it is seen as implying a strong ontology, as Abbey
suspects—and his commitment to pluralism. To that end, I will offer a
sketch of how Taylor's theistic commitments unfold within his larger project in ways that are not only fully reconcilable with his pluralism, but also
best understood in terms of weak ontology. This requires an exploration
of how Taylor's conception of transcendence plays a constructive moral
and anthropological, and not just ideological, role in his moral and political program, and an account of how the kenotic structure of his theism
calls into question the possessive movements of strong ontology.

One of the ultimate objectives of this chapter is an analysis of Taylor's
moral ontology, but it is important to note that his conception of the good
is inextricable from his philosophical anthropology. Thus, it is prudent
and necessary first to consider his discussion of selfhood because of the
extent to which his moral theory is founded on the premise that our conceptions of the self and the good are deeply implicated in one another.

## Expressivism, Articulation, and the Good

A principal thesis in *Sources of the Self* concerns the ways in which the modern self emerges centrally from three sources comprising the modern moral order: naturalism, expressivism, and theism.[12] Naturalism—which holds that the human is best understood in scientific, instrumentalist, atomistic terms—often functions as a hegemony, consistently accorded as it is a de facto or paradigmatic status in the defining of models by which to understand the human.[13] On Taylor's reading of the modern moral order, this "stripped-down" scientistic perspective by itself is unable to meet the self's intrinsic need for a wide range of strong moral sources while simultaneously giving an overly narrow account of subjectivity. Notably, until the relatively recent religious turn in his work—which becomes most explicit, I would suggest, with *A Catholic Modernity?*—Taylor's main overt opposition to naturalism has been articulated in terms of expressivism, which is a conception of human subjectivity rooted in the thought of Rousseau, Goethe, Humboldt, and Hegel, but which finds its clearest expression for Taylor in Herder. It stresses that the human subject reaches its highest potentialities through acts of expression that are irreducible to scientific objectification.[14] For Taylor, the modern subject is self-defining and can only fully know her nature by articulating or *expressing* that which exists within—the subject's "inner voice."

Taylor's attraction to expressivism, as mentioned, is at least partly motivated by his view that naturalist moral sources alone render a dangerously shallow account of human subjectivity, and that the expressivist constellation of sources serves as an important corrective to dominant naturalistic anthropologies. Correlatively, Herder's expressivism is perhaps best understood as a reaction against the conventional naturalistic anthropological account of the Enlightenment. This Enlightenment anthropology, which continues to exert significant influence today, has had a tendency, historically, to objectify human nature, to partition the human mind into discrete (and often opposing) faculties, and to envision the human as instrumentally rational, independent of emotion and will.[15] As Taylor succinctly puts it, Herder's expressivism "can be seen as a protest against the mainstream Enlightenment view of man—as both subject and object of an objectifying scientific analysis."[16] The Enlightenment model of self-defining subjectivity is characterized by a tendency to objectify the world of phenomena and, correspondingly, to stress the dichotomy of subject and object. This dualism, Taylor argues, essentially prohibits any conceptions such as "meaning," "expression," and "purpose" from being used as descriptors for objective reality, since such notions tend to be understood purely noetically, restricted to the mind of the human subject.[17] Expressivism, on the other hand, can be seen as an attempt to generate a renewed anthropology that allows for meaning, purpose, and expression beyond the *mental* life of human subjects. The central idea in expressivism is that human life is fundamentally the *realization* of a *self* and of purpose through unique acts of expression. In Taylor's words, expressivism "added the epoch-making demand that my realization of the human essence be my own, and hence launched the idea that each individual (and in Herder's application, each people) has its own way of being human, which it cannot exchange with that of any other except at the cost of distortion and self-mutilation."[18] Herderian expressivism maintains that humans are able to reach their "highest fulfillment in expressive activity," and this enables human lives to be conceptualized narratively as "expressive [unities]."[19] The expressivist view of subjectivity attempts to unite the human with the natural world, rejecting the Cartesian bifurcation of mind and body in favor of a conception of subjectivity as an expressive unity. By rejecting this dualism, expressivism resists the Cartesian objectification of nature and the body. Expressivism recognizes that subjective expression requires the context of *nature* to be actualized and that the relationship between embodied humans and the natural world must be understood in terms of complementary expressivity.[20]

For Taylor, it is only through an understanding of the historical significance of expressivism that we can begin to come to grips with the philosophical roots of our moral commitment to ideals such as authenticity, individualism, and creative expression. Taylor also traces how particular dispensations of expressive individuation contribute to the relatively recent turn to the often shallow "ethics of authenticity."[21] In these more shallow modalities of expressivity, one's own way of being or "measure" may be reduced to choices about style or fashion that are "expressed" largely through consumptive activity—purchasing the fashions that say something about who I am, driving a certain automobile because it communicates something about my aesthetic sensibilities as well as my affluence (or refusal to pursue affluence, as the case may be), and so on. But what should be emphasized here is that Taylor perceives a very *deep, powerful* animating moral force at the heart of the expressive account of human subjectivity, whereas what is encountered in the more shallow modes of the ethics of authenticity, though they emerge from expressivism, represents a degeneracy of the original ideal as articulated by the likes of Herder. Taylor's study of expressivism helps to uncover the foundational and inescapable role that language, interpretation, and articulation play in ontological accounts of the human. And, according to Taylor's chronicle of the development of modern selfhood, these anthropological categories are entirely inescapable for moderns and must be at the center of any anthropological account that seeks to be meaningful to the modern subject. Expressivity, with its fundamental ideals of interpretation and articulation, must be given serious consideration in any attempts at a full account of the modern subject.

Influenced as it is by expressivism, Taylor's own philosophical anthropology is deeply hermeneutical and illuminates the centrality of interpretation and self-understanding as the means for humans to access and cultivate meaning. This hermeneutical stance assumes "that our interpretation of ourselves is constitutive of what we are, and therefore cannot be considered as merely a view on reality, separable from reality, nor as an epiphenomenon, which can be by-passed in our understanding of reality."[22] And predictably, given the focus on meaning, articulation, interpretation, and self-understanding, the philosophy of language (following Herder) is central to Taylor's own anthropological account. Herder's linguistic theory emphasizes that words do not simply represent and designate the objects that they identify, because language must be recognized fundamentally as the means by which a human subject reflects on the world and simultaneously a medium through which she expresses herself. Meaning is generated through interpretation, and the hermeneutical stance cannot be understood in terms of a simple linearity, for there is no obvious direct line between an object of meaning and an interpreting subject.[23] Interpretation relies on the webs of interlocution that provide the subject with the intersubjective languages and frameworks required to make sense of the world, to interpret the world's significance and meaning for the self.

Indeed, one can accordingly approach *Sources of the Self* as Taylor's own articulation, his "best account," of the nature of moral consciousness for modern subjects. His articulation begins genealogically, through a historical recovery and reclamation, and thus Taylor understands *Sources* to be a regenerative work aimed at reviving the articulacy of often disregarded (but still powerful and necessary) modern moral sources—and surely an analogous methodology is employed in *A Secular Age*.[24] The process of articulation is for Taylor both imperative and inescapable if moderns wish to avoid the descent into either a psychopathological or a nihilistic abyss. According to Taylor, moral inarticulacy can cause us to "lose all contact with the good, however conceived," and through this loss of contact we "would cease to be human."[25] Articulation is a constitutive part of moral consciousness, a basic feature of the human condition, but Taylor also contends that the gravity of the process of articulation is qualitatively different for moderns in their quest for meaning than it was for our premodern predecessors, since the latter faced a "fundamentally different existential predicament." A paradigmatic example here (for Taylor) is Martin Luther, whose "intense anguish and distress before his liberating moment of insight about salvation through faith" was a consequence of a "sense of inescapable condemnation, irretrievably damning himself through the very instruments of salvation, the sacraments. However one might want to describe this, it was not a crisis of meaning. This term would have made no sense to Luther in its modern use."[26] Taylor observes that the widespread experience of meaninglessness within modernity has been accompanied by a perhaps not unrelated shift in the "dominant patterns of psychopathology"—from disorders of phobia, hysteria, and fixation to afflictions characterized by "'ego loss,' or a sense of emptiness, flatness, futility, lack of purpose, or loss of self-esteem."[27] Taylor does not map out any direct links between this shift in pathological patterns and the historical variation in existential predicaments, but he does suggest that it is "overwhelmingly plausible a priori that there is some relation; and that the comparatively recent shift in style of pathology reflects the generalization and popularization in our culture of that 'loss of horizon.'"[28] The palpable increase in the pathologies of ego loss makes the work of articulation even more urgent on Taylor's account, since powerful and illuminative articulations of our moral sources represent important bulwarks against the nihilistic slide that has become widespread in modernity.

Taylor's moral philosophy, as we see most clearly in *Sources of the Self*, revolves around a moral ontology, an account of the "background picture which underlies our moral intuitions," and his analysis of the structure of these sorts of undergirding realities leads him to a discussion of the "frameworks which articulate our sense of orientation in the space of questions about the good."[29] Taylor underscores the importance of our moral intuition as a point of access to the moral sources that in turn shape the "inescapable frameworks" or "horizons" that enable us to find our moral bearings, giving us a sense of where we stand in relation to the good. In Taylor's words, "we should treat our deepest moral instincts, our ineradicable sense that human life is to be respected, as our mode of access to the world in which ontological claims are discernible and can be rationally argued about and sifted."[30] In other words, an account of the good is preceded by a moral intuition of a source that has a hold on us. Throughout *A Secular Age*, Taylor points out how the moral significance of these gut responses is poignantly exemplified in the Gospels, wherein Jesus "is portrayed as being moved 'in the bowels' by compassion (*splangnizesthai*)."[31] An analogous depiction is found in the Gospel of Luke, where Jesus's parable of the good Samaritan depicts a love that is enacted out of pity, a moral discernment that has visceral, intuitive roots: "Agape moves outward from the guts."[32]

This intuitionist depiction in the Gospels is important for Taylor as it relates to the grounds for ethical pluralism. The fact that one's access to the sources that animate and sustain enactments of Christian love is situated within *intuition*, "in the guts," means that such moral truths exceed any single account (though exceptionality and exclusivity may often be claimed), since moral intuition cannot be located within a single perspective or discourse—it cannot be captured by a rule or a code. Instead, a moral intuition's hold on a moral agent is fleshed out and given increased power through the process of articulation in a *best* account *amongst a pluriformity of others*. Notably, it does not follow from this that we cannot talk about correctness; indeed, the articulation that more correctly expresses, illuminates, formulates, or makes sense of an intuited moral source should be talked about as the *best* (or, at least, a *better*) account. Taylor's formulation assumes a plurality of accounts, all of which are better or worse at correctly articulating a particular vision of the good, but it also assumes that even the worst account can say *something*, however inchoately, about the sources that animate it. But it is the *best account* that illuminates the good most fully or clearly for us, and such an account is best precisely in terms of its correctness and its power to move us.

It should be clear in light of the foregoing discussion that Taylor does not talk about moral goods independent of the ways in which they are experienced and articulated by subjects. However, this does not mean that Taylor is some sort of Humean subjectivist, for he does not believe that our moral judgments are simply statements of approbation and disapprobation. Taylor acknowledges that expressivism and the ethics of authenticity, as well as post-Romantic art, consist of a high degree of self-reflexivity and a slide to "subjectivation," but he also distinguishes between a subjectivation of "manner" and a subjectivation of "matter" and argues that a movement toward one does not ipso facto imply a movement toward the other.[33] Similarly, Taylor often talks about our assessments of moral sources in terms of "strong evaluation," wherein our moral judgments comprise "discriminations of right or wrong, better or worse, higher or lower, which are not rendered valid by our own desires, inclinations, or choices, but rather stand independent of these and offer standards by which they can be judged."[34] Strong evaluation, for Taylor, centers on the assertion that moral goods are "normative for desire"—that "they are seen as goods which we ought to desire, even if we do not, goods such that we show ourselves up as inferior or bad by our not desiring them."[35]

One can at this point understand the suggestion that such destinations can indeed *seem* to be pointing to a strong ontology. But I want to suggest instead that careful attention must be paid to the unique character of Taylor's theism here. For it is in fact his grounding of all of this in a particular kind of theism that shows that it need not entail a strong ontology, against which the kind of pluralism he is advocating would be undermined.

## THE CATHOLIC ROOTS OF TAYLOR'S PLURALISM

As Abbey rightly points out, the creationist nature of Judaism, Christianity, and Islam contributes to the substructure of Taylor's ontological moral pluralism.[36] Taylor asserts that one of the most significant discernments of Abrahamic monotheism is "that God as creator himself affirms life and being, expressed in the very first chapter of Genesis in the repeated phrase: 'and God saw that it was good.'"[37] It is because life is good that martyrdom is sacrificial—a fundamental part of the witness of the martyr is the dispossession of life itself, an unfathomable good given up in love and obedience. Taylor outlines how this basic fact of the goodness of life distinguishes the death of Jesus from the death of Socrates, regardless of the comparisons that abound. Taylor suggests that Socrates's death represents no real loss for the Platonic protagonist. It is for this reason that Socrates's last words have him asking Crito to pay a debt to Asclepius, the god of healing. The implication is that, for Socrates, "life is an illness of which death is the cure."[38] The Socratic death scene is incompatible with Christ's anguish in Gethsemane. As Taylor puts it, "Jesus suffers agony of soul in the garden, and is driven to despair on the cross, when he cries, 'Why hast thou forsaken me?' At no point in the passion is he serene and untroubled."[39] Whereas the Socratic or Stoic renunciation of life is a renouncing of something that is external to the good, the Christian renunciation of life in martyrdom, exemplified in Jesus's cruciform sacrifice, endorses as a valuable good the very life that is being relinquished. Taylor argues that the surrendering of life by Christian martyrs gives rise to the paradox that "Christian renunciation is an affirmation."[40] Moreover, it is because creation is good for Jew, Christian, and Muslim that these religious traditions must also affirm the pluriformity that characterizes creation. The very nature of creation in its diversity demands an attunement to difference, since this heterogeneity is constitutive of the creation that God affirms as good in Genesis.

In addition to this creationist influence, Taylor's pluralism is also guided by his Trinitarianism, and it is his discussion of the Trinity that represents the most explicitly Christian formulation of how (Christian) transcendence implies pluralism. In *A Catholic Modernity?* Taylor underscores how the Greek *katholou* "compris[es] both universality and wholeness; one might say universality through wholeness," and that this dual nature of Catholicity enjoins Catholics, and presumably all Christians, to resist the coercive and often violent drive toward univocity, which "strive[s] to make over other nations and cultures to fit it."[41] This formulation of universality through wholeness has clear resonances with his discussion of the goodness of creation, but it is the correlation that Taylor traces out in this lecture between Catholicity (comprising universality and wholeness) and the way in which humans are created in *imago dei* that is of present interest. According to Taylor, "unity-across-difference, as against unity-through-identity, seems the only possibility for us, not just because of the diversity among humans, starting with the difference between men and women and ramifying outward. . . . [It] seems that the life of God itself, understood as trinitarian, is already a oneness of this kind. Human diversity is part of the way in which we are made in the image of God."[42] So, just as Father, Son, and Holy Spirit are a relationality *and* a unity, so paradoxically, or perhaps better put, *mysteriously*, do humans embody simultaneously both diversity and unity.

This Trinitarian conception of human relationality adds a compatible theistic element to Taylor's wider anthropology, insofar as both imply a multiplicity of individual and cultural expressions.[43] This notion of the triunity of the Godhead as a referent for human unity-across-difference also ramifies into Taylor's more communitarian formulations of what it is to have a social existence characterized by fullness. Taylor's Trinitarianism implies a deep pluralism (especially combined with the pluriformity of expressions that follow from his anthropology), but as the following quotation suggests, it also places our access to the good life in our communal nature: "When you get to the point of seeing that what is important in human life is what passes between us, then you are coming close to the Trinity. It is not so surprising that the fullness of human life is what passes between humans, if the fullness of divine life is what passes between persons, and we are made in God's image."[44] So Taylor's Catholicism supplies him with yet another anthropological fortification against the monological conceptions of the human that are presumed in most atomistic sociopolitical accounts.

Furthermore, in addition to the communitarian implications of this formulation, it would seem that there is also a powerful link here between Taylor's Trinitarian perspective and his expressivism. Just as Father, Son, and Spirit are not *things,* but are constituted by the *way* they relate to each other in love, so too human beings constituted *expressively* represent a sort of "passing between" (between selves, between selves and nature, etc.) that reflects the Trinitarian relationality. Thus, in the foregoing discussion, we see how Taylor's theistic commitments complement, or perhaps more precisely *help shape* (ontologically), his understanding of modern pluralism while also contributing to a sociopolitical vision alternative to those radical individualist accounts that envision society as a fragmented conglomerate of self-interested individuals bound together by some sort of contractual obligation.

My argument is that there is a compelling case that Taylor's normative moral vision is best categorized as weak ontology. Taylor himself asserts that the sorts of "qualitative distinctions" that we make when we consider how the self is oriented in moral space inevitably produce "contestable answers to inescapable questions," a formulation that echoes very clearly White's description of the tendencies of weak ontology.[45] Still, at least on first glance, Taylor's utilization of theistic arguments, and in particular his Trinitarian formulation, seems to fall within the realm of strong ontology. Recall White's definition of strong ontology quoted at the opening of this chapter: "Strong are those ontologies that claim to show us 'the way the world is,' or how God's being stands to human being, or what human nature is." Surely, *when taken on its own*, Taylor's account of how our being created in the image of God leads to the twofold claim that unity-through-diversity is the only available option, and that the fullness of human life is to be found in what passes between humans, seems to meet the basic criteria of strong ontology. However, his theistic formulations must be contextualized within his wider anthropological and moral vision. He consistently discusses Christianity and scripture, and even theism in general, as a best account of what it is to be human and to live the good life, an account that issues forth from the hermeneutical stance and that takes history seriously.[46] White surely has philosophies like Taylor's in mind when he ascribes "deep historical interpretation and existential analytic" to weak ontology.[47] Thus, Taylor's Catholicism also seems to meet the requirements of weak ontology when it is taken in the larger context of his moral ontology.[48]

Surely, it is because of these kinds of textures in Taylor's philosophy that White's early work described Taylor as a "border runner between strong and weak ontology."[49] After all, Christian theism does provide Taylor with the formulation that the diversity-cum-unity of social life reflects how we are created in God's image, although Taylor's hermeneutical and historical sensibilities (central as they are to his moral ontology and anthropology) would seem to anchor his ontology on the weak side of the spectrum. However, more needs to be said about how Taylor conceptualizes transcendence as a moral source before we can correctly come to any judgment here, because, as I will suggest, a "weak" notion of transcendence lies at the very center of Taylor's religious ethics. This conception of transcendence will be described as weak, both because it is attentive to the demands of religious pluralism and because it is kenotic or dispossessive in form.

One of Taylor's fuller descriptions of transcendence is found in *A Catholic Modernity?*, where the transcendent is identified as being "beyond life." The reality of transcendence means that

> the point of things isn't exhausted by life, the fullness of life, even the goodness of life. This is not meant to be a repudiation of egoism, the idea that the fullness of my life (and perhaps those of people I love) should be my only concern. Let us agree with John Stuart Mill that a full life must involve striving for the benefit of all humankind. Then acknowledging the transcendent means seeing a point beyond that. One form of this is the insight that we can find in suffering and death—not merely negation, the undoing of fullness and life, but also a place to affirm something that matters beyond life, on which life itself originally draws. . . . What matters beyond life doesn't matter just because it sustains life; otherwise it wouldn't be 'beyond life' in the meaning of the act.[50]

While this formulation has deep resonances with Taylor's Catholicism, it is also compatible with accounts of the transcendent beyond orthodox Christian ones. Some branches of Buddhism might take issue with the notion that the transcendent is something "on which life itself originally draws," which on first glance is suggestive of some form of creative force, prime mover, or even deity—formulations that do not obviously resonate with many Buddhist notions of transcendence, especially as they are articulated within the Theravada tradition. But we need only think of how Emmanuel Levinas, for example, talks about transcendence in a way that is not obviously theistic, but which has some correspondence with Taylor's formulation as it is presented in this passage. For Levinas, it is through the encounter with transcendence through the face of the other that the ego or self is put into question, "call[ing] the freedom of the ego] to responsibility and found[ing] it."[51] Though the ego itself does not find its origins in the encounter with the face, it is the irreducibility of the face of the other that opens "a new dimension," that of the ethical, thereby establishing the self in freedom and responsibility.[52] As such, the "moral summons" of the face-to-face encounter brings about the establishment of a new "life," the *ethical* life, and thus Levinas's conception of transcendence resonates with Taylor's, demonstrating that the formulation Taylor offers is not limited to explicitly theistic accounts.[53]

A further point regarding Taylor's formulation and how it corresponds to Buddhism concerns the relation with the Millian exaltation of the "fullness of life" alluded to in the passage quoted above. Arguably, the calculative nature of the utilitarian perspective, especially as it understands itself to be concerned with pure immanence, must find mere disutility both in the cruciform sacrifice of Jesus and the self-immolation of Buddhist monks, nuns, and laypeople seeking Buddhahood through an overcoming of enfleshment. This has to be the case because the immanentist utilitarian move that brackets off everything that does not contribute to the fullness of life understood immanently cannot recognize any good or utility in selfless sacrifice or the "somatic path" to enlightenment that becomes possible through self-immolation.[54] Within the Christian perspective, the recognition of the transcendent as it is present in Jesus opens up the possibility for an understanding of both how Incarnation and crucifixion call the fullness of life into question and how, through that calling into question, they actually affirm the fullness of life through cruciform love. Viewed through the calculative utilitarian lens, the gospel ethic, according to which our access to the highest form of love is found in self-sacrifice, is nonsensical. Similarly, the historical practice of self-immolation within Buddhism turns the economy of utility on its head, but the encounter with ultimate reality, with the transcendent, as one reaches enlightenment makes possible a life of *metta* and *karuna*, as we see most saliently in the figure of the Bodhisattva.[55]

Taylor argues that Buddhism and Christianity present us with complementary notions of how an encounter with transcendence initiates a decentering movement away from the self or atman that leads to an inevitable return to immanence that upholds human flourishing. So, even though the structure of the moral source in each of these traditions may vary, Taylor underscores that diverse transcendent sources can motivate us, move us, to the dispossession of the self, or kenosis, that Taylor holds is vitally important for practical agape. He describes this dispossessive movement as "acknowledging the transcendent means being called to a change of identity. Buddhism gives us an obvious reason to talk this way. The change here is quite radical, from self to 'no self' (*anatta*). But Christian faith can be seen in the same terms: as calling for a radical decentering of the self, in relation with God. ('Thy will be done.')"[56]

Taylor's basic point is that the radical decentering of the self through an encounter with transcendence initiates both an "aiming beyond life" and the opening of the self to a "change in identity." This movement can have vital ethical implications for how the decentered self understands immanence and human flourishing. Taylor acknowledges that there are many examples of "reformers" in most religious traditions who have denied the potentially "symbiotic, complementary relationship between renunciation and flourishing" and thus have pursued renunciation "disintricated from the pursuit of flourishing."[57] However, Taylor argues that this disintrication cuts against the grain of the "central thrust" of religions such as Christianity and Buddhism. In these two religious traditions, "Renouncing— aiming beyond life—not only takes you away but also brings you back to flourishing. In Christian terms, if renunciation decenters you in relation with God, God's will is that humans flourish, and so you are taken back to an affirmation of this flourishing, which is biblically called agape. In Buddhist terms, Enlightenment doesn't just turn you from the world; it also opens the floodgates of *metta* (loving kindness) and *karuna* (compassion)."[58]

Contra those critiques of religious life, which hold that the acknowledgment of transcendence results in a negation of life, the kenotic decentering of the self does not simply aim beyond life, but actually lays the grounds for a reinvigoration of human flourishing through practical agape, enacted in charity and ethics as benevolence. It is this kind of response to self-dispossession that Taylor's ethics emphasize, since after all even Nietzsche's philosophy has a kenotic component, but with a different response. The use of kenotic language is no clearer in Nietzsche than at the beginning of *Thus Spoke Zarathustra*, where the Nietzschean protagonist exclaims, "'This cup wants to become empty again, and Zarathustra wants to become man again.' Thus Zarathustra began to go under."[59] And nowhere in Nietzsche is the emptying and decentering more climactic than in Zarathustra's affirmation of the eternal recurrence, in which Zarathustra affirms the perpetual return of the last man. Through this decentering act, Zarathustra renounces a vital part of himself—his affinity for strength, which is manifested in his loathing of the banality of the last man—but this renunciation is essential for him to relate himself properly to eternity and thereby to become the creator, the child who "lusts after eternity." But whereas Taylor's formulation of the decentering move that precedes agape is a response in *obedience*—"Thy will be done"—Nietzsche's "kenosis" manifests itself not in obedience, but in resolute, violent, *autonomous* willing. This is in stark contrast to Taylor, who is not concerned with the moral import of all kinds of self-dispossession, but rather with self-emptying and self-abnegation that is a response *in obedience manifested in love of the neighbor*. The decentering of the self before God makes possible an obedient response in love to the radical unconditionality of the fact that the neighbor is created in *imago dei*.[60] Thus, unlike the Nietzschean perspective that affirms the strength of the human and advocates the destruction of the weak, Taylor affirms the alternative "pattern" found in the philanthropy of Mother Theresa and Jean Vanier.[61] Taylor suggests that the careers of both exemplify models of benevolence moved by agape, and that these agapeic models stand in stark contrast to those ethical models that hinge on the vitality or potentialities of the other—these latter, in other words, affirm the other *conditionally*.[62] For Taylor, the agapeic model opens up a comportment to the other that reaches out to the other even (or perhaps, *especially*) in the other's brokenness. Taylor asserts that Christian love prompts "us to extend help to the irremediably broken, such as the mentally handicapped, those dying without dignity, fetuses with genetic defects"—a claim with which Nietzsche would contemptuously agree.[63]

We also find a kenotic formulation of transcendence in *A Secular Age*. Consider the following portrayal from Taylor of the transformative power of cruciform transcendence, which captures once again the important role of kenosis in his religious thought:

> Now Christ's reaction to the resistance [to God] was to offer *no counter-resistance*, but to continue loving and offering. This love can go to the very heart of things, and open a road even for the resisters. . . . Through this *loving submission*, violence is turned around, and instead of breeding counter-violence in an endless spiral, can be transformed. A path is opened of *non-power*, limitless *self-giving*, full action, and infinite openness. On the basis of this initiative, the incomprehensible healing power of this suffering, it becomes possible for human suffering, even of the most meaningless type, to become associated with Christ's act,

and to become a locus of renewed contact with God, an act which heals the world. The suffering is given a transformative effect, by being offered to God.[64]

Obviously this passage is Taylor's Christian iteration of love as kenotic, whereas the formulation in *A Catholic Modernity?* is more straightforwardly pluralist, toggling back and forth between Buddhism and Christianity. But as Taylor explicitly asserts in that essay, his aspiration is to say something about transcendence that goes beyond the Christian.[65] Arguably, that same pluralist aspiration underlies the more prescriptive portions of *A Secular Age* as well, including especially his affirmation of Illich's critique of nomolatry, the modern fetishization of rules. A central significance of the parable of the Good Samaritan and the gut reaction is that the enfleshed character of agape means that it cannot be contained by a single discourse. Because of the moral intuition's locus in the body, we can recognize its importance for a kind of human normativity. Since the moral response described in the Samaritan (*splangnizesthai*) is bodily—in "the gut," a site that is universal for all moral agents—it would seem to follow that no single theological account can fully capture all that the parable illuminates. Christianity cannot claim sole proprietorship in this regard, though the example of Jesus—for Taylor and for all Christians—may be understood to disclose something unique and fundamental about what it is to love thy neighbor, an agapeic movement that is necessarily self-emptying. So while charity and kenosis are central components of Taylor's best account (which centers around his Catholicism), their inclusion is not a consequence of Christian triumphalism, but rather a concern about what is owed to the other—and my suggestion here is that his formulation of transcendence is not only kenotic—self-dispossessive—but also attentive to the rigorous demands of religious pluralism.

In light of the foregoing discussion of the kenotic nature of transcendence, which I would argue resides at the very center of Taylor's religious ethics, my suggestion is that it is not possible to understand Taylor's moral enterprise properly in terms of a strong ontology, insofar as Christian kenosis is by definition "weak," *dispossessive* of "being," always giving itself up, never seeking power. Indeed, if the "universal" and transcendent normativity it claims to express can be called ontological at all, then it must be called a "weak" ontology. Such an ontological formulation is difficult to reconcile with those strong ontologies that "carry an underlying assumption of certainty that guides the whole problem of moving from the ontological level to the moral-political," the kinds of strong ontology that share a filiation with and often animate those self-assured religious movements that seek to make over the *saeculum* to fit their particular normative understanding of how things ought to be.[66] Surely, on Taylor's account, such Constantinian modes of making over the world should be given a wide berth. Our situatedness in the world, in history, does not allow us to claim this kind of exceptionalism: "My community, my history, exceptional models, and my own reflection, have all combined to offer me a language in which I make sense of all this" *in a best account*.[67] But an equally important point for the present discussion is the nature of Constantinianism, which runs against the grain of transcendence as kenosis. Taylor's vision of the good, insofar as it is centrally animated by a kenotic conception of transcendence, cannot lay the groundwork for any kind of discourse that seeks power—as strong, foundationalist ontologies often tend to do. And though what might be called "discursive Constantinianism" may seem less overtly political than the actual making over of the world by governments, militaries, and other institutions, the discursive modality of the Constantinian must be recognized as an attempt to seek coercive power over other discourses. Such an agonistic battle of ideologies is arguably a part of any Constantinian activity, but surely kenotic moral sources, which resist power and instead seek abasement and love of neighbor, cannot be the sources for such an ideological striving for possession. Taylor's moral philosophy is not motivated by any kind of Constantinian triumphalism, but is interested instead in carving out the ontological space (in a "weak" mode) necessary for moderns to function as moral beings. For Taylor, this means resuscitatively bringing "the air back again into the half-collapsed lungs of the spirit" through a rearticulation of the transcendent sources that move us. As I have suggested here, both the *mode* in which Taylor talks about transcendence and the *nature* of the transcendent source that Taylor draws from in his best account are compatible with the political demands of pluralism and the ontological demands of a postfoundationalist world. Given the importance of language for Taylor's account—including especially how language is so important for his anthropology—the way in which we talk about the good, transcendence, and moral sources is cru-cially important. If the good is dispossessing, then it would follow that our articulations of the good be similarly dispossessive. Thus it seems to be the case that Taylor, for not only philosophical, anthropological, and method-ological, but also *theological* reasons, would want to underscore the *how* of weak ontology.[68] The demands of weak ontology require a similitude of word and deed, with the form of both reflecting the contestability of weak ontology.

## Notes

A version of this paper was presented at the 2009 Society of Christian Ethics Annual Meeting in Chicago, Illinois. I thank Ruth Abbey, P. Travis Kroeker, and Paul D. Janz for their comments on the version I presented in Chicago.

1. In the NRSV translation, the passage reads: Jesus "*emptied* himself, taking the form of a slave, being born in human likeness" (emphasis added).

2. Stephen K. White, *Sustaining Affirmation: The Strengths of Weak Ontology in Political Theory* (Princeton: Princeton University Press, 2000), 6–8.

3. There is an obvious connection between White's Teflon subject and the Carte-sian disengaged subject and the Lockean "punctual" self discussed throughout *Sources of the Self*, as well as the "buffered self" of *A Secular Age*. See Charles Taylor, *Sources of the Self: The Making of the Modern Identity* (Cambridge, MA: Harvard University Press, 1989), 49, 143–76, 320; Charles Taylor, *Hegel* (Cambridge: Cambridge University Press, 1975), 6–7; and Charles Taylor, *A Secular Age* (Cambridge, MA: Belknap Press, 2007), esp. 37–42, 134–42, 300–7. See also White, *Sustaining Affirmation*, 4–5.

4. Stephen K. White, "Weak Ontology: Genealogy and Critical Issues," *The Hedgehog Review* 7, no. 2 (Summer 2005): 17; White, *Sustaining Affirmation*, 9.

5. Ruth Abbey, "Turning or Spinning? Charles Taylor's Catholicism: A Reply to Ian Fraser," *Contemporary Political Theory* 5 (2006): 172. See also Ruth Abbey, "Pri-mary Enemy? Monotheism and Pluralism," in *How Should We Talk about Religion?*, ed. James White (Notre Dame, IN: University of Notre Dame Press, 2006), 211–29.

6. White, *Sustaining Affirmation*, 8.

7. Ibid.

8. Ibid., 9. It is worth noting that Ruth Abbey suggests that Taylor also offers a set of anthropological universals. See her chapter on selfhood in *Charles Taylor* (Prince-ton: Princeton University Press, 2000).

9. Abbey, "Turning or Spinning?," 172–73. Though Abbey discusses White's in-terpretation of Taylor in earlier work, it is only in her more recent reply to Fraser that she casts doubt on whether Taylor's theism is in fact best understood as weak ontology.

In that more recent work her critique runs as follows: "While White's supple analysis of the role of theism in Taylor's thought is highly illuminating, it seems to either overlook or accord insufficient attention to the powerful link between Taylor's theism and his pluralism. Once a theistic ontology appears as the foundation for pluralism, at least in certain important respects, we might find ourselves back in the land of strong ontology, according to which there is a clear and direct relationship between ontological claims and ethical prescriptions. Perhaps what Taylor offers is a strong ontology with important pluralist components that issues in an ethics and politics with important pluralist components." Abbey, "Turning or Spinning," 172–73.

10. White, *Sustaining Affirmation*, 6.

11. It is worth underscoring that Abbey does not suggest anywhere in her work that the relationship between ethics and (strong) ontology in Taylor is problematic. I thank Abbey for her clarification on this point.

12. Taylor, *Sources of the Self*, 495–521.

13. Charles Taylor, *Human Agency and Language: Philosophical Papers 1* (Cambridge: Cambridge University Press, 1985), 2.

14. See Taylor, *Hegel*, 13–29; and Charles Taylor, *Hegel and Modern Society* (Cambridge: Cambridge University Press, 1979), 1–14.

15. Taylor, *Hegel*, 13.

16. Taylor, *Hegel and Modern Society*, 1.

17. Taylor, *Hegel*, 14.

18. Ibid.,15.

19. Taylor, *Hegel and Modern Society*, 2.

20. Ibid., 3.

21. This theme is a central focus of Taylor's *Malaise of Modernity* (Toronto: Anansi Press, 1991)—so central, in fact, that the American release of the book (originally delivered as a Massey lecture) is entitled *The Ethics of Authenticity*.

22. Taylor, *Human Agency and Language*, 47.

23. Ibid., 9–10. For the formulation of Taylor's hermeneutical stance as a circular rather than a linear model, see Gregory Millard and Jane Forsey, "Moral Agency and the Modern Age: Reading Charles Taylor through George Grant," *Journal of Canadian Studies* 40, no. 1 (Winter 2006): 185.

24. Taylor, *Sources of the Self*, 520.

25. Ibid., 97.

26. Ibid., 18.

27. Ibid., 19.

28. Ibid., 19.

29. Ibid., 41.

30. Ibid., 8.

31. Taylor, *Secular Age*, 115; cf. 554, 640, 741. This insight comes to Taylor through Ivan Illich. See David Cayley, *The Rivers North of the Future: The Testament of Ivan Illich as Told to David Cayley* (Toronto: Anansi Press, 2005), 207, 222.

32. Taylor, *Secular Age*, 741.

33. Taylor, *Malaise of Modernity*, 87–91.

34. Taylor, *Sources of the Self*, 4. See also Taylor's "What is Human Agency?" in *Human Agency and Language*; and Charles Taylor, "Understanding and Ethnocentricity," in *Philosophy and the Human Sciences: Philosophical Papers 2* (Cambridge: Cambridge University Press, 1985), 120.

35. Taylor, "Understanding and Ethnocentricity," 120.

36. See Abbey, *Charles Taylor*, 13.

37. Taylor, *Sources of the Self*, 218.

38. Ibid., 219.

39. Ibid.

40. Ibid.; *Secular Age*, 17–18.

41. Charles Taylor, *A Catholic Modernity? Charles Taylor's Marianist Award Lecture, with Responses by William Shea, Rosemary Luling Haughton, George Marsden, and Jean Bethke Elshtain*, ed. James L. Heft (Oxford: Oxford University Press, 1999), 14. In light of this formulation, it is unsurprising that a little further into the piece Taylor warns against "the project of Christendom," which though "inspired by the very logic of incarnation" is "doomed" as a historical project because of the coercion involved in governing; see 17.

42. Ibid., 14–15.

43. Taylor himself notes how Herder's own conception of complementarity has "an explicitly Christian source, even if not explicitly rooted in Trinitarian theology"—so the continuities between Taylor's expressive anthropology and the more theistic anthropological components should be unsurprising in light of Herder's influence. See Taylor, *Catholic Modernity?*, 114.

44. Ibid. Elsewhere, Taylor discusses the *ecclesia* as a "sacramental communion" and a "mystical body" and suggests that radically individualist conceptions of Christianity have difficulties accommodating the ways that corporate life mediates belief and worship. See Charles Taylor, *Varieties of Religion Today: William James Revisited* (Cambridge: Harvard University Press, 2002), 23–26.

45. Taylor, *Sources of the Self*, 41.

46. For a discussion of the Bible as a best account, see Taylor, *Sources of the Self*, 91, 97.

47. Stephen K. White, "Weak Ontology and Liberal Political Reflection," *Political Theory* 25 (August 1997): 509.

48. The presence of these "stronger" ontological formulations in a paper delivered to the Society of Mary should be unsurprising. As Taylor himself notes at the beginning of the piece, theistic issues "have been at the center of [his] concern for decades," but have remained implicit because of the "nature of philosophical discourse . . . which has to try to persuade honest thinkers of any and all metaphysical or theological commitments." Taylor recognizes some of the difficulties that arise when theistic perspectives are introduced into philosophical debate, and thus his more theistic claims in a text such as *Sources of the Self*, which has a readership that goes beyond the confessional, arise when considering how theism can indeed be the best account to talk

about moral life—over and above, say, utilitarianism. Because *A Catholic Modernity?* was delivered to an audience that already shares some theistic affinities, Taylor is able to articulate his normative moral and political vision without having to make the case that theism is the best account—his audience (for the most part) would already be convinced that Christian theism offers a better account of the good than utilitarianism ever can. This is not to say that Taylor does not recognize the contestability of theism in a confessional context; the assumption is that members in a Marianist society are participants in the contestation over whether Christian theism *is* the best account—and thus he says elsewhere that "'my' best account . . . may just as easily be 'our' best account. No one thinks totally alone; the Cartesian ideal is unrealizable integrally." See Charles Taylor, "Charles Taylor Replies," *Philosophy in an Age of Pluralism*, ed. James Tully (Cambridge: Cambridge University Press, 1994), 227. The task Taylor sets forth for himself when addressing the Marianist society is to give a best account of Christianity, to give a Christian account that best describes what it is to live a good life, to live agapeically—a best account that to a large extent is already shared. See *Catholic Modernity?*, 13 ff.

49. See White's "Weak Ontology and Liberal Political Reflection," 506. It should be noted that further study of Taylor's moral and political program brought about a shift in White's interpretation of Taylor's theistic and ontological commitments, with White finally concluding that Taylor's "Christian sources might actually qualify as weak ontology." See White, "Weak Ontology: Genealogy and Critical Issues," 14.

50. Taylor, *Catholic Modernity?*, 20.

51. Emmanuel Levinas, *Totality and Infinity* (Pittsburgh: Duquesne University Press, 1969), 203.

52. Levinas, 197.

53. Levinas, 196.

54. In an interesting 2007 book, James Benn examines the historical practice of self-immolation. Benn claims "that self-immolation, rather than being an aberrant practice that must be explained away, actually offers a bodily (or somatic) path—a way to attain awakening and, ultimately, buddhahood. This path looks rather different from those soteriologies that stress practices of the mind (such as meditation and learning), which have probably received the most attention from Western scholars in Buddhist studies. Nonetheless, as we shall see, it was a path to deliverance that was considered valid by many Chinese Buddhists." It is worth noting that self-immolation in Benn's book does not refer to "auto-cremation" alone. He notes that "in its strictest sense, it means 'self sacrifice'" and he therefore uses it to refer to "the broader range of practices [that include] drowning, death by starvation, feeding the body to animals or insects, and so forth." See his *Burning for the Buddha: Self-immolation in Chinese Buddhism* (Honolulu: University of Hawaii Press, 2007), 8.

55. This is not to say that there are not significant, and perhaps even insurmountable, differences between Christian and Buddhist notions of transcendence. One that comes to mind concerns the ineluctable relation between transcendence and the world of immanence within Christianity. Theologian Paul D. Janz describes

the connection between transcendence and immanence in Christian thought as follows: "Revelation per se is to be seen as a divine self-disclosure which is essentially communicated to *whole* sensibly embodied and rationally self-aware human beings in the real world of space and time, which is to say dynamically and causally at the center of life." For Buddhists, on the other hand, the phenomenal world is illusory—a view that is hard to reconcile with the central place of causal authority in Christian thought, particularly as it relates to Incarnation, "the weaving of God's life into human lives" (to use Taylor's words). Paul D. Janz, "Divine Causality, World, and Reason," Plenary Paper, Society for the Study of Theology, 2007. See also his "Divine Causality and the Nature of Theological Questioning," *Modern Theology* 23, no. 3 (July 2007), 317–38. See also Taylor, *Catholic Modernity?*, 14.

56. Ibid., 21; cf. *Secular Age*, 17.

57. Taylor, *Catholic Modernity?*, 21.

58. Ibid., 21–22; cf. *Secular Age*, 16–18.

59. Nietzsche, *Thus Spoke Zarathustra*, in *The Portable Nietzsche*, trans. and ed. Walter Kaufmann (New York: Penguin, 1954), 122.

60. Taylor, *Catholic Modernity?*, 35.

61. It is worth mentioning that the depiction of Nietzsche's ethics given here represents Taylor's own depiction of Nietzsche, a depiction that Taylor employs as a foil to his own moral and political program. There are readings of Nietzsche that are at odds with such an interpretation of Nietzschean ethics. Two notable examples of this kind of interpretation of Nietzsche can be found in the work of William Connolly and Romand Coles.

62. Though the examples of Vanier and Mother Theresa are Christian ones, Taylor also discusses "exceptional people, whom [he calls] for short saints" who "refract" the nature of transcendence and its agapeic implications for ethics. Taylor acknowledges that by talking about saints and love he is giving a "Christian 'spin'" to his account, and that "exceptional individuals, showing very similar spiritual strengths, will account for their lives very differently in other spiritual traditions." Taylor, "Charles Taylor Replies," 226–30. If we consider this discussion of the analogous nature of these exceptional people in light of the discussion of transcendence in *A Catholic Modernity?*, presumably a basic feature of what makes them analogous is this: they understand their ethical responses to be evoked by the dispossessive encounter with a transcendent source, thus giving rise to an unconditional—agapeic or karunic—comportment to the other.

63. Taylor, *Sources of the Self*, 517.

64. Taylor, *Secular Age*, 654; emphasis added.

65. Taylor, *Catholic Modernity?*, 105.

66. White, *Sustaining Affirmation*, 6–7.

67. Taylor, "Charles Taylor Replies," 227.

68. In her article "Faith Beyond Nihilism: The Retrieval of Theism in Milbank and Taylor," Alexandra Klaushofer describes how a kind of contestability is built into Taylor's philosophy. The article compares Taylor's philosophical approach with the

work of the Radical Orthodox theologian John Milbank and suggests that the form of Taylor's best account is such that it effectively brings together his Christianity and pluralism, a move that, on her reading, is unavailable to Milbank because of the form of his account. Klaushofer argues that

> [Milbank's] brand of communitarianism . . . stays within the perspective of his own spiritual community, retaining an inward-looking focus on the internal features of Christianity that impacts on the status of his central claim, which reads something like "I am a Christian because Christianity *is* the best account." In contrast, Taylor's might be restated as: "I recognize that what I see as the best account is only so because of my contingently constituted identity," thus dropping the exclusivist claim that tends to superiority. In other words, his external move, in conjunction with his internal position, engenders the holding in balance of two options which might previously have seemed incommensurable: nurturing one's own while remaining open to the stranger. . . . [Unlike Taylor] Milbank fails to acknowledge the fact of pluralism in contemporary reality and the way in which it impinges on the internal dynamics of each belief-system and the status of its claims (147).

Whether Klaushofer's depiction of Milbank's position is accurate or not is outside the scope of this work, but it is worth considering how the "brand of communitarianism" that Klaushofer ascribes to Milbank is arrived at methodologically via strong ontology. Taylor's ontological account is at odds with this kind of perspective, precisely because of the self-assured form that Klaushofer describes in Milbank's formulation. Such self-assuredness is problematic from the Taylorian perspective I have described here, both because it does not take full account of the modern epistemological predicament that limits us to best accounts articulated by historically situated interpreting subjects, and because as a Christian account it does not discernibly embody the "discursive abasement" that corresponds to transcendence as kenosis. The suggestion in this paper is that the shape of Taylor's normative political vision is fundamentally cruciform and kenotic, taking a form analogous to the moral source that animates it, and thus resists the drive for power, whether it is discursive or institutional. The nature of moral experience within modernity as understood by Taylor means that the form of his best account must steer clear of the exceptionalism or triumphalism that Klaushofer ascribes to Milbank—such a position is unavailable to him for theological, anthropological, and moral ontological reasons. See Alexandra Klaushofer, "Faith Beyond Nihilism: The Retrieval of Theism in Milbank and Taylor," *Heythrop Journal* 40 (1999): 137–49.

# CHAPTER FOUR

# Theorizing Secularity 3
## Authenticity, Ontology, Fragilization

RUTH ABBEY

*Life in a secular age (in sense 3) is uneasy and cross-pressured, and doesn't
lend itself easily to a comfortable resting place.*

—Charles Taylor, *A Secular Age*

One of Charles Taylor's ambitions—perhaps even his central ambition—
in *A Secular Age* is to shed light on Secularity 3, as he calls it, or the current
conditions of religious belief and experience in Western societies. This is
what, in Taylor's eyes, sets his approach apart from other analyses of secularity, which see the term as referring either to the evacuation of religion
from the public and other social spheres—which he calls Secularity 1—or
to the decline in the number of people expressing allegiance to traditional
religious views and in particular Christianity—which he dubs Secularity 2.
While Taylor's preferred approach to secularity cannot ignore either of

these developments, it is distinguished by its preoccupation with experience, with what it is like to be a religious believer or nonbeliever in contemporary Western societies.[1]

This chapter begins by identifying the conceptual tools Taylor employs to understand religious belief and nonbelief in contemporary Western societies. The second section discusses the phenomenon of religious authenticity, while the third section raises a number of questions about Taylor's cross pressures and fragilization thesis: what it means, how it affects people, how widespread it is. The fourth section contends that underlying Taylor's diagnosis of a secular age is an ontological claim that some orientation toward religion or transcendence is lodged in human nature. It is important to note here that Taylor counts any perspective or worldview that remains open to transcendence of the human, all too human, as religious. What matters is whether an outlook has a transcendent axis and whether its sense of the transcendent returns to inform its conception of human flourishing.[2] By this logic, the category of religion embraces more than theism—theism is but one form of religion.

A chapter of this length can, of course, deal with only a sliver of a work as formidable as *A Secular Age*. This chapter draws from those sections discussing the conditions of contemporary religious belief and experience without engaging the historical material that constitutes a large slice of the book. My comments therefore pertain primarily to material from the introduction and from chapter 13, "The Age of Authenticity," to the book's end.[3] An immediate objection to limiting the parameters of my discussion to those sections of *A Secular Age* dealing with the conditions of contemporary religious experience comes from Taylor's insistence that the history he weaves is inseparable from the present he presents. "Our past is sedimented in our present, and we are doomed to misidentify ourselves, as long as we can't do justice to where we have come from. This is why the narrative is not an optional extra, why I believe that I have a story to tell here."[4] Much later in the book he declares one of its "structuring principle[s]" to be the conviction that "the story of how we got here is inextricably bound up with our account of where we are."[5]

Despite these remarks, I focus on contemporary conditions for two reasons. The first is practical: in a paper of this size, it is impossible to do justice to the book as a whole. The second justification is my sense that, *pace* Taylor, it is possible to analyze his comments about the contemporary condition without constant reference to his historical narrative.[6] Whatever the details of that narrative, and whatever its value as a history of Christianity, my sense is that Taylor uses history in this book for three major purposes.[7] One is to show that Western societies were not always secular (in senses 1, 2 or 3) and thus that there is nothing natural or inevitable about the contemporary condition. It has to be explained rather than taken for granted. The second major purpose is to encourage readers to take some imaginative distance from the present and try to see it from a perspective somewhat different from that in which we are immersed when living it. In both cases, the awareness of history has an exoticizing function, and it is this shift in perspective on the present, rather than the particular details of the history, that seems crucial to Taylor's task of examining Secularity 3.

A third function of history is connected with this aim of enhanced self-understanding, but here the danger is not that of forgetting the past and taking the present for granted as natural or necessary. Rather, Taylor claims that the self-awareness of modern unbelievers is inescapably historical; that this sense of self is inherently contrastive. Unbelievers compare where they are now favorably to where Western civilization once was and see the present as progress, as an achievement, as the overcoming of an inferior earlier condition.[8] But, for Taylor, this contrastive historical awareness is based on an impoverished view of the past and a limited view of the present. Offering a richer and fuller account of then and now helps to weaken the grip of this view. A particularly limited account of the relationship between past and present that Taylor strives to combat appears in what he calls "subtraction stories."[9] This is the general name he gives to views that see modernity in general and religious nonbelief in particular as involving a sloughing off of old ideas and beliefs to make space for options and possibilities that were waiting in the wings.[10] For subtraction stories, "modernity or secularity—is to be understood in terms of underlying features of human nature which were there all along, but had been impeded by what is now set aside."[11] As Arto Laitinen points out, subtraction stories presume a distinction between the immanent and the transcendent or the natural and the supernatural. Yet Taylor shows that this very separation is a product of history.[12]

Indeed, Taylor goes to great lengths to display how much creative intellectual and normative work has been expended to arrive at the conditions of contemporary religious belief and nonbelief. He demonstrates persuasively that "Western modernity, including its secularity, is the fruit of new inventions, newly constructed self-understandings and related practices."[13] But we can grant Taylor this point—that the current condition is much more than what is left over when older views fade away—without having to constantly refer back to the particular ways in which current beliefs and possibilities have been forged. I concede that his more general claim—that some current secular self-understandings are nourished by limited views of the past—makes it harder to separate the historical exegesis from the analysis of contemporary conditions. But as these are not my focus in what follows, its separation of historical narrative from analysis of the present is not detrimental.

## What is Secularity 3?

Taylor's aspiration to shed light on what it is like to be a religious believer or nonbeliever in contemporary Western societies is a massive task. Indeed, his own reference to "the strange and complex conditions of belief in our age" testifies to his awareness of the magnitude of the challenge he has set himself.[14] It is therefore not surprising that he approaches this difficult question from a number of angles: it is as if he is trying out a series of formulations for capturing what is unprecedented about life in a secular age. I discern four major entrées into this question about what is distinctive about the current conditions of modern religious belief and practice in Western societies. These are: 1) the phenomenon of religious authenticity; 2) the experience of cross pressures and fragilization; 3) the three-cornered contest between exclusive humanism, the immanent counter-Enlightenment, and theism; and 4) the immanent frame. Of these, the idea of the immanent frame is the only conceptual innovation in that portion of *A Secular Age* treating contemporary religious experience. Versions of all the other ideas have appeared in Taylor's earlier works, including *A Catholic Modernity?* (1999), *Varieties of Religion Today* (2002), and *Modern Social Imaginaries* (2004).

In what follows, I pay close attention to the first two items, investigating what Taylor has in mind by the phenomenon of religious authenticity and scrutinizing his cross pressures and fragilization thesis. I consider how these features relate to one another as well as asking what their contribution is to the distinctive nature of the secular age as Taylor portrays it.

## Religious Authenticity

Chapter 13 of *A Secular Age*, "The Age of Authenticity," opens with the announcement that "something has happened in the last half-century, perhaps even less, which has profoundly altered the conditions of belief in our societies."[15] Here Taylor explores the extension to religion of an ethos described in *Sources of the Self* and *The Malaise of Modernity* (aka *The Ethic of Authenticity*).[16] Those earlier works portrayed the ethic of authenticity as a uniquely modern and hugely influential ideal animated by the injunction that each individual choose a way of living that is in tune with his or her unique self. This ideal of "expressive individuation"[17] sees each person as having his or her own mode of being human and enjoins each to discover and live according to this, rather than conform to some model devised by others and imposed from outside.[18]

In *Varieties of Religion Today*, Taylor proposes that this ideal has now penetrated conceptions of religious belief in Western societies, ushering in "a rather new phase of religious life."[19] Examining this phenomenon would seem, therefore, to be a crucial component of his quest to divine what is distinctive about a secular age. The major consequence of the penetration of religious life by the ethic of authenticity is the demand that "the religious life or practice that I become part of not only must be my choice, but must speak to me; it must make sense in terms of my spiritual development."[20] However, being true to oneself in one's religious life need not have spiritual atomism as its corollary: as Taylor points out, "The new framework has a strongly individualist component, but this will not necessarily mean that the content will be individuating. Many people will find themselves joining extremely powerful religious communities, because that's where many people's sense of the spiritual will lead them."[21]

*A Secular Age* reprises this earlier analysis of religious authenticity and offers the example of Taizé to illustrate this blend of openness and authenticity in religious belief on the one hand, with the urge to collaborate with others in one's spiritual quest on the other.[22] Young people from a range of countries are drawn to this interfaith Christian center in France because they "want to meet their counterparts from other lands, and explore Christian faith without any preconditions as to the outcome."[23] As the Taizé example intimates, Taylor finds the quest for religious authenticity to be especially powerful among young people.[24]

Findings from a recent Pew survey of religion in America are also in keeping with Taylor's depiction of the quest for religious authenticity, especially among younger people. Just over 12 percent of the adult population in the Pew sample claimed to be unaffiliated with any particular religion. However, this figure doubles for those between the ages of 18 and 29, with 25 percent of that cohort saying that they are not currently affiliated with any religion. The number of people aged 70 and older who report nonaffiliation is, by comparison, 8 percent.[25] Yet *nonaffiliated* need not mean nonreligious. Among those who report themselves as not affiliated with any particular religious tradition, 41 percent say that "religion is at least somewhat important in their lives, seven-in-ten say they believe in God and more than a quarter (27 percent) say they attend religious services at least a few times a year."[26]

Taylor implies that the penetration of religious belief by the ethic of authenticity is an irreversible development. It will, however, be resisted by some believers, indicating that the ethic of authenticity has not permeated all forms of religious belief. Critics of this approach to religion portray it as self-absorbed, self-indulgent, superficial, trivial.[27] Extending his earlier position on the ethic of authenticity, Taylor argues that this is a misperception—or, rather, that it is inappropriate to tar all quests for authenticity with the same dismissive brush.[28] Critics of the thirst for religious authenticity are missing something crucial about what he calls the post-Durkheimian religious dispensation. Religious identities are increasingly becoming unmoored from national ones, and more individuals are seeking their own ways of exploring and expressing religious faith. As noted above, this need not mean that they will do so in solitude: however, their communities will be forged and found rather than arriving ready-made in the form of national or institutional religion.[29] Elsewhere Taylor suggests that the misunderstanding can cut both ways, for those who prize religious authenticity can have trouble understanding traditional religions and their followers' adherence to orthopraxy.[30]

This tension between orthodoxy and authenticity is depicted by Taylor as a difference between religious people's view of authority. Those with a more traditional view place authority first, whereas those embarking on quests for religious authenticity prize wholeness first and, in pursuing this, may or may not find some form of authority to be necessary.[31] In presenting the debate in this way, Taylor further claims that this new development—the quest for religious authenticity—is not so new after all. This dispute among religious believers about how central authority should be "has some affinities with a division which goes back 500 years in our civilization, to about the time of the Reformation."[32] So what is initially depicted as novel—the quest for religious authenticity—actually has a long pedigree, and the battle among believers over whether to trust oneself or some external authority first proves to be an old one. When it comes to the United States in particular, Taylor again identifies religious authenticity as predating the last fifty years. The United States' "whole religious culture was in some way prepared for the Age of Authenticity, even before this became a facet of mass culture in the latter part of the twentieth century."[33]

These longer views on religious authenticity are noteworthy for three reasons. They suggest, firstly and most obviously, that while religious authenticity has become more widespread, it is not a completely novel aspect of contemporary religious life. They point, secondly, to a slightly different function for the historical aspect of A Secular Age, for here the longer view reveals continuity rather than change—at least in the phenomenon itself, if not its dispersion. Thirdly, and most importantly, its pedigree suggests that the rise of religious authenticity is not dependent on the existence of exclusive humanism. It becomes possible to imagine, counterfactually but not counterintuitively, a society in which everyone is a religious believer but in which the quest for religious authenticity takes place among some or many believers. This, in turn, casts doubt upon the constitutive role Taylor accords to exclusive humanism in defining the secular age.[34]

## CROSS PRESSURES AND FRAGILIZATION

Another of the concepts advanced in *A Secular Age* to illuminate contemporary religious experience was also articulated in *Varieties of Religion Today*, viz the idea that the rise of nonbelief combined with increased religious pluralism in Western societies creates cross pressures for, and fragilization of, religious belief and nonbelief. In Western societies, believers and nonbelievers alike realize that they are surrounded by a wide array of religious and nonreligious positions, and that reasonable people adhere to these. As Taylor explains early in *A Secular Age*, a large part of what distinguishes this age is the fact that "faith, even for the staunchest believer, is one human possibility among others. I may find it inconceivable that I would abandon my faith, but there are others, including possibly some very close to me, whose way of living I cannot in all honesty just dismiss as depraved, or blind, or unworthy, who have no faith (or at least not in God, or the transcendent). Belief in God is no longer axiomatic. There are alternatives."[35]

Another of Taylor's formulations holds that "This mutual fragilization of all the different views in presence, the undermining sense that others think differently, is certainly one of the main features of the world of 2000."[36] In this secular age, "the dwellers within each [milieu] are very aware of the options favored by the others, and cannot just dismiss them as an inexplicable exotic error."[37] As this suggests, the existence of exclusive humanism is not all that fragilizes belief. Different religious positions are mutually fragilizing: "It is a pluralist world in which many forms of belief and unbelief jostle, and hence fragilize each other."[38]

Taylor's diagnosis of the cross pressures and fragilization that mark a secular age goes beyond simply pointing to the fact of religious pluralism. As the previous paragraph intimates, what matters is not just that a dizzying array of religious and nonreligious options exists, but also that individuals feel the pull of those and can imagine making some of them their own, whether they actually do so or not. At the very least, the existence of alternative religious and nonreligious positions makes it hard for people in modern Western societies to take it for granted that their own position is unquestionably correct. In a seminal statement of the cross pressures and fragilization thesis, Taylor portrays the present as

marked by an unheard of pluralism of outlooks, religious and non-
and anti-religious, in which the number of possible positions seems
to be increasing without end. It is marked in consequence by a great
deal of mutual fragilization, and hence movement between different
outlooks. It naturally depends on one's milieu, but it is harder and
harder to find a niche where either belief or unbelief go without saying. . . . Religious belief now exists in a field of choices which include
various forms of demurral and rejection; Christian faith exists in a
field in which there is also a wide range of other spiritual options.[39]

In keeping with the work's accent on experience, the cross pressures–
fragilization thesis thus tries to capture something about how this pluralism is lived.[40]

It seems, moreover, that these two key features—religious authenticity on the one hand and cross pressures and fragilization on the other—
are complementary components of Taylor's theoretical framework for
Secularity 3. If more believers are moving away from traditional conceptions of religion to seek a style of spirituality that resonates with their individuality, they could be influenced by neighboring religious conceptions
and practices in this process. As part of their spiritual search, it could make
perfect sense to find out what religious alternatives are available in one's en-
vironment and try them on for size. After all, there is nothing in the ethic of
authenticity that precludes such borrowing: what matters is that the individual chooses it, that it fits, and that it not be imposed from outside.

In the long passage just cited, Taylor seems to suggest that the mere
presence of multiple religious and nonreligious possibilities generates
fragilization ("it is marked in consequence by"). He reiterates this later in
the book, claiming that "the existence of an alternative fragilizes each context, that is, makes its sense of the thinkable/unthinkable uncertain and
wavering."[41] A later formulation contends that "the salient feature of Western societies is . . . a mutual fragilization of different religious positions, as
well as of the outlooks both of belief and unbelief."[42] However, despite
these remarks, Taylor does not always suggest that fragilization is a universal experience generated by the mere existence of alternatives. On other
occasions, the fragilization effect shows up as more contingent. The passage cited above, for example, includes the concession that its power "nat-

urally depends on one's milieu."[43] Later we read that "the cross pressures are experienced more acutely by some people and in some milieux than others."[44] Such qualifications of the cross pressures–fragilization thesis with regard to milieux could imply that hard-core believers and unbelievers alike are less likely to be touched by this and are more prone to regard other positions with suspicion and hostility, finding them threatening, offensive, or stupid rather than attractive or viable alternatives. Taylor's quip about the default position in the Bible Belt compared to that "in certain reaches of the academy"[45] suggests that when he portrays occupants of some milieux as more entrenched in their beliefs than others, he is thinking of extremes.[46]

However, to complicate this interpretation of the cross pressures and fragilization effect being less potent at the extremes, Taylor also claims that "most people may be ensconced in a relatively untroubled way in one or other position, *whether extreme or middle*."[47] He later states that "cross pressure doesn't mean that all *or even most* people in this culture feel torn."[48] Such qualifications suggest that it is not only those occupying hard-core positions who remain immune to the influence of other beliefs. They also cast doubt on how widespread the experience of fragilization is supposed to be. If most people remain untouched by other positions, cross pressures and fragilization cannot be an inescapable part of contemporary belief and nonbelief in the way that Taylor otherwise says they are. This further implies that the mere presence of the exclusive humanist option need not ramify across the whole spectrum and need not change the field of experience for some, and perhaps even many, people. On the basis of such questions, we are left wondering whether the phenomenon of cross pressures and fragilization really is such an important feature of Secularity 3.

On closer examination, further questions appear about the meaning of Taylor's cross pressures and fragilization thesis. Two versions seem to be at play in the book, one structural and the other psychological. On the one hand, this thesis seems to describe a structural feature of the conditions of modern belief: with such a wide array of alternatives, many possibilities present themselves to believers and nonbelievers alike. Early in the chapter entitled "Cross Pressures," Taylor explains that "*The whole culture experiences cross pressures*, between the draw of narratives of closed immanence on the one side, and the sense of their inadequacy on the other, strengthened by encounter with existing milieux of religious practice, or just some intimations of the transcendent. The cross pressures are experienced more acutely by some people and in some milieux than others, but *over the whole culture*, we can see them reflected in a number of middle positions, which have drawn from both sides."[49]

As the italicized sections indicate, Taylor seems to be describing cultural conditions. In another passage, part of which is cited above, he seems again to focus on the structural conditions of belief—that is, the fact of religious and nonreligious pluralism.

> My claim that *the culture* is suspended between the extreme positions [orthodox religion and materialist atheism] in no way involves that all, or even most, of its members are. Most people may be ensconced in a relatively untroubled way in one or other position, whether extreme or middle. That is not the point, which is rather that these positions themselves are defined in a field in which the extreme ones, transcendental religion on one hand, and reductive materialism on the other, are crucial reference points.[50]

Here it seems that the culture can be cross-pressured while "most people" remain untouched by this. Yet it is unclear how a culture can be characterized by something that leaves most of its members unaffected. This also calls into question Taylor's claim to be saying something about the *experience* of religious belief in modern Western societies, for if many or most people are oblivious to these forces, how do they count as a central component of their experience? However, as noted above, there are times when the cross pressures and fragilization thesis makes a psychological claim about how people experience their religious (or nonreligious) beliefs in a secular age. Taylor seems unable to decide how widespread the effects are, saying at one point that "*all* see their option as one among many"[51] but at others that only some people feel it. But irrespective of the numbers, in these portrayals cross pressures and fragilization are felt directly by individuals rather than just being a generic feature of the culture.

In propounding the cross pressures and fragilization thesis, Taylor seems to move without notice between two standpoints. One is the agentic perspective of those who live in a secular age and who might (or might not) feel the pull of different religious or nonreligious options. The other is the structural or God's eye perspective, which sees the wide variety of religious and nonreligious options available in that culture but makes no claim about how those on the ground experience these. At one point Taylor imputes this bifocalism to all who live in a secular age: "We learn to navigate between two standpoints: an 'engaged' one in which we live as best we can the reality our standpoint opens us to; and a 'disengaged' one in which we are able to see ourselves as occupying one standpoint among a range of possible ones, with which we have in various ways to co-exist."[52]

But, given Taylor's repeated admissions that not everyone in a secular age undergoes cross pressures and fragilization, it is more accurate to see this bifocalism as describing the author's own shifting stance. The disengaged perspective observes the wide variety of religious positions in modern Western cultures and imagines them rubbing up against one another and jostling for adherents. The engaged stance, by comparison, strives to capture people's actual experiences and concedes, as noted above, that "most people may be ensconced in a relatively untroubled way in one or other position."[53]

Yet if, with the cross pressures and fragilization thesis, Taylor is taking a disengaged stance—if he is making a claim about the wide and varied spectrum of religious and nonreligious possibilities available in a secular age without saying anything about how these are felt—it is hard to know why the language of cross pressures and fragilization is introduced, for these terms seem to refer to experience. Why not stay with the language of religious pluralism or a religious mosaic or, in Taylor's own terms, the nova effect?[54] If the very terminology of cross pressures and fragilization beckons toward an engaged perspective that attends to actual experience, it is hard to know why Taylor imputes this condition to the culture as a whole. At one point he says that "life in a secular age (in sense 3) is uneasy and cross-pressured, and doesn't lend itself easily to a comfortable resting place."[55] But how can a "whole culture" be cross-pressured and find its life uncomfortable?

It seems, moreover, that someone with Taylor's ambition—to shed light on Secularity 3—must be concerned with psychological questions, with how individuals experience their religious or nonreligious beliefs.

As we have seen, in making his distinctive contribution to an understanding of secularity, Taylor wants to "shift the focus to the conditions of belief, experience and search."[56] At the work's outset he declares his intention to "focus attention on the different kinds of lived experience involved in understanding your life in one way or the other, on what it's like to live as a believer or an unbeliever."[57] Readers familiar with Taylor's thought will recognize this as an extension of his career-long concern with self-interpretations. In his landmark "Interpretation and the Sciences of Man," Taylor insists that we "think of man as a self-interpreting animal. He is necessarily so, for there is no such thing as the structure of meanings for him independently of his interpretation of them."[58] Self-interpretations are crucial components of human identity and, therefore, of social reality. Given Taylor's enduring insistence on incorporating meaning into the social sciences, it seems that a discussion of religion must include reference to how people live their beliefs, to what those beliefs mean to them. My claim that the concept of fragilization sometimes includes a psychological component is not, therefore, intended as a criticism, but rather as eliciting one of its necessary features.[59] But this makes it hard to understand and integrate those versions of the thesis in which Taylor suggests that this is a property of the culture as a whole and need not be felt by many individuals within it.

Assuming that the best way of reading it is to include a psychological or agentic dimension to the cross pressures and fragilization thesis, further confusion arises when Taylor specifies that fragilization does not refer to people holding their views with less conviction: it is simply a function of the wide array of alternatives. Quite late in *A Secular Age* we read that "greater proximity of alternatives has led to a society in which more people change their positions, that is, 'convert' in their lifetimes, and/or adopt a different position than their parents. Lifetime and intergenerational switches become more common. But this has nothing to do with the supposed greater fragility of the faith they end up with (or decide to remain with). . . . On the contrary, the faith arising in this contemporary predicament can be stronger, just because it has faced the alternative without distortion."[60]

This might be true: those who have changed beliefs once or more across their lifetime might arrive at a religious outlook that does not depend for its appeal on demeaning other religious or nonreligious positions. But Taylor provides no evidence about whether changing religious belief affects the way a person holds his or her new beliefs. He is conjuring possibilities, and competing possibilities can be conjured just as readily.[61] Nothing rules out the possibility that those who change their religious positions will hold their newer beliefs more tenuously than do people who have adhered to the same position all their life, and whose parents and children occupy that location as well. Changing one's religious beliefs need not have the effect of fragilizing the position one ultimately holds, but then again, it might. What is needed to make Taylor's claims on this issue more plausible is information from people who have undergone such transformations. How do converts in contemporary Western societies relate to their new and their old religious or nonreligious views?

Taylor's insistence that the fragilization thesis does not refer to the tenacity with which a person holds a view at any particular time is, however, undermined by the fact that elsewhere he contends that fragilization *can* make people more tentative. He accepts that "these cross pressures can lead to a condition where many people hesitate for a long time in their attitude to religion . . . a movement to and fro, and/or a long term hesitancy can also result."[62] Cross pressures can lead "to prolonged uncertainty or havering."[63] Taylor again seems to contradict his own claim that fragilization does not weaken conviction when shortly after he says that fragilization is increased "by the fact that great numbers of people are not firmly embedded in any such context, but are puzzled, cross-pressured, or have constituted by bricolage a sort of median position."[64] Rather than elaborating on this, he goes on to talk about the way in which those who are puzzled and cross-pressured affect those who are more settled in their beliefs, suggesting that their effect is to raise doubts among those who are supposedly more assured.[65] So it seems that Taylor himself havers on the question of whether fragilization makes one likely to hold new religious beliefs with less commitment than would someone who had cleaved to the same position all their life. Perhaps his equivocation illustrates that this is not a question to be answered in the abstract: what is needed, as just suggested, are encounters with the experiences of people who have undergone such religious realignment.

Indeed, if we look for some evidence of the phenomenon Taylor is trying to capture with his cross pressures and fragilization thesis, we find it in the aforementioned Pew study of religion in America. One measure of fragilization comes in an individual's receptivity to changing his or her religion: as Taylor says, "cross-pressured, we are prone to change, and even multiple changes over generations."[66] The Pew study reveals that "religious affiliation in the U.S. is both very diverse and extremely fluid,"[67] vindicating Taylor's point about the great variety and mobility in contemporary religious experience—at least with regard to the United States. It would be unwise to extrapolate too freely from the United States to other Western societies.[68]

Yet, beyond pointing to the increased prevalence of religious change by individuals, it is hard to determine exactly what Taylor is claiming with this cross pressures and fragilization thesis, which he presents as one of the defining features of a secular age. It is unclear where, how, and how widely the cross pressures and fragilization make themselves felt. It seems, moreover, that the frequency of religious change on the part of individuals could be explained by the quest for religious authenticity, making that thesis redundant in this case.

The second section concluded with the proposal that the phenomenon of religious authenticity is not in itself dependent on the existence of exclusive humanism. The same can be said of cross pressures and fragilization. Again one can imagine, counterfactually but not counterintuitively, a society in which everyone is a religious believer and in which cross pressures and fragilization occur. Indeed, this dynamic could be even more intense in a society where everyone evinced some sort of religious orientation. If religious authenticity and cross pressures and fragilization do not depend on the presence of exclusive humanism, uncertainty prevails about how central to Taylor's depiction of the secular age they really are. They might be crucial for his sociology of contemporary religious experience, but it remains unclear how vital they are to understanding the secular dimension of the secular age.

Moreover, the language of cross pressures and fragilization plays an additional role in *A Secular Age*. As well as attempting to capture something distinctive about religious experience in modern Western societies, Taylor presses this language into the service of advocacy. He aims to shift the terms of debate about the role of religion in Western modernity and, as part of this project, seeks to destabilize the (apparent) extremes in the debate about religion's place in Western societies.[69] In a quintessentially

Taylorean move, he tries to show that the supposed antagonists who seem to, and seem to themselves to, occupy polarized positions have more in common than either realizes. Moving the exchange in a more productive direction thus involves fragilizing its extremes.[70] The dilemmas each side faces include whether all forms of transcendence can really be eschewed; how to make sense of violence; how to understand death; and how to strive for high ethical standards without mutilating the ordinary goods of human life.[71] Fragilizing the rigidity of these apparent extremes not only begins to deconstruct the supposed binary opposition of belief and nonbelief, but also wedges open a space for articulating the experience of many people who recognize themselves in neither of these opposing positions. At the moment, partisans of polarized standpoints define themselves against one another, largely ignoring this middle, cross-pressured ground.[72] Viewed from this advocacy perspective, cross pressures and fragilization is something that Taylor is trying to bring about and enhance. As Michael Warner, Jonathan VanAntwerpen, and Craig Calhoun observe, Taylor's claim about the mutual fragilization of religious and nonreligious options "is both an analytic point and a rhetorical posture . . . the major rhetorical burden of the book is to persuade us to understand this mutual fragilization more deeply, and thus to de-dramatize some of the conflicts that have been inflamed in so many ways around the world."[73]

## WHAT LIES BENEATH

Part of Taylor's purpose in writing *A Secular Age* is to show that religion is neither dead nor dying in the modern West and to make room for the recognition of religious faith and orientations toward transcendence in all their variety and motility. As he says, "the developments of Western modernity have destabilized and rendered virtually unsustainable earlier forms of religious life, but . . . new forms have sprung up. Moreover this process of destabilization and recomposition is not a once-for-all change, but is continuing."[74]

Underpinning this observation, however, is a view that goes beyond the characterization of religious experience in contemporary Western societies toward the question of what it means to be human. Just as Taylor suggests that subtraction stories understand secularity "in terms of underlying features of human nature,"[75] so his own position on the status of religion in modernity is also undergirded by (different) ontological presuppositions.[76] Although Taylor remains, for the most part, reticent about claiming ontological status for humans' orientation toward transcendence, such a position seems to underlie and inform his analysis of the current conditions of religious belief and nonbelief in Western societies.

Consider Taylor's belief that a view of human existence that remains open to transcendence is better qualified to describe and explain aesthetic and ethical experience. Refusing to speak of interpellation by outside forces, closed immanence is poorly equipped to make sense of "the specific force of creative agency; or ethical demands, or . . . the power of artistic experience."[77] *A Catholic Modernity?* submitted that an understanding of humans as made in God's image and likeness and a Christian commitment to agape provide a more durable foundation for the very demanding modern ethic of universal solidarity and assistance. *A Secular Age* reiterates this position, that theism supplies a richer and more robust moral source for this ethic.[78] Closing a discussion of this issue, Taylor concludes that "this kind of response to the image of God in others . . . can be real for us, but only to the extent that we open ourselves to God." Such opening provides "a path towards a much more powerful and effective healing action in history."[79] Here he seems to be arguing in favor of the attractions and advantages of living the immanent frame in an open way.[80]

Taylor maintains that views that see humans as having some orientation toward the transcendent are superior to those lacking this idea. That exclusive humanism denies what Taylor takes to be part of the human condition — the yearning for transcendence[81] — appears in his remarks about why the immanent counter-Enlightenment will always trouble exclusive humanism: "The perennial human susceptibility to be fascinated by death and violence is at base a manifestation of our nature as *homo religiosus*."[82] This ontological view also seems to inform Taylor's response to the possibility, evoked by Steve Bruce, that widespread indifference to religion could eventually reign in Western societies. Deeming this scenario "deeply implausible," Taylor declares himself unable to "see 'the demand for religion' just disappearing like that." While there could be many reasons for this skepticism, the one Taylor offers is his sense that "our situation

(the perennial human situation?) is to be open to two solicitations." The
solicitation muted by Bruce's scenario is "the draw to a transformation
perspective." The other solicitation, which beckons away from religion, is
caused in part by "abuses and distortions" of the call to transformation
and in part from the fear that some valued forms of human flourishing
will be compromised or abandoned should the call to religion be heeded.[83]
Although Taylor puts the ontological claim—"the perennial human
situation"—in parentheses and places a question mark over it, it is noteworthy that the call to transformation is presented as a good or a power in
its own right. The call away from religion, on the other hand, is explained
through distortion and fear. It helps to remember that part of what Taylor
is doing in *A Secular Age* is outlining how this second call even became au-
dible in modern Western societies. The existence of the first call—toward
religion or transcendence—does not have to be explained—it is presented
as simply persisting, albeit in changed and changing forms.

A little further on, Taylor explicitly rejects the view "that the human
aspiration to religion will flag."[84] Later he refers to the "irrepressible need
of the human heart to open . . . and first look, then go beyond [the tran-
scendent] window."[85] Exclusive humanism has not only slammed this window shut, but also blacked it out. Of course, it could be that here Taylor is
merely framing the debate from the side of transcendence rather than endorsing this position. But the fact that he has already rejected the possibility of a flagging in the human aspiration to religion renders him unable
to claim the status of neutral arbiter at this point. Notwithstanding his dis-
claimer that he is not "arguing either for or against an open or closed reading [of the immanent frame], just trying to dissipate the false aura of the
obvious that surrounds one of these," Taylor is no impartial mediator in
this dispute.[86] Indeed, at other times he admits to taking the side of transcendence against closed immanence, "freely confess[ing]" that "my own
view of 'secularization' . . . has been shaped by my own perspective as a
believer."[87] He later describes himself as speaking "from out of this religious understanding."[88] Invoking and rejecting once again Bruce's sketch
of religion's fate, Taylor foresees another future, based on the supposition
that "in our religious lives we are responding to a transcendent reality. We
all have some sense of this." This means, as he goes on to point out, that
forms of exclusive humanism that deny such transcendence are fatally

flawed, misrecognizing as they must the reality of transcendence.[89] On the following page he reiterates his general and particular positions on transcendence, claiming that "our sense of fullness is a reflection of transcendent reality (which for me is the God of Abraham)."[90]

While the remarks canvassed here strongly suggest that Taylor takes the orientation toward transcendence to be ontologically grounded, this becomes clearer in an interview conducted at the time of *A Secular Age*'s publication. There he says that "it is just evident that human beings are religious animals. There's something that intrinsically strikes people about spirituality, and that's part of the motivation. It's part of the reason why it goes on. And it [*sic*] you try to circle around that, you go nowhere."[91] This largely tacit ontological position also helps to explain the problems and limitations that arise from attempts to live the immanent frame in a closed way. Taylor concedes that the immanent frame is biased in the direction of closure: it tilts its inhabitants toward living without reference to or regard for the transcendent. This is the default position in modern Western societies: the "notion of a closed immanent order" is "culturally hegemonic."[92] Yet this bias is just that—a bias—and Taylor strives to correct for it by showing that the presumption that the immanent frame is closed to transcendence is a picture that holds us captive.[93] Trying to loosen the grip of that picture, he proposes that the immanent frame "allows of both readings, without compelling us to either."[94] In arguing that the immanent frame does not require the closing of the transcendent window, Taylor refers to the cross pressures generated by attempts to live in closed immanence. Using the term in yet a different sense from those analyzed above, he claims that just as the immanent frame draws its inhabitants toward closure, their experiences of the transcendent resist this, pulling them back from this conclusion.[95] In an earlier passage, Taylor uses the term *cross-pressured* in this same way, writing of "the cross-pressure felt by the modern buffered identity, on the one hand drawn towards unbelief, while on the other, feeling the solicitations of the spiritual—be they in nature, in art, in some contact with religious faith, or in a sense of God which may break through the membrane."[96]

Others have drawn attention to the religious inflection of *A Secular Age*,[97] but I suggest that there is also an ontological one, and that in order to fully appreciate its argument about Secularity 3, we need to recognize

Taylor's belief in humans' intrinsic orientation toward transcendence.[98] Taylor's claim about humans having an orientation toward the transcendent should, moreover, be understood with the aid of "best account" reasoning. This is a style of argument Taylor has deployed elsewhere in discussions of ethics and ontology. Despite its use of the superlative, a "best account" is not final or definitive but is based upon the things we find it hard to eradicate from, or explain away in, a depiction of human experience. His remarks in *Sources of the Self* are apposite here: "The world of human affairs has to be described and explained in terms which take account of the meanings things have for us. And then we will naturally, and rightly, let our ontology be determined by the best account we can arrive at in these terms."[99] Best-account reasoning thus allows for the possibility that a better account will one day come along that overturns the best one currently available. But it seems clear that Taylor deems any such supersession unlikely in the case of humans' orientation toward religion.

NOTES

Some of these arguments were first made in a paper presented at the American Political Science Association Annual Conference in Boston in 2008. I thank Michael Gibbons for convening the panel and Jean Bethke Elshtain for her comments as respondent. Bill Dodge, Joe Nawrocki, and Paul Weithman also provided helpful comments on that version of the paper.

1. Charles Taylor, *A Secular Age* (Cambridge, MA: Belknap Press, 2007), 2–3; cf. 423. Arto Laitinen calls these three types of secularity "political," "sociological," and "existential," respectively. See his review of *A Secular Age* in *Ethical Theory and Moral Practice* 13, no. 3 (June 2010): 353.

2. Taylor, *Secular Age*, 15; cf. 16, 20, 510, 544.

3. The introduction runs from pages 1–22, while chapter 13 to the end occupies pages 473–776. This is a companion paper to my "*A Secular Age*: The Missing Question Mark," in *The Taylor Effect: Responding to* A Secular Age, ed. Ian Leask, with Eoin Cassidy, Alan Kearns, Fainche Ryan, and Mary Shanahan (Newcastle, UK: Cambridge Scholars Publishing, 2010), 11–28. Both papers critically examine the meaning of Secularity 3. The first asks how secular the age we are said by Taylor to live in really is, proposing that Taylor's own framework can be used to show that religious belief is not as marginal to the lives of most contemporary Westerners as many of his remarks suggest. Both papers converge on an interrogation of what Taylor is saying about experience in a secular age.

4. Taylor, *Secular Age*, 29.

5. Ibid., 772; cf. 768.

6. In Michael Morgan's view, "we can best understand the book as having two parts, a diachronic or narrative one and a dialectical or synchronic one." See his review of *A Secular Age*, by Charles Taylor, *Notre Dame Philosophical Reviews* 2008-08-10, http://ndpr.nd.edu/review.cfm?id=13905. Morgan does not, however, indicate how detachable those parts might be from one another.

7. Others have offered assessments of the book's historical aspects. Jonathan Sheehan makes some critical remarks in his contribution to *The Immanent Frame* blog, "Framing the Middle," January 14, 2008, http://www.ssrc.org/blogs/immanent_frame/2008/01/14/framing-the-middle/. Elizabeth Shakman Hurd, by contrast, writes that "Taylor convincingly argues that historical processes associated with secularization were deeply intertwined with Reform within Christianity, concluding that the movements drawing the largest masses of people into the 'slipstream of disenchantment' were religious ones." See her contribution to *The Immanent Frame* blog, "The slipstream of disenchantment & the place of fullness," October 29, 2007, http://blogs.ssrc.org/tif/2007/10/29/the-slipstream-of-disenchantment-the-place-of-fullness/. In her contribution to the same blog, Wendy Brown criticizes Taylor's history for excluding "every stripe of outsider to Latin Christendom, from Jews and Muslims in Europe to colonized natives and other outsiders, as well as dissident voices, reversals and disruptions to what he calls his 'story.'" See her "Idealism, materialism, secularism?" October 22, 2007, http://www.ssrc.org/blogs/immanent_frame/2007/10/22/idealism-materialism-secularism/. Hurd echoes Brown's criticism of defining the West without reference to its constitutive other in her review of *A Secular Age* in *Political Theory* 36, no. 3 (June 2008): 490–91. For other objections to treating the West in isolation, see, in *Varieties of Secularism in a Secular Age*, ed. Michael Warner, Jonathan VanAntwerpen, and Craig Calhoun (Cambridge, MA: Harvard University Press, 2010), José Casanova, "A Secular Age: Dawn or Twilight?"; Nilüfer Göle, "The Civilizational, Spatial, and Sexual Powers of the Secular"; and Saba Mahmood, "Can Secularism Be Other-wise?". A number of contributors to William Schweiker et al. "Grappling with Charles Taylor's *A Secular Age*," *Journal of Religion*, 90, no. 3 (2010): 367–400, question Taylor's depiction of the history of Christianity. See also Schweiker's own review of *A Secular Age* in *American Journal of Theology and Philosophy* 30, no. 3 (September 2009): 323–329.

8. Taylor, *Secular Age*, 29, 268–9, 289, 301, 589.

9. References to this appear throughout the book—see the index entry for "subtraction stories" in Taylor, *Secular Age*, 871.

10. Taylor, *Secular Age*, 571–72.

11. Ibid., 22; cf. 157. I see this as analogous to Foucault's rejection of the repressive hypothesis—i.e., the idea that power simply negates and represses, and that if we could remove power's effects, a pristine, natural, preexisting self would emerge.

12. Arto Laitinen, review of *A Secular Age*, by Charles Taylor, *Ethical Theory and Moral Practice* 13, no. 3 (June 2010): 354. See also Taylor, *Secular Age*, 773.

13. Taylor, *Secular Age*, 22; cf. 294, 572–73. Taylor is similarly dedicated to the task of rebutting subtraction stories in his *Modern Social Imaginaries* (Durham, NC: Duke University Press, 2004), 18, 64.

14. Taylor, *Secular Age*, 727.

15. Ibid., 473; cf. Charles Taylor, *Varieties of Religion Today: William James Revisited* (Cambridge, MA: Harvard University Press, 2002), 79–80.

16. Eoin Cassidy argues, however, that the tenor of Taylor's discussion of authenticity has changed between these earlier works and *A Secular Age*. See his "'Transcending Human Flourishing': Is There a Need for Subtler Language?" in *The Taylor Effect: Responding to* A Secular Age, ed. Ian Leask, with Eoin Cassidy, Alan Kearns, Fainche Ryan, and Mary Shanahan (Newcastle, UK: Cambridge Scholars Publishing, 2010), 38–41.

17. Charles Taylor, *Sources of the Self: The Making of the Modern Identity* (Cambridge, MA: Harvard University Press, 1989), 376.

18. Ibid., 375–77; Taylor, *The Malaise of Modernity* (Concord, ON: Anansi Press, 1991), chapter 3.

19. Taylor, *Varieties of Religion Today*, 80.

20. Ibid., 94. This paragraph is reproduced in *A Secular Age*, 486.

21. Ibid., 112. This is repeated verbatim in *A Secular Age*, 516, except for a minor change in punctuation.

22. Much of the material from *A Secular Age*, 484–92, replicates material from the second half of chapter 3 of *Varieties of Religion Today*.

23. Taylor, *Secular Age*, 517. Further information about Taizé is available at http://www.taize.fr/en.

24. Cf. Taylor, *Varieties of Religion Today*, 88. From the work of Mikhail Epstein, he also finds some evidence of the spread of religious authenticity in post-Soviet Russia. Taylor, *Secular Age*, 533–35.

25. Pew Forum on Religion & Public Life, "The U.S. Religious Landscape Survey Reveals a Fluid and Diverse Pattern of Faith," February 25, 2008, http://pewresearch .org/pubs/743/united-states-religion.

26. Pew Forum on Religion & Public Life, "U.S. Religious Landscape Survey: Summary of Key Findings," 2008, http://religions.pewforum.org/. Casanova, "Dawn or Twilight?," 280, also cites this Pew study in discussing Taylor's work.

27. Taylor, *Secular Age*, 508.

28. Ibid., 512.

29. Taylor, *Varieties of Religion Today*, 95, 111–12; Taylor, *Secular Age*, 516. Peter Steinfels reads Taylor differently, saying that "In a development Taylor calls 'post-Durkheimian,' faith is uncoupled from any collectivity, whether the religious community or the civic order." See his "Modernity & Belief: Charles Taylor's 'A Secular Age,'" *Commonweal* 135, no. 9 (May 9, 2008): 18. This point about religious communities being made rather than given does not address the question sociologists of religion pose about how these more personal, less orthodox religious views and practices will be relayed to future generations. See, for example, Danièle Hervieu-Léger,

"Religion as Memory," in *Religion: Beyond a Concept*, ed. Hent de Vries (New York: Fordham University Press, 2008), 257–58. While these forms of religious life might be shared, in the absence of greater institutionalization, it is unclear how they can be preserved and transmitted over time.

30.   Charles Taylor and Gerard Bouchard, *Building the Future: A Time for Reconciliation*, Report of the Consultation Commission on Accommodation Practices Related to Cultural Differences (Quebec: Government of Quebec, 2008), 145–46. For a fuller discussion of this report, see my "Plus ça Change: Charles Taylor on Accommodating Quebec's Minority Cultures," *Thesis Eleven* 99, no.1 (November 2009): 71–92.

31.   Taylor, *Secular Age*, 510.

32.   Ibid., 510; cf. 512.

33.   Ibid., 529. Casanova concurs that the age of religious authenticity began much earlier in the United States than in other Western countries. Casanova, "Dawn or Twilight?," 272.

34.   Taylor, *Secular Age*, 19–21, 322, 423.

35.   Ibid., 3.

36.   Ibid., 303–4.

37.   Ibid., 21.

38.   Ibid., 531.

39.   Ibid., 437; cf. 21, which says that "Naiveté is now unavailable to anyone, believer or unbeliever alike." See also 30. Peter Berger sees contemporary religious pluralism as having similar consequences. As he says, "On the level of consciousness, this [pluralism] means that religion is no longer taken for granted, but becomes the object of reflection and decision." See his "Religion and the West," *The National Interest* (Summer 2005): 114. Berger adds that "The loss of the taken-for-granted status of religion in the consciousness of individuals means that they are forced to make choices. . . . But even an individual who declares adherence to a very conservative version of this or that religious tradition *has chosen to do so* and will be at least subliminally aware of the possibility of reversing that decision at some future time" (115; emphasis original).

40.   Modernity's homogenizing dynamic contributes to this situation, for while the pressures of modernity make people more alike, religious attachments separate and distinguish them. The modern presumption of social and political equality thus shines a light on religious differences, throwing them into question. In Taylor's estimation, modernity's "homogeneity and instability work together to bring the fragilizing effect of pluralism to a maximum." Taylor, *Secular Age*, 304.

41.   Taylor, *Secular Age*, 556.

42.   Ibid., 595.

43.   Ibid., 437; cf. 12, 531, 557.

44.   Ibid., 595.

45.   Ibid., 595; cf. 13, 531.

46.   It also suggests that he thinks of the typical university as a province of exclusive humanism. See, for example, Taylor, *Secular Age*, 525, 549.

47.   Taylor, *Secular Age*, 598; emphasis added.

48. Ibid., 676; emphasis added.

49. Ibid., 595; emphasis added.

50. Ibid., 598; emphasis added; cf. 676.

51. Ibid., 12; emphasis added.

52. Ibid., 12.

53. Ibid., 598.

54. Taylor's coinage, "the nova effect," refers to contemporary religious plural-ism; Taylor, *Secular Age*, 599. Indeed, early in Part III of the book, entitled "The Nova Effect," we read that "we are now living in a spiritual super-nova, a kind of galloping pluralism on the spiritual plane"; Taylor, *Secular Age*, 300; cf. 727. Yet there are times when Taylor's conception of the nova effect builds into itself the experience of cross pressures and fragilization. Casanova contends that the supernova description does not apply to western Europe, which manifests much greater religious homogeneity than the United States; "Dawn or Twilight?," 280. Hans Joas agrees that Taylor exaggerates re-ligious pluralism in Western societies, but on different grounds. Joas points out that the (small) number of people adhering to some of these new forms of religion and the (short) period for which they do so diminishes their significance for understanding contemporary religious experience. See his "Die säkulare Option. Ihr Aufstieg und ihre Folgen," Symposium zu Charles Taylor: *A Secular Age, Deutsche Zeitschrift für Philoso-phie* 57, no. 2 (2009): 293–300.

55. Taylor, *Secular Age*, 676.

56. Ibid., 4.

57. Ibid., 5; cf. 8, 13–14.

58. Charles Taylor, "Interpretation and the Sciences of Man," in *Philosophy and the Human Sciences: Philosophical Papers 2* (Cambridge: Cambridge University Press, 1985), 26; cf. 54. For a fuller discussion of Taylor's views on these issues, see Ruth Abbey, *Philosophy Now: Charles Taylor* (Princeton: Princeton University Press, 2000), 58–62; and Nicholas H. Smith, *Charles Taylor: Meaning, Morals and Moder-nity* (Cambridge: Polity, 2002), 120–28. A more systematic approach to the study of self-interpretations inspired by some of Taylor's insights appears in Hartmut Rosa, "Four levels of self-interpretation," *Philosophy & Social Criticism* 30, no. 5–6 (2004).

59. The sort of distinction I am suggesting also appears in Taylor's separation of agent and observer: "This universal category [meaning] doesn't belong to the agent's perspective, but rather appears to the (generally disenchanted) observer. . . . [T]his general theory of religion as motivated by the search for meaning . . . belongs so clearly to the observer's perspective"; *Secular Age*, 679–80. Taylor intends it as a criticism of the idea of religion as meaning when he points out that it is not the way an agent would describe his or her experience.

60. Taylor, *Secular Age*, 833–34, note 19. As this note indicates, in explaining that fragilization need not entail holding views with less conviction, Taylor is trying to preempt the sort of criticism Joas leveled at a similar claim by Berger.

61. The idea that facing "the alternative without distortion" can strengthen one's faith echoes a point made in Taylor's 1990 essay, "Comparison, History, Truth,"

reprinted in Charles Taylor, *Philosophical Arguments* (Cambridge, MA: Harvard University Press, 1995), 146–64. Although the focus of that article is the challenge of cross-cultural understanding, Taylor concludes it by pointing to the advantages that come from understanding the other undistortively: "Most of the great religions or secular world views are bound up with a deprecatory view of others in contrast to which they define themselves." Coming to understand another position nondistortively, "and hence to see its spiritual force," changes not only the way in which one views the alternative(s), but also the way in which one holds one's own beliefs. One's own beliefs no longer rely on deprecation of rival positions. Faith that cannot survive without such condemnation of alternatives will wither, whereas that with more positive bases "will be free to nourish itself on better food, on something like the intrinsic power of whatever the faith or vision points us toward" (164). For a fuller discussion of this essay, see Ruth Abbey, "Comparativists and Cosmopolitans on Cross Cultural Conversations," *Revista de Filosofía* 121, no. 40 (January–April 2008): 45–63

62. Taylor, *Secular Age*, 598.

63. Ibid., 599.

64. Ibid., 556.

65. Ibid., 556–57.

66. Ibid., 304; see also 437.

67. Pew, "Fluid and Diverse," 1.

68. In an interview published after *A Secular Age*, Taylor invokes this Pew study and concludes that it "does indeed say something about the nature and future of Western societies"; see "The New Atheism and the Spiritual Landscape of the West: A Conversation with Charles Taylor," interview by Ronald A. Kuipers, *The Other Journal.com An Intersection of Theology and Culture* 11, "Atheism" (June 12, 2008), http://theotherjournal.com/print.php?id=375. I would, however, not assume that American religious experience can be too readily transported to other Western societies.

69. Indeed, according to Cassidy, "the whole purpose" of *A Secular Age* is "to reinvigorate public discourse on foundational beliefs and values for twenty-first century Western society." "'Transcending Human Flourishing,'" 29.

70. Taylor, *Secular Age*, 618, 624–25, 656, 674–76, 726–27.

71. Ibid., 630, 656; 639, 668, 673, 688–89; 720–27; and 623–24, 627, 640–41, 656.

72. Ibid., 431, 627. A slightly different characterization of the debate appears on pages 556–57, where Taylor seems to be saying that those at one extreme can write their opposite number off as "just mad or bad," whereas "the intermediate positions can sometimes not be as easily dismissed." This suggests that the extremes are more likely to be fragilized by positions closest to them.

73. See their "Editors' Introduction" in *Varieties of Secularism in a Secular Age* (Cambridge, MA: Harvard University Press, 2010), 23.

74. Taylor, *Secular Age*, 594; cf. 437.

75. Ibid., 22; cf. 157.

76. As Stephen White has said, "One of Taylor's major interventions in contemporary social and political theory has been to stress the importance of underlying,

and sometimes obscure, ontological considerations." Stephen K. White, *Sustaining Affirmation: The Strengths of Weak Ontology in Political Theory* (Princeton: Princeton University Press, 2000), 42.

77. Taylor, *Secular Age*, 597; cf. 589.

78. At the end of one of these discussions (*Secular Age*, 677–78), Taylor directs readers to *A Catholic Modernity?* I assume the material he has in mind appears at Section IV, pages 30–36. Questions are raised about this view by Smith (*Charles Taylor*, 227–42), while Taylor's position is strongly criticized by Ian Fraser in *Dialectics of the Self: Transcending Charles Taylor* (Exeter, UK: Imprint Academic, 2007), 31–59. Fraser's book also has a chapter criticizing Taylor's concept of transcendence (62–77). Mark Redhead mounts some criticisms of Taylor's religious views in *Charles Taylor: Living and Thinking Deep Diversity* (Lanham, MD: Rowman and Littlefield, 2002), 175–209.

79. Taylor, *Secular Age*, 703. At the start of this discussion (695), Taylor refers to the final chapter of *Sources* in which he makes the claim that "high standards need strong sources" (516). However, most of this section of *A Secular Age* (695–99) replicates portions of *A Catholic Modernity?* verbatim. See Charles Taylor, *A Catholic Modernity? Charles Taylor's Marianist Award Lecture, with Responses by William Shea, Rosemary Luling Haughton, George Marsden, and Jean Bethke Elshtain*, ed. James L. Heft (New York: Oxford University Press, 1999), 30–35.

80. According to Colin Jager, "unofficially . . . Taylor seems to argue for the existential validity of Christianity as the best response to the secular age"; see his "This Detail, That History: Charles Taylor's Romanticism," in *Varieties of Secularism in a Secular Age*, ed. Michael Warner, Jonathan VanAntwerpen, and Craig Calhoun (Cambridge, MA: Harvard University Press, 2010), 177.

81. Taylor, *Secular Age*, 638.

82. Taylor, *Catholic Modernity?*, 28.

83. Taylor, *Secular Age*, 435.

84. Ibid., 515.

85. Ibid., 638.

86. Ibid., 551.

87. Ibid., 437; cf. 436.

88. Ibid., 653.

89. Ibid., 768.

90. Ibid., 769. Michael Warner, Jonathan VanAntwerpen, and Craig Calhoun see *A Secular Age* as "a personal book . . . Taylor speaks here of questions in which he has a powerful motivating interest"; "Editors' Introduction," 3. For some indication of Taylor's lifelong commitment to Catholicism, see Redhead, *Charles Taylor*, 13–16.

91. Interview with Charles Taylor, "Spiritual Thinking," Templeton Foundation, n.d., http://www.templetonprize.org/ct_thinking.html.

92. Taylor, *Secular Age*, 774. See also 14, 291, 555–57, 727.

93. Ibid., 291, 548–49, 555–57, 565.

94. Ibid., 550; cf. 551, 566, 594, 600.

95. Ibid., 555.

96. Ibid., 360.

97.  In descending order of generality, Sheehan reads it as "an *explicit* brief for a theological critique of secularism and the immanent frame"; see his "Framing the Middle." For Morgan, in his review of *A Secular Age,* it is "a philosophical paean to one form of Christian moral and political life." In Jager's estimation, "the phenomenology in which Taylor is most interested is the phenomenology of a Christian in a secular age — the person who must live with the knowledge that his or her faith is an option"; "This Detail, That History," 177. Charles Larmore sees it as "written by a Catholic for Catholics" in "How Much Can We Stand? Review of *A Secular Age,*" *The New Republic,* April 9, 2008, 40.

98.  In 2000 I detected that this was beginning to appear in Taylor's work: Abbey, *Charles Taylor,* 212. It has since grown stronger. On the basis of *A Secular Age,* 679, Simon During imputes to Taylor the view that "what he calls 'spiritual hunger' is integral to human beings . . ."; see Simon During, "Completing Secularism: The Mundane in the Neoliberal Era," in *Varieties of Secularism in a Secular Age,* eds. Michael Warner, Jonathan VanAntwerpen, and Craig Calhoun (Cambridge, MA: Harvard University Press, 2010), 107.

99.  Taylor, *Sources of the Self,* 69; cf. 57–62.

PART III

MIDDLE DWELLERS

CHAPTER FIVE

# Humanism and
# the Question of Fullness

WILLIAM SCHWEIKER

Throughout his writings, Charles Taylor has insisted that any adequate account of human action and social relations must attend to the meanings that sustain and motivate human beings. Against the aspiration of some political thinkers to analyze social life on the model of the natural sciences, Taylor has resolutely and tirelessly advocated a hermeneutical turn in thought. Further, because of his commitment to moral and political reflection, he has argued, unlike some hermeneutical thinkers, that human "meanings" always entail evaluations, what he has called strong evaluations, by means of which human beings guide their lives. The question of the good is thereby properly basic in human life. We exist in some "moral space," as he calls it, and thus understand and orient life within that context of evaluations.[1]

Granting these commitments, it is crucial, if one wants to understand the shifting patterns of human self-understanding and social existence, to examine the evaluations used by people, how they picture the moral space of life, and how they believe they ought to orient existence. This threefold examination widens reflection to its most comprehensive moral and even religious scope. In *A Secular Age*—a book based on Taylor's 1998–1999 Gifford Lectures entitled "Living in a Secular Age"—Taylor's ideas about human beings as self-interpreting animals moved by strong evaluations come to focus on the question of fullness in human life and also the ways certain forms of secularism flatten life and threaten fullness.

The idea of fullness and its relation, if any, to humanism is the subject of these reflections. I begin by indicating the purpose and standpoint of the inquiry.

IN LIGHT OF THE GENERAL outline of his thought just noted, it would appear on first blush that Taylor is a committed humanist of some form, since for him strong evaluations are linked to ideas about *human* flourishing or wholeness. Yet while obvious humanistic ideas about history, human action, flourishing, and self-understanding permeate Taylor's work, he has in recent writings undertaken an attack on what he calls "exclusive humanism." What is one to make of the attack on exclusive humanism by a thinker apparently committed to at least some features of a humanistic outlook? Unless one imagines that Taylor has somehow abandoned ideas that underwrite his entire philosophical output, then two things seem at stake: (1) competing conceptions of human fullness relate to different types of humanism, and (2) the possibility of a properly nonexclusive type of humanism, even if Taylor has not himself articulated the position. The purpose of this essay is, on the one hand, to reconstruct Taylor's argument by sorting through conceptions of the relation between types of humanism and ideas about fullness, and, on the other hand, to isolate and to identify a type of humanism that avoids the criticisms of exclusive humanism. The outlook advanced in the following pages is called "theological humanism" for reasons that will become clear later.[2] What is at stake, I judge, is how to preserve a humanistic focus within religious life, and thus to put moral constraints on what the religions can rightly do to human beings, while at the same time avoiding the reductions of "exclusive humanism."

There is of course some irony in me as a theologian raising the question of humanism. The irony springs from standpoints of reflection. A philosopher and political thinker, Taylor has nevertheless long held religious commitments that are consistent with his overall framework of thought. These commitments have become more explicit in works such as *A Secular Age* and his *Varieties of Religion Today: William James Revisited*, even while his criticism of secularism parallels worries about narrowly naturalistic accounts of human action.[3] The prohibition of religion, as Gianni Vattimo has noted, is over.[4] Social scientists, literary critics, political theorists, and even economists are exploring "religion." Like many other contemporary philosophers, Taylor too is talking about religion. Some might consider him a Catholic thinker.

The standpoint of this essay is admittedly theological. I am a Christian, Protestant theologian who holds that one must counter reductionist forms of secularism but also understand that one basic task of religious thinking is the *criticism* of religion. Religion is not merely some brute feeling or sense of "God," although it includes those sensibilities. Every religion we know about is some interpretation of reality through ritual, symbolic, and narrative forms as well as a way of orienting life. Theology is then an interpretation of an interpretation of reality. As a kind of second-order discourse, it seeks to articulate the meaning and show the truth of a religious outlook. More pointedly, theological thinking seeks to articulate and analyze the structures of lived reality for the sake of orienting life in relation to God. And this theological inquiry entails answering a range of other questions: What is religion? How should it be studied? What relation, if any, is there between a general concept of religion and the claims of specific communities and traditions? How—if at all—can one make judgments about the truth and goodness of religious convictions? Theology as a form of critical and constructive reflection must be suspicious of supposedly undistorted knowledge of the divine, including claims made by one's religious community, found in experience, or advanced by theologians, philosophers, and religious leaders. Call this a prophetic or an ethical impulse, but it is a central ingredient in Christian thought. Christ insisted that the Sabbath was made for human beings and not human beings for the Sabbath. Religious ritual and practice ought to respect and enhance the integrity of life. In Christian theology the two great commands, to love God and to love the neighbor, are thus necessarily intertwined and inseparable. This fact should guide reflection on God and human existence. It is at once a methodological principle about how to undertake theological thinking and an idea of fullness that is neither exclusively humanistic nor a kind of hypertheism. Later in this essay, I return to this point in light of engaging Taylor's work on religion and humanism.

This claim about different standpoints—philosophic and theological—can be made more generally and in terms of the topic of the present inquiry. If human beings are creatures unavoidably oriented by what they hold as good and right, and so by some idea of fullness, as Taylor properly notes, then, religiously speaking, they are beings who always find something to worship. Strong evaluators, understood theologically, are worshipping beings. As G. K. Chesterton is said to have observed, "When people stop believing in God they do not believe in nothing; they believe in anything." The theological question is about the right and proper, the truly divine, object of devotion. The very meaning of "God" in Christian thought thereby requires the critique of religion and the criticism of idolatry. The ground of criticism from a Christian perspective is the link between love of God and love of neighbor. So, from a theological perspective, we live not only in an age in which there are different forms of the "secular," but also in a supercharged religious age. The agenda of theological humanism working within a religious tradition is to provide orientation in ways that escape exclusive humanism and also forms of "hypertheism," in which human flourishing is sacrificed to religious piety or unquestioned orthodoxy. We will see later that Taylor agrees on this point and thus would seem to be committed to a form of religious humanism.

On the way to that conclusion, I want next to reconstruct the outlines of Taylor's position in order to clarify his criticism of exclusive humanism. I call this a reconstruction because Taylor's thoughts about religion and humanism run through several works but are not given direct or systematic presentation. That is the job of the reader. Two main points will become salient: the intrinsic connection between a conception of fullness and where it is "located," and, further, how to understand the possibility of human transformation in relation to ideas about fullness. Those matters in hand, I can identify what appears to be tension in his religious thought. I conclude by working beyond the strictures of his position to indicate the meaning and purpose of theological humanism.

READERS OF *A SECULAR AGE* know that it is a massive study of Western culture and the place of religion within it. At the core of the book

is an observation. "We have moved," Taylor writes, "from a world in which
the place of fullness was understood unproblematically outside or 'beyond'
human life, to a conflicted age in which this construal is challenged by
others which place it . . . 'within' human life."[5] Four interlocking questions
are thereby involved. What do we mean by *fullness*? Where is it "located"
(within human life or somehow beyond it)? How, if at all, can human beings attain some measure of fullness? Finally, how has the shift from one
conception and location of fullness to another taken place? Most of the
book is preoccupied with the last of these matters, and so with historical and
social transitions. Taylor seems to have a couple of points to make about
the shift. One is a normative intent to counter the narrowing of fullness
under the pressure to reform life, to make people better within the immanent frame of history. As he puts this later in the book, "The urge to reform
has often been one to bring all of life under the sway of a single principle or
demand: the worship of the one God, or the recognition that salvation is
only by faith, or that salvation is only within the church."[6] The worry is
about an overarching moralism and what I called above "hypertheism,"
each driven to reform human beings with respect to beliefs about fullness
and how best to guide human interactions.

Taylor's other point about the shift in modernity is more historical
and interpretive. The target is what he calls the "subtraction theory," that
is, the claim that modernity is best understood by subtracting religion.
The theory—of which there are many versions—asserts a "uniform and
unilinear effect of modernity on religious belief and practice."[7] Taylor
wants us to look again and to see how complex our secular age really is.
He knows that whoever tells the story defines the terms of debate. If religion was part of modernity all along, then it is, per definition, admissible
to contemporary discussion, and the subtraction theory is wrongheaded.[8]
This insight is also an opening to the first point about the shift in modernity, since one can then challenge on descriptive and phenomenological
grounds the narrowing of fullness and where it is supposedly located. Taylor's historical account strives to be error-reducing, as he has called it in
other writings, on the "subtraction thesis" and thus to show the validity of
his account. More importantly, on my reading, he wants to explain why
"exclusive humanism" is the product and yet also the driver of the link between these points: it locates fullness solely within human life and incites
a rage for order to remake life so that human beings might "flourish."

Rather than engaging the historical objective of the book in detail, I will consider now the meaning of *fullness* and where it is located. Later I will pick up the theme of personal and social "transformation," but first it is necessary to gain clarity about fullness. The idea, again, is that human identities are always tied to convictions about the meaning of reality rooted in strong evaluations. We cannot abstract from those beliefs in order to reach some supposedly neutral perspective if we wish to understand ourselves. In *A Secular Age*, Taylor notes that "every person, and every society, lives with or by some conception(s) of what human flourishing is: What constitutes a fulfilled life? What makes life really worth living? What would we most admire people for?"[9] Of course, so formulated, the claim is purely formal; it is simply about the necessary connection between human self-understanding and some orienting good. Thinkers such as Plato or, more recently, Iris Murdoch have made the point, but so too has a long history of theological reflection from St. Augustine to Luther and Schleiermacher, and then in the twentieth century from the likes of Paul Tillich, H. Richard Niebuhr, and many others. Every human being has some ultimate concern about the meaning of being (Tillich). One's ultimate trust is one's "god" (Luther). There is a "whence" to self-consciousness and a related highest good (Schleiermacher). Each human life is marked by a decisive love of self (*amor sui*) or love of God (*amor Dei*), in relation to whom self and others are loved (Augustine). Everyone must have some center of value (Niebuhr).

Of course this concern, trust, or love can be misguided, misplaced, and distorted—that is, theologically speaking, the condition of sin. The point remains: human beings are evaluative creatures. Even Nietzsche—hater of both Plato and Christianity—made a similar argument. Human beings always and necessarily live within some "table of values," as he called it, in relation to the constitutive feature of reality, the will to power.[10] The contention that human beings are evaluative and thus moral/spiritual creatures is crucial to sustain in the face of attempts to explain morality soley in terms of brain functions or, as Taylor challenged in earlier work, merely as the analysis of human action as events and natural processes. The argument is also, as noted, a kind of ontological reflection, that is, inquiry into the meaning of being drawing on the moral sources of a culture or civilization. The space of human existence—our ontological condition—is shaped by these sources.

Whether the *formal* claim about human beings as evaluative creatures can be sustained is not the point of the present inquiry, although I readily agree with Taylor and others about it. More germane to this argument is the *content* that a thinker or even a culture gives to its ideas of "fullness," and that is, as previously mentioned, the real target of Taylor's argument in *A Secular Age*. About this matter, I think one needs to pull apart positions that, if I read him rightly, are sometimes collapsed within the flow of his narrative. The battle over fullness and its location is more complex than it first appears. What do I mean?

Taylor's contention is that present conditions of experience, and so one kind of "secularity," tend toward exclusive humanism and therefore a truncated idea of fullness. Fullness, on this outlook, is to be found solely within the immanent framework of historical existence and, because of the pressure to attain it, gives rise to a rage for order to remake human beings to this end. In terms of Christianity, the drive for reform and the rage for order, especially among Protestants, has given rise to a homogenous conception of fullness, an "excarnation," that is the "steady disembodying of spiritual life, so that it is less and less carried in deep meaningful bodily forms, and lies more and more 'in the head.'"[11] This move inward, as it were, is a connection to secularism. "In fact, a striking feature of the Western march toward secularity is that it has been interwoven from the start with this drive toward personal religion."[12]

What is lost is a sense of belonging to a group—what Taylor has elsewhere called the post-Durkheimian condition—in the drive toward the personal and the desire for authenticity. More specifically, what is lost to individualism are forms of embodied communal religion.

The burden of Taylor's argument is to show that a different account clears up confusions and reduces errors in exclusive humanism (religious or not) even while it resonates with actual life and our experiences of transcendence and fullness. However, it is also salient that, according to Taylor, the two points are connected: how fullness is conceived is related to where it is believed to be "located." Exclusive humanism conceives of fullness as the ordering of human life for maximal flourishing within the flow of historical time. The problem with modern (mostly Protestant) religion is, on his account, that it locates the connection to the divine solely in the individual.[13] Insofar as "fullness" can be attained nowhere else than within mundane history or in authentic selves, and there is no power other than human power to attain it, the rage for order is both demanded and justified. However, in order to grasp the force of this argument and also to isolate yet another option, we need to probe further the modern moral order.

The moral/spiritual landscape of human life, according to Taylor, is three-dimensional: there is, first, a sense of fullness that reaches beyond our ordinary experience to a depth or power in existence; second, there are moments of exile or brokenness from that fullness; and third, there is a kind of middle condition between fullness and exile. In various writings he has noted that too often the critics of religion reduce it to either other-worldly renunciation or, as noted above, repressive moralism. However, Taylor argues that there are various ways of being religious that link fullness to something "beyond" the human. There is a saintly or monastic path that includes acts of renunciation in order to bring long life, health, and benefits to the community of believers. On this way of being religious, "the supreme achievements of those who went beyond life have served to nourish the fullness of life of those who remain on this side of the barrier."[14] There is, likewise, the path of purity that is a more extreme ascetic or puritanical stance. Religious reformers in every tradition, such as Protestants within Christianity, may demand that everyone pursue the path of renunciation, not just the saints. This is, of course, the rage for order in religious form, and it can be seen in fundamentalisms around the world and in other widely popular forms. The path of purity may lead to a denial of modern humanitarian concern and gives rise to the idea that religions are repressive and moralistic.

A final way of being religious, and one favored by Taylor, is the path of self-giving love that is characterized by a more complex relation between renunciation and flourishing. The believer renounces her or his flourishing in the service of a transcendent good, but this renunciation, ironically, makes possible a renewed affirmation of what has been renounced. As Taylor describes it, "Renouncing, aiming beyond . . . , not only takes you away but also brings you back to flourishing."[15] Enlightenment in Buddhism "does not just turn you from the world; it also opens the flood-gates of . . . loving kindness . . . and compassion."[16] Christians renounce flourishing by praying that "God's will be done, on earth as it is in heaven." Yet because God wills human fullness, renunciation makes it possible to regain what was renounced. "He who would gain his life must lose his life for my sake," as Christ put it. Or, "What would it serve a man to gain the whole world and lose his soul?" In this respect, flourishing, for Christians, has a paradoxical character. Love of God and love of neighbor—even of the enemy—means that fullness for one's life cannot be directly aimed at, but is found by acting for the sake of God and others. In this respect, Christian renunciation means forgoing the direct pursuit of one's own flourishing with the faith and the hope that the life of love is the fullness of human existence.

The vital question is how one conceives and inhabits the middle condition, the fact of our longing and yet also finitude and exile. Further, there are different religious ways of inhabiting this condition. Despite these different paths, what religious people share is a faith and hope in fullness beyond the mundane world, as well as experiences of the in-breaking of a fullness graciously received under its own power. This in-breaking can take various forms, ritualized or not, and they also denote a "higher time," as Taylor calls it, amid historical time. It might happen in festival, an epiphany, or in what Tillich called "kairotic events," that is, events in which the fullness of time is present within the flow of chronological time. Religion includes a higher good beyond human perfection, a higher power that transforms human life, and "life as going beyond the bounds of its 'natural' scope."[17] Taylor grants that some of the great spiritual visions of humanity have been "the causes of untold misery and even savagery."[18] Many religious people believe, in terms of saintliness or purity, that true fullness requires "a profound inner break with the goals of flourishing in their own case; they are called on, that is, to detach themselves from their own flourishing, to the point of the extinction of self in one case, or to the renunciation of human fulfillment to serve God in the other."[19] Yet that is only one way of being religious. Taylor insists that rejecting transcendent ideals in toto because of the dangers of strident renunciation exacts too high a price, a "stifling" of "some of the deepest and most powerful spiritual aspirations that humans have conceived."[20] Human beings cannot be content with an affirmation of the everyday goods of human life. They "have an ineradicable bent to respond to something beyond."[21] As noted above, people are driven to "worship" something. Denying the religious impulse thus amounts to a kind of suffocation that flattens as well as constricts moral experience and leads to concealing that impulse, not to its destruction in human life.

This reconstruction of Taylor's argument has complicated the picture of ways of inhabiting the middle condition that links some form of renunciation with flourishing. First, there are a variety of ways of being religious, ways of connecting human fullness to something beyond the immanent frame of worldly life. Second, within ways of being religious, Taylor is keen to isolate the dangers of the way of purity and the saint as well as the rage for order and excessive renunciation. He marshals his own "criticism of religion." In light of that criticism, he advocates another path that entails the paradoxical relation of renunciation and fullness. But, finally, there are thinkers who insist that the religious way is always moralistic and repressive and either demeans or destroys finite human life. For them, it is a human possibility to dwell within the middle condition, with the conviction that human flourishing is to be found here and nowhere else and that the power of that fullness is wholly a human power.[22] Thinkers of this ilk agree that human beings always live with strong evaluations and live in the middle condition. They insist, as Martha Nussbaum puts it, on an innerworldly or lateral kind of transcendence, which asks us "to bound our aspirations to the constitutive conditions of human existence" and so to delve deeply into the realities of finite life and human excellence.[23] Whatever transcendence is available can be found only there, because otherworldly transcendence elides (so they claim) concern for actual life and can breed disgust of finite existence, with its many imperfections. This last outlook is, in Taylor's terms, the path of exclusive humanism; it entails its own strong evaluation and also a specific innerworldly moral ontology.

Taylor finds the roots of exclusive humanism in the axial religions, Western Christendom and especially Protestantism, with its claims about the sanctity of everyday life and everyday vocations. Yet the implications of exclusive humanism are more profound and contestable than its ostensive historical origins. The outlook led to the "buffered self," a self closed off from more radical kinds of transcendence, and thus an "exclusive" humanistic way to live in the middle condition, driven by the quest for authenticity. Socially speaking, exclusive humanism requires the reordering of social life in ways that maximize utility. What counts as "good" can be made roughly equivalent among people, and what protects people's rights can be

measured. Further, experience is coded around certain moral principles—
basically those of utility and rights—that somehow are to guide social existence. According to Taylor, code fetishism cannot meet the actual dilemmas of existence even if it can—and has—warranted aggressive policies
of restructuring life. Not surprisingly, his story of the "secular age" is about
the debate over the kind of "fullness" that human beings can and ought to
seek and also what kind of transformation of existence is needed for that
fullness.

By reconstructing Taylor's account of our religious condition, we have
lent nuance to those readings of his work that pit religious experience
against exclusive humanism. To be sure, most of the debate over his recent
work has been on this point and has led to the perception, noted at the beginning of this inquiry, that he now apparently rejects any humanistic outlook even if that endangers other features of his thought. That is not the
case. Taylor has his own criticism of religion. What he rejects is exclusive
humanism and a specific way of being religious, the path of purity. Further,
Taylor seemingly equates the two: the path of purity and exclusive humanism are essentially linked. It is that equation which I now want to examine
in order to move toward theological humanism, first historically and then,
second, by probing the question of the power of transformation.

First, a historical observation: one can challenge the story Taylor tells.
As stated above, he finds the roots of the modern rage for order in reform
movements within Christianity. This is a surprising argument, and it is one
that theologians—who are conspicuously underrepresented in *A Secular
Age*—need to assess. I imagine that by isolating the roots of the rage for
order within Christianity, Taylor hopes to move Christians beyond that account of their faith and back to something closer to Jesus and the Gospel.
Yet the point of Christian faith has always been that human beings cannot
utterly transform or save themselves. It is why the Reformers rejected medieval Catholicism, with its monastic orders and ideas about condign and
congruent merit. The path of the saint or the monk was seen to be hu-
manly impossible and even idolatrous in its quest for purity. The magisterial reformers such as Luther and Calvin, and much later others such as
John Wesley, insisted that God and not human codes or human actions
redeem human beings. In their outlook, Protestants were being biblical.
After all, the Bible has the Decalogue and the Holiness Code in Leviticus,

and also Jesus's Torah teaching in the so-called Sermon on the Mount (Matt. 5–7). This is hardly code fetishism; it is about liberation, emancipation, and freedom. So, the roots of modern code fetishism ought to be sought in nonreligious sources, monastic movements, and medieval penitential rites as well as with the Reformers who proclaimed God's free grace accepted in faith and sought to lessen human suffering by renewing the social order. Taylor knows this, of course. Yet the argument of the book, it must be said, lays most of the blame for the rage for order, the buffered self, and also the origins of exclusive humanism at the feet of Protestants. There are historical questions to pose to that account.

Given that my concern is with "fullness" and humanism, I leave aside the historical worry just mentioned. More crucial for the present argument is the question of human transformation and whether or not this can be seen in purely human terms. Taylor's insight is to see that the problem of moral change cannot be outside of politics and ethics, nor—and this is crucial—simply within the moral and political order. What does this mean?

I HAVE BEEN ARGUING THAT Taylor's position is a complex defense of a basic thesis about the meaning of fullness and where it is located in human life. The defense is offered through an excavation of the modern moral order, both historically and broadly, in hermeneutical and phenomenological terms.[24] So far I have been exploring his depiction of our "religious" condition. But the thesis also has moral and political dimensions. Under that heading, the claim is that we find ourselves in a cultural and political situation in which it is hard if not impossible to rise above consequentialist calculations and rigid ideas of reciprocity in the attempt to overcome legacies of human conflict or even conflicts between goods. In other words, we are in a situation in which what counts as a "valid" and persuasive moral or political argument is one that supposedly "works" by making things better. Further, what is "better" is determined on nonmoral grounds so that "goods" can be made roughly equivalent and people's rights measured. This also means that we have to make people better so that they will work to make things better in the way so defined. This is the moral/political backbone of code fetishism and also exclusive humanism and the rage for order.

So, the moral and political order of modern Western cultures entails the belief that a code will settle disputes based on ideas about the commensuration of goods, personal rights, set procedures, and also a certain kind of moral formation so that we will live by these ideals. One hallmark of the modern world is this kind of secular redemption rooted in a rather one-dimensional view of human beings and moral situations. Given this, modern societies lack the epistemic and affective resources to rise above the mundane in order to reorient commitments. Yet code fetishism and exclusive humanism rest on a still deeper element in the current moral order, namely, the loss of a vibrant sense of religious transcendence that provides the perspective and motive to address and overcome seemingly intractable social and political problems, especially those about violence and war.[25] Taylor's idea about human transformation is that the contribution religion can make to social life is crucial. Religious resources, through ideas such as "forgiveness" and "sanctification," provide the epistemic distance and motivation needed to overcome conflict.

Anyone mindful of the history of modern ethical thinking from Kant onwards knows that one of its profound weaknesses is how to deal with human evil and moral change.[26] This has led some thinkers back to virtue theory in ethics. It has led others to insist that the problem of moral change is simply outside the ambit of ethics and politics. It has also led to social engineering, code fetishism, or longing for the Übermensch. There is little doubt that high modern societies truncate human experience and seek purely procedural answers to social problems. Here, too, some reconstruction of Taylor's argument is in order. We can isolate a parallel distinction with respect to conceptions of transformation and the various ways of inhabiting the "middle condition." Clarifying these distinctions, which Taylor himself does not do, is a crucial step in these reflections because it helps to articulate a way of being religious that is also humanistic. Can one isolate different kinds of the rage for order, just as we indicated differences in being religious?

A quick survey of modern—and even ancient—social thought discloses at least three different "types" of thinking about human transformation. Despite profound differences among thinkers, a first type of prominent modern outlooks, found in various ways in Rousseau, Marx, Durkheim, and others, sees the human problem in terms of the relation between persons and society or social structures. In order to change the human condition, it is necessary to alter social structures and thereby address the forms of repression, inequality, and alienation that scar social life. The "rage for order" is directed at social structures (institutions, classes, etc.) rather than at individuals precisely because the problem is specified in terms of the relation between human beings and society. Most of these arguments either see religion as illusion and repressive ideology (Marx) and thus locate the power of transformation purely within historical processes, or, conversely, isolate that power in the "general will" and some "civil religion" (Rousseau) or identify the religious with the community itself (Durkheim). Given Taylor's worries, in *A Secular Age* and *Varieties of Religion Today*, about a post-Durkheimian world where spiritual life would be totally private and in line with procedural liberalism, it will be crucial in a moment to return to this point.

A second, virtually opposite, type of thinking—again despite differences among those who hold the account—locates the human problem not between people and society, but in the core of human existence itself. Old ideas about the war between the flesh and the spirit or religious conceptions about the depth of sin or illusion mean that in order to overcome our plight, we have to be changed, ontologically as well as morally. Once human existence is changed, social structures will follow suit. The rage for order is quite different from the first type. Monastic and meditative practices, ascetic disciplines, and certain conceptions of divine redemptive action and human sanctification characterize this outlook. The account, we should note, can take religious and nonreligious forms. That is, one might hold, as many Christians do, that the "power" of sanctification is God's action or some cooperation between divine and human action, as Thomas Aquinas might put it. Currently, there are proposals about the church as a counter-society and the need to resocialize people through the story of God's action in Christ. Others argue this idea on purely naturalistic grounds, say, Nietzsche's idea of the will to power and the emergence of the Übermensch, or Kant's transcendental argument, in *Religion within the Limits of Reason Alone*, about moral transformation with respect to the image an agent forms of the "redeemer."

These two types of social thought about human transformation and where the "power" of that transformation is "located" do not exhaust the possibilities, although many, and sometimes Taylor as well, argue such. For example, one can hold a third type—as many Christians do—that the power of human transformation is "beyond" human capacities, and yet it is possible for human beings to develop institutions and structures that work to ameliorate, if not overcome, forms of innerworldly want and injustice. Transformation is possible to some degree in social life, but fallen and alienated human beings are not capable of radical self-transformation. Further, the kind of transformation that is possible in social life finds its norm in justice, but this is at best an approximation of Christian love. Individuals can act out of love for others, but societies, as Reinhold Niebuhr reminds us, do not have the same capacity for self-transcendence. This outlook thus has a double edge: persons can and do sometimes act in love, but they can never transform their own being; social life is open to some measure of transformation, but human collectivities are bound by self-interest and thus not open to genuine transcendence.[27] This type of position might lead to a kind of "rage for order," but it is decidedly limited rage given the conception of the human plight. On the one hand, human beings need a fundamental transformation beyond their own capacities if they are to attain real fullness. Salvation is a matter of grace. On the other hand, the capacities we do have can and ought to be used to lessen want, protect the innocent, and work for justice. Acknowledging that the power to attain fullness is not one's own and that some renunciation of endless striving for it is religiously required enables one to labor for the sake of others through which, paradoxically, fullness is yet received.

This account of the distinction and yet relation of personal and social transformation is deeply embedded in the Christian tradition. It is overlooked by Taylor, although as far as I can tell, his position might be a version of it. The oversight might be explained by the fact that his main target, along with exclusive humanism, is procedural liberalism. Secular liberal social thought sees no problem within human beings and so is naïve about the depths of human sin, much like the first type noted, but it hopes to ameliorate social problems based on rights, private preferences, and procedural justice. That argument, I submit, is decidedly different from this third type of thought about transformation just isolated. It is why, in my judgment, a robust Protestant or Catholic liberal social thought is not open to criticisms leveled against its secularized forms.

I have now drawn some distinctions among accounts of human transformation. By doing so, we uncover a puzzle that must be explored. Taylor seems to endorse the first type under the rubric of a Durkheimian outlook, stressed by him, no doubt, in order to counter the buffered self, expressive individualism, and private religion. Yet he also endorses the third type, since the power working for human transformation is not limited to human or social powers. Solving this puzzle should clarify the relation between the religious and the moral/political sides of Taylor's position and move us toward theological humanism. How to solve the puzzle?

Actually the puzzle is not too difficult to solve, or so it seems. First, against typically modern accounts of religion that stress the individual and faith, Taylor argues that "the religious connection, the link between the believer and the divine (or whatever), may be essentially mediated by corporate, ecclesial life. . . . Let us imagine further that these ways are in some respect inherently social: say, that we are called upon to live together in brotherly love, and to radiate outwards such love as a community. Then the locus of the relation with God is (also) through the community and not simply the individual." This is, as he admits, a Catholic vision of the church as a sacramental community. And, further, it entails the "idea of God's life interpenetrating ours, and of this interpenetration being made fuller, more intense and immediate through our own practices."[28] On one level, then, Taylor wants to show that a way of inhabiting the middle condition, one way to connect to a higher power, is neither saintly nor the path of purity, with problems of renunciation and moralism, but, rather, a more collective, sacramental one. This argument accords with the first type of social thought noted above, in which the main problem is between people and their community. However, Taylor gives an explicitly Catholic account of this outlook because the power of transformation is not the community qua community. That power is from God, mediated sacramentally through the community and made intense by Christian practice. Part of his claim is that the modern moral order is one in which we cannot return to a premodern, paleo-Durkheimian world in which connection to the community was not only necessary but also sufficient. Taylor sees the problem of the loss of a vibrant religious life, yet he is sure that we do not want to retreat into religious enclaves and attack "modern" commitments to democracy or human rights. This is why he distances himself from movements such as Radical Orthodoxy or those who would bash everything modern.

What, then, about the third type of social thinking that also seems present in his argument, at least at times? Precisely because he seeks to isolate a "Catholic" option within the modern moral order, and thus to isolate different ways of being secular, something like that third type is also needed. In one passage, Taylor notes strands in French Catholic spirituality, specifically "*l'humanisme dévot.*" The idea is that "we try to come closer to God, or center our lives on him, where we proceed in a fashion that trusts and builds on our own inner élan, our own approach to God." This can be contrasted, as he goes on to show, with forms of religious practice "which consist in following the Law, or God's command, as these are prescribed in the tradition or Revelation, without necessarily relying for guidance on one's own inner sense of these things."[29] He concludes that these two are not necessarily opposed. Ideally, they complement each other. Importantly, he confesses that is the leaning of his thought. In other words, there is a kind of humanism, devout humanism, that can and must be complemented by the more communal outlook as a way of inhabiting a "secular age" and thus avoiding exclusive humanism and expressive individualism, but also social or religious tyranny. How does this solve the puzzle, since, after all, it was about conceptions of "transformation"?

While Taylor is worried about the dangers of a post-Durkheimian world in which social life is reduced to expressive individualism, procedural justice, and code fetishism, he likewise insists that this condition thankfully disconnects more and more the relation to the spiritual from political society. This opens the possibility of different kinds of spiritual connection that one can have and how they are or are not mediated by a community, but it does so, thankfully, by desacralizing society and national identities. That fact is, one must say, crucial in our hyperreligious age, in which forces seek to resacralize ethnic and national identities around the world. In terms of transformation, Taylor seems to seek a vision in which some inner élan, inner desire for God, is formed by religious practices and disciplines even as the connection to the divine is mediated by a sacramental community but not the secular, political order. This position would seem to be, I suggest, a version of the third type of transformation noted above. The social order is understood in purely mundane terms, and it is possible and necessary to work to ameliorate suffering and injustice, but the capacity for that kind of social labor is not sufficient to account for real religious transformation. Religious transformation, and the fullness that can come with it, requires the mediation of connections to God coupled with sustained religious practices that shape and guide the desire for God. Trouble arises when these are disconnected. The collapse of the distinction between social and human transformation leads to a rage for order. Trusting only one's personal religious desires and breaking the collective connection to God leads to excessive individualism and an "excarnation" of religion.[30] The denial of deep experiences and the desire for God finds its consequence in the triumph of exclusive humanism over a devout humanism. Our current condition, religiously speaking, is precisely to dwell within these disconnections. That is the force of the shift traced in *A Secular Age* and the reality of living in the middle condition as I have developed it above.

By reconstructing Taylor's argument, using the relation between humanism, fullness, and transformation as the means to connect his account of our religious condition with moral/political reflection, I have isolated versions of an option missing from the story he tells, and yet a version that appears to be his own. In light of the modern religious situation, it is possible to balance "devout humanism," with its focus on human desires for God, and a more communal focus where the connection to God is mediated by the practices and sacraments of the church. In order to avoid exclusive humanism and the rage for order in religious ways of living in the middle condition, these two claims cannot be opposed. That insight can then be formulated as a theological principle for determining adequate and justified religious claims that are consistent with the double love command: the stress on communal practice and sacramental mediation cannot demean or thwart the personal élan and desire for God, and, conversely, the personal religious quest cannot rightly deny or distort the communal mediation of connection to God. There are, it seems to me, both Catholic and Protestant versions of this principle that differ in how its elements are balanced and related. Yet the task is to balance them. The balancing is precisely the ongoing work of the religious life.

In terms of the modern moral/political condition, I have isolated an outlook that sees the depth of the human problem *within* human existence, and thus any transformation to fullness is by and with grace, how-ever that is mediated. Conjointly, this position still holds, on moral and religious grounds, that it is possible and morally required to ameliorate human want and suffering through the transformation of social insti-tutions. If these are collapsed, then there is a rage for order to transform human beings through either a hypertheistic appeal to God's sovereignty over life or an exclusively humanistic belief in the power of human self-transformation, individually and socially. The key is to avoid collapsing claims. That insight can be formulated as a social/moral principle also consistent with the love commands. And, again, there are Catholic and Protestant versions of the social/moral principle: the idea of subsidiarity among Catholic social thinkers and Protestant ideas about the balance of powers within differentiated and interacting social spheres or domains. These are also ways to thinking about and inhabiting social life religiously in our "secular age."

My present task is not to explore the details of Protestant and Catho-lic accounts of these principles, but merely to isolate them. They provide distinct options for thinking socially/morally and theologically about the relation between religious commitments and the order of human life. I hope I have shown that there is more commonality between Taylor's proj-ect and some versions of Protestantism than he admits. Likewise, there are points for fruitful disagreement within wider shared commitments about how to counter exclusive humanism and the rage for order in its various forms. I will not explore these matters further; the real insight is that, taken together, the theological and the social/moral principles allow us to return to the question of humanism. That is to say, if I have given a fair reconstruction of Taylor's position and isolated forms of thought not examined in his work, then, importantly, in order to be fully articulate about possible ways of life in the secular age, we need a type of religious humanism.

DESPITE GIVING A HISTORY of the conditions of modern experience, Taylor's own position remains rather formal. His story does not explore in detail the *content* of any religious interpretation of reality and thus remains mostly on the level of a general conception of "religion." This gives the impression that traditional forms of religion—say, conservative Catholic

piety—can remain with their forms and authorities and legitimately claim
to be just one more way of living in the secular age. There is, of course,
a degree of truth to that judgment, insofar as we are living amid multiple
modernities, as Taylor has shown. Nevertheless, the forms of religious life
now seen on the world scene beg for critical and constructive theological
reflection on the actual meaning and truth of religious practices, symbols,
and forms. Taylor has avoided the theological task, and that is because,
as I noted at the outset, he takes a philosophical and political standpoint.
If space allowed, it would be possible to provide theological interpretations of various religious accounts of reality, and so (say) Christian claims
about Christ as redeemer, eschatological events, salvation and creation,
and so on. That is not the purpose of the present essay.

What has been noted by neither friend nor foe of Taylor's project is that,
if my reconstruction is right, the *norm* for viable and valid religious life is
not drawn from traditional authorities or "revelation," but rather developed
by articulating the conditions of experience. This conceptual move, in which
norms for theological reflection on religious interpretations are not derived
solely from religious sources and authorities, opens the possibility, I suggest, of a way of being religious in the post-Durkheimian world in which
people can freely inhabit religious sources. In order to make sense of these
points it is helpful, and I think necessary, to speak of theological humanism.
Let me explain.

It should be clear at this point that by *theological humanism* I mean
a way of living freely within a religious tradition and thus inhabiting its
symbolic, ritual, and narrative interpretation of reality, with respect to the
theological and social/moral principles I have isolated by reconstructing
Taylor's argument. That way of life can take different forms: a Christian
theological humanist (Catholic, Orthodox, or Protestant) is different from
a Muslim one (Sunni or Shia) or, for that matter, a Buddhist theological
humanist (Zen or otherwise). The humanism is "theological" because it
understands human fullness in a religious way and yet with respect to a
principle for making judgments about the meaning and truth of a religious
outlook. To recall, theology is a second-order normative interpretation of
first-order religious interpretations of reality and human life. Theology is
an interpretation of an interpretation. It is concerned with the meaning
and truth of a religious interpretation of life and reality. In this respect, a

Buddhist, no less than a Christian—or Muslim or Jew or Hindu—can practice theological reflection and adopt a theological outlook, even if the first-order religious interpretation (as, say, in some forms of Buddhism) does not speak of "gods." Yet this outlook remains a kind of humanism because its social/moral principle is about the complex nature of human flourishing and transformation with respect to human beings as moral agents motivated by strong evaluations. A viable way of inhabiting a religion freely must balance the desire for God and the communal mediation of religion to God; this avoids an invidious opposition between human longings for what is divine and the necessarily communal mediation of religious life. It aims to save religion from hypertheism. By the same token, one should not collapse the insight into the depth of the human problem within human existence itself and the demand, on religious and moral grounds, to ameliorate want and suffering. This aims to avoid exclusive humanism and also a destructive rage for order. Theological humanism, then, is a name for a way of life deeply informed by and freely inhabiting religious sources, and oriented by these principles, as we have called them; a life so lived aims to incarnate these in actual existence. The belief is that such a life is marked by genuine fullness. It is, therefore, a practical, lived response to the secular age.

What does this mean for the Christian life, since, as noted at the outset, it is the tradition within which I think and live? For Christian tradition—and, perhaps, the outlook of other religions too—the idea of human fullness, the highest good, interrelates actual human flourishing with ideas about what is righteous, just, holy, or virtuous. A Christian vision interweaves a robust Jewish commitment to justice with strands of thought, Hellenistic and otherwise, that focus on human flourishing. Yet that is not quite right, either. Those traditions—Jewish and others, as well as nonreligious outlooks—also have ways of thinking about these connections between flourishing and justice, albeit in different ways. In other words, the highest good is not just one transcendent otherworldly standard, as the critics claim, but actually a complex, synthetic idea. This perspective on the highest good entails, at least in a Christian vision, an account of our condition. The travail of history is marked by a longing for the resolution of the collision between flourishing and righteousness, the fact that in this world, those who flourish are not always righteous and the righteous too often suffer. Since the "space" of human existence in the middle condition is the complex reflexive interaction of institutions, communities, beliefs, and values, as well as human fault and viciousness and also natural processes, the longing for resolution is at best ambiguously satisfied.

This fact, even aporia, in a Christian interpretation of reality is an engine of creativity, the stage for human despair and fidelity, and also the source of endless human folly and humor. Accordingly, any idea of fullness that is not constitutively about the relation of flourishing and righteousness is too trimmed down—either too otherworldly or too innerworldly. Trimmed-down visions lack urgency, depth, and a realistic assessment of our condition, or they stunt human aspiration. Purely innerworldly or ardently otherworldly accounts of fullness thereby lack the depth of insight and power of motivation actually to orient life. Any Christian account of our condition that denies the tension is naïve about human possibilities, despairing of ameliorating any woe or injustice, or driven by a rage for order to change the world. Christians hope for the resolution of this conflict pictured in the eschatological reign of God. It is not a product of human striving alone. Yet it frees one to labor responsibly and joyfully for justice and flourishing, since together this is what is meant by fullness.

If that is the case—at least, a lot of Christians and others seem to adopt an outlook like this—then the quest for fullness cannot be divorced from convictions about what is right and holy, any more than the love of God can be separated from the love of neighbor. This perspective thereby indicates another take on the moral and spiritual shape of the "middle condition" between fullness and exile, namely, the irresolvable tension in history between flourishing and righteousness, happiness and holiness. The challenge of a secular age, maybe of any age, is how to live within the middle condition without despair, defiance, resignation, or naïve idealism, but with a resolute and joyous commitment to the integrity of life with and for others. It is a way of living religiously in a secular age that does not rage for order or truncate human transcendence, even as it clarifies the domain of responsibility and how religious convictions might help fashion a humane future in a time when the rush to flourish too often trammels human hope, struggles for what is just, and endangers the integrity of realms of life.

I am hinting at an outlook that parallels Taylor's account but entails as well a decidedly different perspective on how to conceive and to inhabit the middle condition, at once religious and humanistic. It involves ontological reflection because a conception of the highest good is used to articulate conditions of experience and the variety of responses to it. This perspective has found different expressions throughout the Christian tradition. And it is one, I think, that we need to cultivate in an age in which, too often, exclusive humanistic ideals trammel religious longings, and the religions too easily demean and mutilate the goodness and dignity of finite human life.

## Notes

1. A number of thinkers have recently addressed the connection between beliefs about the meaning of reality and their place in the formation of human identities. See, for example, Stephen K. White, *Sustaining Affirmations: The Strengths of Weak Ontology in Political Theory* (Princeton: Princeton University Press, 2000); William Connolly, *Neuropolitics: Thinking, Culture, Speed* (Minneapolis: University of Minnesota Press, 2002); and, of course, Charles Taylor, *Sources of the Self: The Making of the Modern Identity* (Cambridge, MA: Harvard University Press, 1989). See also *The Hedgehog Review* 7, no. 2 (2005). It is interesting that these theorists are now discovering insight of earlier Christian theologians, such as Paul Tillich and H. Richard Niebuhr, and, still earlier, Luther and Augustine on the constitutive relation between self and community and some ultimate concern about the meaning of being (Tillich) or a center of value (Niebuhr) or trust of the heart (Luther) or a decisive love (Augustine). I return to this point later in this essay.

2. See David E. Klemm and William Schweiker, *Religion and the Human Future: An Essay on Theological Humanism* (Oxford: Wiley-Blackwell, 2008).

3. Charles Taylor, *A Secular Age* (Cambridge, MA: Belknap Press, 2007); and Charles Taylor, *Varieties of Religion Today: William James Revisited* (Cambridge, MA: Harvard University Press, 2002).

4. Gianni Vattimo, "The Trace of the Trace," in Jacques Derrida and Gianni Vattimo, *Religion* (Stanford, CA: Stanford University Press, 1998), 79–94. I owe this reference to Klaus Tanner.

5. Taylor, *Secular Age*, 15.

6. Ibid., 771.

7. Ibid., 461.

8. It is important that one line of modern social thought, owing to the work of Max Weber and Ernst Troeltsch, never accepted anything like the "subtraction theory," but always understood that religion in some form would be present even in highly rationalized and seemingly secular societies.

9. Taylor, *Secular Age*, 16.

10. For a fine discussion of these issues, see Robert B. Pippin, *Nietzsche, Psychology and First Philosophy* (Chicago: University of Chicago Press, 2010).

11. Taylor, *Secular Age*, 771.

12. Taylor, *Varieties of Religion Today*, 13.

13. This is of course a longstanding Catholic criticism of Protestant thought and life, but it is one that has been widely rejected by contemporary Catholic theologians. The fact that Christian faith always entails some personal or existential relation to the living God does not mean that faith is reducible to a private, subjective relation.

14. Charles Taylor, "Iris Murdoch and Moral Philosophy," in *Iris Murdoch and the Search for Human Goodness*, ed. Maria Antonaccio and William Schweiker (Chicago: University of Chicago Press, 1996), 21.

15. Ibid.

16. Ibid.

17. Taylor, *Secular Age*, 20.

18. Taylor continues, "From the very beginning of the human story, religion, our link with the highest, has been recurrently associated with sacrifice, even mutilation, as though something of us has to be torn away or immolated if we are to please the gods." Taylor, *Sources of the Self*, 519.

19. Taylor, *Secular Age*, 17.

20. Ibid., 520.

21. Taylor, "Iris Murdoch and Moral Philosophy," 25.

22. Recall Martin Heidegger's insistence on resoluteness in being towards death, Hans Blumenberg on self-assertion and the legitimacy of the modern age, or current advocates such as Tzvetan Todorov of neohumanism and innerworldly transcendence. See Martin Heidegger, *Being and Time*, trans. J. Macquarrie and E. Robinson (New York: Harper & Row, 1962); Hans Blumenberg, *The Legitimacy of the Modern Age*, trans. R. M. Wallace (Cambridge, MA: MIT Press, 1983); and Tzvetan Todorov, *Imperfect Garden: The Legacy of Humanism* (Princeton: Princeton University Press, 2002).

23. Martha Nussbaum, "Transcending Humanity," in *Love's Knowledge: Essays on Philosophy and Literature* (New York: Oxford University Press, 1990), 379.

24. Taylor has addressed some of these issues elsewhere. See Charles Taylor, *Modern Social Imaginaries* (Durham, NC: Duke University Press, 2004).

25. For related but different account, see Jonathan Glover, *Humanity: A Moral History of the Twentieth Century* (New Haven, CT: Yale University Press, 2000); and Raimond Gaita, *A Common Humanity: Thinking about Love and Truth and Justice* (New York: Routledge, 2000).

26. No doubt the most profound thinker standing in the line of Kant to address the problem is Paul Ricoeur. See his *The Symbolism of Evil* (Boston, MA: Beacon Press, 1986).

27. One finds this argument in Luther's claims about the freedom of the Christian in love, in Calvin's depiction of the Christian life, with John Wesley and his conception of perfection in love, and, most recently, in the work of so-called Christian Realists such as Reinhold Niebuhr. For a recent discussion of Christian Realism and

its importance for social and ethical thought, see Robin W. Lovin, *Christian Realism and the New Realities* (Cambridge: Cambridge University Press, 2008).

28. Taylor, *Varieties of Religion Today*, 23–25.

29. Ibid., 15, 16.

30. This is another place where historical nuance is needed. The magisterial reformers and many others as well were critical of claims by "enthusiasts" such as Thomas Muentzer to having individual revelations from God. While Catholic polemics like to lump all Protestants into that camp, it is clear that Luther, Calvin, Anglican divines, and leaders such as Wesley insisted on the social mediation of spiritual connection—through scripture, the church, preaching, and sacraments—as well as deep personal piety.

# Chapter Six

# The "Drive to Reform" and Its Discontents

## CHARLES MATHEWES AND JOSHUA YATES

> *The modern world is not evil; in some ways the modern world is far too*
> *good. It is full of wild and wasted virtues. When a religious scheme is*
> *shattered (as Christianity was by the Reformation), it is not merely the vices*
> *that are let loose. The vices are, indeed, let loose, and they wander and do*
> *damage. But the virtues are let loose also; and the virtues wander more*
> *wildly, and the virtues do more terrible damage. The modern world is full*
> *of the old Christian virtues gone mad. The virtues have gone mad because*
> *they have been isolated from each other and are wandering alone.*
> —G. K. Chesterton, *Orthodoxy*

*A Secular Age* offers many lessons, but perhaps the most interesting is one that, ironically, challenges the book's very title. For in the book, Taylor suggests that the defining characteristic of modern times is not the much-

debated rise of the secular, but the universalization of the drive to Reform—
the imperative to take active responsibility for the progressive improvement of the world. All those who live within the orbit of the modern West
and its dominant institutions, which are now global in scope, live under
the relentless glare of this commanding impulse. However much we fail
to satisfy this impulse in practice, however much we manipulate it to suit
our respective interests and inner longings, we, as Western modern people,
cannot lead our lives without paying homage to it, even when that homage comes indirectly in the form of resistance, evasion, or escape. Believers
and unbelievers alike, we cannot avoid the burden of taking responsibility
for ourselves or the world.

Evidence of this is everywhere. Today, examples abound of people trying to enhance the human condition by reforming social relations on a yet
more prosperous, just, sustainable, and peaceable footing. Such examples
are at once extraordinary and routine, geographically ubiquitous and historically unique. Consider the armies of the humanitarian, development,
public health, refugee, human rights, environmental, educational, and social justice INGOs that today cover the surface of the globe. Think of the
cadres of experts, advocates, practitioners, celebrities, and philanthropists
who have dedicated themselves to various causes, from ending extreme poverty and global pandemics such as HIV/AIDS to fighting climate change
to promoting the rights of indigenous peoples. Their activism is predicated on a powerful and historically distinctive ideal: that we can and
should work for the betterment of other humans, even strangers beyond
our shores, as well as the welfare of other species and the health of the
planet; that neither the natural nor the social and moral condition of
humankind is static or determined, but rather subject to our own creative
and interventionary powers.[1]

These are only the most conspicuous of examples. The animating impulse reaches still deeper and is more pervasive. Francis Bacon's classic formulation of humanitarianism as the "relief of man's estate" has long func-
tioned as an *ideological* rationale for modern organizations of all kinds,
from universities and hospitals to scientific bodies and international organizations. But it is *ontologically* constitutive as well, stamped into the
DNA of the modern organization itself. Consider the persistent need modern organizations have to articulate their world-reforming aims through

constitutions, charters, and mission statements, as well as their (and our) persistent desire to monitor their effectiveness in meeting their constitutional aims. Is GDP going up or down? Are malaria rates or childhood obesity rates rising or falling? What about literacy? Maternal mortality? Infant natality? Internal population displacement? Biodiversity? Teen pregnancy? Violent conflict? Modern organizational structures act in this way as vast accounting mechanisms that, taken together, provide a barometer on how well we are doing and where we are still failing to improve the world. The modern social order is thus organized and legitimated around managing and solving a universe of discrete social problems in the name of improvement and reform. To rework an apt analogy from the sociologist Peter Berger, this imperative to improve the world is the shadow cast by the "sacred canopy" of the modern West upon the entire world.

Taylor is right to identify the imperative to Reform as so fundamental. He is also right to diagnose this imperative as riddled with tensions and contradictions. Through the fissures of repeated frustration and failure, in the unbridgeable gaps between our idealizations of the world and the world of actual experience, a host of questions emerge, as vexing as they are abiding: How can we take care of our neighbor, let alone the entire world? Why do we feel compelled to care for the world at all, let alone in the particular ways we do—for example, giving primacy to the means of life as primary elements of human flourishing? Does the pursuit of human flourishing so understood lead to a full life, a life of coherence and meaning, a life well-lived? Is this pursuit the surest path to personal "fullness"? Or is there something more, something greater that the preoccupation with the primacy of life obscures or denies, something that might include a fuller range of human experience, including self-assertion, even if that means a rejection of life's primacy? Do the efforts to secure the mundane primacy of human flourishing actually depend upon some adherence to a metaphysical source? Feeling the weight of these and similar questions is, for Taylor, inevitable for, inescapable within, intrinsic to, and crucially constitutive of our condition in this secular age.

And here is the irony: the very energy at the center of what Taylor labels our "secular age" has its origins, and perhaps its still-motivating energies, in fundamentally *religious* impulses. For him, both the "drive to Reform" and the search for "fullness" emerge out of developments within Christianity, and it is their emergence within the matrix of Christendom that has led to the process commonly labeled "secularization." The biblical warrant for seeing the fallen world as the "theater of God-willed activity in one's calling," as Weber once put it, has driven the rise of the secular age in which we now live and is central to the ethical predicament at its heart.[2] We misconstrue the "secularity" of our secular age unless we understand the specific history of its emergence. Christianity remains central to the unfolding story; indeed, Taylor even suggests that Christians today may possess a potential antidote to the inhuman demands and disenchanting effects of "the drive to Reform," albeit only if Christianity can recognize its own captivity to that drive.

*A Secular Age* weaves together ideas Taylor developed over the course of his career into a vast, many-stranded narrative tapestry. But what makes this work stand out from his previous writings is that it is at once deeply learned and profoundly personal. As he says, "In a way, this whole book is an attempt to study the fate in the modern West of religious faith in a strong sense," where "faith in a strong sense" means belief in transcendent reality and the connected aspiration to a self-transformation "which goes beyond ordinary human flourishing."[3] In this book Taylor appears as one of the most sensitive and discerning religious thinkers of our time, plumbing the depths of the modern spiritual condition in ways that most honest-minded readers, believers or not, will recognize in some measure as their own. But this religious inquiry is enabled—empowered, oriented, and profoundly informed—by an equally deep acquaintance and engagement with social theory. Indeed, it is Taylor's profound engagement with social theory that we suspect many theologians and philosophers miss in his work, much to their detriment in understanding, appreciating, and building upon his proposal. For it is at the intersection of his social theory and his religious reflections, we think, that religious communities have the most to learn from Taylor's work.

In this essay we explore Taylor's analysis of the drive to Reform and assess its normative and descriptive fruitfulness for helping religious communities more faithfully and vitally inhabit the contemporary world. First we sketch Taylor's ambivalent assessment of our modern condition, focusing especially on the philosophical anthropology underlying his assessment. Then we explore how this account helps religious believers understand their situation, in part by applying it to the experience of one of the largest Christian movements abroad today—namely, Evangelicalism—in order to learn how religious believers in general, and Christians in particular, should act in light of this ambivalent condition. We conclude with some comments meant to suggest how this example may help religious believers, and the rest of us as well, appreciate aspects and implications of Taylor's work that would otherwise go unnoticed.

## TAYLOR'S GRAND THEORY OF WESTERN MODERNITY

Taylor is after no small quarry. He is concerned with understanding both the very particular historical and sociocultural provenance of the imperative to take active responsibility for the world and how this transformation has altered human understandings of reality—from experiencing reality most basically as an external cosmic order that determines human reality and to which we must conform, to experiencing reality as the consequence of the creative and contingent acts of human agents and thus as a "reality" that is increasingly ours to determine.

Nonetheless, Taylor's analysis of modernity is neither triumphalist nor apocalyptic. While he affirms many of the basic aspirations of Western modernity's project, he also points out where he sees it to be, in certain senses, faulty, in some cases aggravating the very problems it is trying to overcome, and in others creating totally new problems. There is something in it, he thinks, that generates profound "cross pressures" that make our stances of deeply held belief (and unbelief) more brittle and fragile than they have been in the past, and to a greater degree than we are usually inclined to admit. In the modern world, more is explicitly demanded of us, but less is granted for our unquestioning reliance than ever before.

## WESTERN MODERNITY'S REVOLUTIONARY MORAL ORDER

Taylor locates the engine of this transformation in the new conception of moral order that initiated and evolved with the emergence of Western modernity.[4] This moral order offers radically new ideals of selfhood and sociality, as well as an unprecedented background picture of how these ideals fit together in time and in the cosmos, and a revolutionary redefinition of "the good" in terms of this-worldly ordinary life. It is helpful to consider each of these key elements briefly in turn.

The new ideal of selfhood is what Taylor refers to as the "free-agent" self. In contrast to premodern conceptions of selfhood, which were putatively more porously related to society and to the cosmos, the modern vision is of a thoroughly "buffered," but also "disciplined," "rational," "disengaged," (and lately) "expressive" self. The modern individual is ultimately understood to be self-determining and deserving of the full respect and protections that flow from this fact. Furthermore, the freely willed intentions of such utterly individuated and rational human beings are to be the prime movers of both history and society. The free-agent ideal of selfhood is, in anthropological terms, the sacred good of Western modernity, the cornerstone upon which the entire edifice of the modern moral order rests.

These buffered selves inhabit a new kind of social existence. The organization of economic and political life is designed to enable individuals (as "free agents") to work toward their mutual benefit—that is, to secure the means of life via material prosperity and security—through association and common action. "The ideal social order," writes Taylor, "is one in which our purposes mesh, and each in furthering himself helps others" (*MSI*, 14). It does this by stressing the various rights and obligations that modern individuals possess prior to the constructed political order. This is a radically nonhierarchical vision of society, one of individuals cooperating, all at the same ontological and evaluative level, for each one's mutual benefit.

Integral to this nonhierarchical social vision is the affirmation of ordinary life of which Taylor has made so much in his writings. In the modern imaginary, humanity's highest aspirations find realization in the quotidian practices of provision and sustenance—for example, the goals of work and family. The organization of society no longer points *upward* to eternity and the perfection of virtue, but instead *outward* to "the basic conditions of existence of free agents" (*MSI*, 13). Borrowing a memorable line from Philip Rieff, in the modern mindset we find "amplitude in living itself."[5]

Together, these evolving dimensions of the modern moral order issue in the ascendance of what Taylor calls "the immanent frame." By this evocative phrase he attempts to describe the constellation of "self-sufficient immanent orders" (*SA*, 543) that today form the dominant horizons of public meaning in the West. In the wake of Hurricane Katrina, to give one telling illustration, public discussion focused on the acute failures of local and federal government agencies in either emergency preparedness or emergency response. No one in any position of official responsibility interpreted the devastation wrought by this massive storm in terms of divine retribution, as they once might well have.[6] Whatever moral one took from it—and there was a variety to choose from—the disaster had only meteorological and sociopolitical significance.

As this example suggests, the immanent frame is distinctively "immanent" because it offers no essential functional role for transcendence in shaping human moral existence. This modern moral order has no organic or functional role for God—God becomes a hypothesis, "an entity," as Taylor says, "which we have to reason towards out of this framework" (SA, 294). At least on its surface, the modern moral order appears to work fine without recourse to the transcendent or the supernatural.

Nonetheless, religious longing for transcendence "remains a strong independent source of motivation in modernity" (SA, 530). That is to say, against declensionist narratives of religion in modernity (whether triumphant or despairing), the transformation of religion in modernity "cannot be captured [simply] in terms of a decline and marginalization of religion" (SA, 530). In fact, the immanent frame can be porous to transcendence, depending upon how it is "spun": it can be either "closed" to it, offering a strict immanence (what Taylor calls "exclusive humanism" [SA, 19]), or "open" to it, as a source of power and motivation beyond the immediate givens that the frame sees as motivating agency. The social, structural, and imaginative conditions of belief and religiosity have changed through modernity; the options for "fullness" have widened beyond traditional religion (SA, 19, 437). Today, "the salient feature of Western societies is . . . a mutual fragilization of different religious positions, as well as of the outlooks both of belief and unbelief" (SA, 595). By *fragilization* Taylor here means that in modernity, for the first time, "belief is an option" (SA, 3), a choice in our culture—not a pre-given, unquestioned reality. Thus there are challenges to belief *and* unbelief in our age; as Taylor says, "Naïveté is now unavailable to anyone, believer or unbeliever alike" (SA, 21; see also 12, 30).[7] Our most fundamental, ontological foundations seem to be up to us, all a matter of our choices, all the way down.[8]

For Taylor, all this represents a revolutionary break from what came before. And the "drive to Reform" is at the heart of it.

The genealogy of this drive is enormously complicated. The rise of the major world religions (in the so-called Axial Age transformations) encoded in each religion's elites an impulse to spiritual reform, to align themselves with the proper transcendent normative order. But in Latin Christendom that elite impulse metastasized into a drive to make over society entirely—to make all classes conform to the higher path of the Christian gospel as it was understood. This is the moment when the reforming impulse became the totalizing "imperative to Reform" in the West.

Ironically, for all its initial religious motivation, this imperative turned out to be an enormously disenchanting force. (Here Taylor drinks deeply at Weber's well.) Aiming to root out all forms of idolatry and pagan contamination in the name of a pure Christian faith and practice, it would eventually usher in a "world shorn of the sacred," in the sense of a dimension of reality qualitatively different from "profane" life (*SA*, 80). It is an energy, moreover, that continues unabated today—only now it is the entire human race and the whole Earth that have increasingly become the object of Reform.[9] At the deepest cultural level, the drive to Reform attempts to overcome the gulf between ideal and actual worlds that was so radically injected into human consciousness by the Axial transformations. Yet this very overcoming operates not by aligning contingent human will with immutable cosmic order, but instead by actively constructing social reality according to the individual's will.

On a practical level, the drive to Reform has enabled ever-greater numbers of individuals to enter the ever-expanding categories of membership in societies that are at least constitutionally premised on mutual benefit. It has arguably resulted in a greater concern with human flourishing than any other force in history. On the other hand, Taylor suggests it brings real costs:

Our age makes higher demands of solidarity and benevolence on people today than ever before. Never before have people been asked to stretch out so far, so consistently, so systematically, so as a matter of course, to the stranger outside the gates. A similar point can be made if we look at the other dimension of the affirmation of ordinary life, that concerned with universal justice. Here, too, we are asked to maintain standards of equality that over wider and wider classes of people, bridge more and more kinds of difference, impinge more and more in our lives (*SA*, 695).

This moral revolution is double-edged in yet another way. The drive to Reform is inherently instrumentalizing, demanding rigorous methodologies of control. This marshals tremendous power, to be sure; but the power originally cultivated to enable us to do good soon becomes *the* good-in-itself. The aim shifts from love to will, and the will to love becomes the love of will, and any force or reality or condition restricting our sheer power becomes, gradually, immoral. As Taylor says, "The higher the morality, the more vicious the hatred and hence destruction we can, indeed must wreak" (*SA*, 709)—first and foremost on ourselves, in our single-minded obeisance to a tightly wound understanding of moral reform. The "great commission" becomes the "great confinement," what Nietzsche and Foucault would call a form of slave morality, oppressing rather than liberating us. The irony for Latin Christendom is profound: rather than leading to a more perfect and faithful realization of its ideals, the drive to Reform leads to its radical transformation, if not outright downfall.

Nonetheless, Taylor does not want to get beyond good and evil. For all its faults, the moral order of Western modernity is a towering achievement; today, he writes, "we live in an extraordinary moral culture, measured against the norm of human history, in which suffering and death, through famine, flood, earthquake, pestilence, or war, can awaken worldwide movements of sympathy and practical solidarity."[10] Moreover, at home, we are daily the beneficiaries of countless goods, including freedom of conscience, self-realization (or authenticity), a fundamental affirmation of life and the reduction of suffering, and most important of all, a profound concern for human dignity. Even in some of modernity's more ambiguous achievements, such as the value we have lately come to place on authenticity, Taylor is quick to point out the goods involved.[11]

Because of this, Taylor believes that the modern moral order is a great advance in the practical penetration of the Christian gospel in human life, one that was not possible in the confines of Christendom itself. Christianity needed the semi-antithesis of Enlightenment and its nonbelieving humanisms to realize crucial parts of its calling. (Taylor even offers up "a vote of thanks to Voltaire" [*CM,* 16].) In this way modernity is related inextricably but complicatedly to the prior era of Christendom.

Today, then, we are heirs to the moral revolution sparked by the Axial Age, to the drive to Reform. But the cultural contradictions of this drive have generated in moderns a particular set of discontents.

## Reform and Its Discontents: The Hegemony of Exclusive Humanism

For all his positive appreciation of the opportunities availed humanity in modernity, the dominant note of Taylor's assessment is ambivalence. After all, he thinks the discontents generated by the drive to Reform are so profound that they threaten to undo whatever good that drive might accomplish. In particular, he focuses on two central problems: the hegemony of exclusive humanism in public culture and the dangers inherent within the drive to Reform when directed solely at human flourishing. According to Taylor, the repeated failure of explicitly Christian attempts at reform played a significant role in opening up the space for the emergence of an exclusive humanism in opposition to Christian belief. More profoundly still, the drive to Reform puts tremendous moral pressure on all inhabitants.

While it is true that all beliefs are self-consciously contingent in our age, some are more self-consciously contingent than others. While the immanent frame does not compel one form of moral understanding, it does seem, for Taylor especially, to encourage one, namely, exclusive humanism. "Exclusive humanism," writes Taylor, "closes the transcendent window, as though there were nothing beyond—more, as though it weren't a crying need of the human heart to open that window, gaze, and then go beyond; as though feeling this need were the result of a mistake, an erroneous worldview, bad conditioning, or, worse, some pathology" (*CM,* 26–27). The rise of the free-agent self, the institutionalization of the mutual benefit society, the eclipse of vertical in favor of horizontal forms of solidarity, and the affirmation of ordinary life, although sought initially for religious reasons, opened the door to the emergence of exclusive humanism.

Yet the exclusive humanist approach has its own problems satisfying the demands of Reform. It has an extremely difficult time articulating the full range of motivations that compel us to pursue the goods it promises. In particular, its monological focus on immanent human flourishing as the highest good denies what many people experience as the source of life and value. The drive to Reform, in other words, has led to the dominant paradigm of "exclusive humanism," only to see that paradigm eschew access to the resources—the transcendent sources of fullness and wholeness— that have traditionally sustained the humanistic enterprise. In Taylor's view, this is self-destructive: "The metaphysical primacy of life is wrong and stifling and . . . its continued dominance puts in danger [life's] practical primacy" (*CM*, 29). It does so because it engenders a profound but not directly expressible resentment about its infinite demands, and that resentment may in turn curdle into cynicism.

This tension—between the depth of the demand and the shallowness of the resources marshaled to meet that demand—is vivid for many people in ordinary life today. An example can be seen in the wrenching soul-searching that has preoccupied much of the humanitarian aid movement over the past few years.[12] The utopian hopes of the post–Cold War era have been lost, replaced by a far grimmer (indeed, despairing) insistence that we simply care for *these* people, *here*, and not ask any larger and fruitless questions about "why" or "wherefore," questions whose asking, it is implied, can only lead to demoralization and apathy.

This defensive response is provoked whenever one seeks a relatively thoughtful account of the limits of the humanitarian worldview. Self-investigation, or a Socratic questioning of one's friends, or research into the websites and in the statements of the humanitarian NGOs and other groups to which moderns are drawn, repeatedly uncovers some version of the following: *There are suffering people out in the world. We will not bother ourselves with merely philosophical questions of whether or not such suffering can ever be eliminated. What matters is simply that we can help them,* here, *and* now, *and refusing to do so would be criminal.*

Is this response really satisfactory to the questioning person? We do not think it is; we think it effectively punts on the fundamental issue. It does not so much answer the question as reject the question itself as somehow tasteless, unworthy of being asked. But this is merely a reaction to a threat, not a thoughtful response to a legitimate worry. Effectively, this response implies that the moral demand to which we are expected to respond cannot find in our articulated worldviews any intelligible wellspring of motivating moral energy—any articulated insight or self-consciously held conviction to which we might return, in the dark nights of our moral souls, for rejuvenation and sustenance. We are commanded, instead, without any satisfactorily expressed rationale, merely to obey.

Of course, it is always possible simply to try harder: to insist that the solution to modernity is more modernity—to believe, that is, that the problem is our residual if partial captivity to archaic premodern notions of self and community and world, and our solution is to more fully accomplish our liberation, make all of us properly free agents and individuals. But such strategies are not, in the end, compelling. If, as George Santayana put it, fanaticism is redoubling your efforts when you have forgotten your aim, such changes suggest that our moral revolution threatens to become fanatical.

It is not surprising, then, that Christians and others in the party of transcendence often experience the dominance of exclusive humanism within the modern moral order as stifling. But Taylor also notes a "revolt from within" the immanent frame, in which many who reject the transcendent still find the terms of exclusive humanism too constraining. This emerges in the Romantic "reaction against the disciplined, buffered self" and climaxes, in a way, with Nietzsche and his contemporary heirs, who want to affirm the whole movement of life, which significantly includes death, or the negation of life. Indeed, from a Nietzschean perspective, the inarticulacy of exclusivist humanism simply makes it the latest iteration of slave morality. "Slave morality" is what happens (in part) when the expressed moral commands of a society are altogether disconnected from, or at best indeterminately related to, the actual energies motivating human life in that society. Nietzsche looks more prophetic every year, as his diagnosis of the fundamental problems of a post-Christian society trying to hold onto a Christian morality comes increasingly to resemble our world.

In this Nietzschean movement, we first see the rise of the "aspiration to wholeness" (SA, 609) framed as a complaint against immanent secularism. Some of this tradition's deepest thinkers, such as Camus and Nietzsche, offer "narratives of self-authorization" (SA, 589) and attempt to sketch an account of such affirmation as providing just the sort of rich and full experience of meaning that secularism lacks, not by attention to some realities *outside* the self, but rather by accessing the deepest wells of the self as furnaces that forge meaning (*SA,* 245, 886–87). But while such antihumanist efforts do recognize the sources of the self's being as beyond the self, their complaint fairly quickly goes off the rails, and they seem by some terrible necessity to only be able to articulate this affirmation of agency through a rhetoric of domination and violence—an essentially violent and even nihilistic language of struggle, conflict, and brutal self-overcoming (*SA,* 637–39). If we are not interested actually in inhabiting the alternative world Nietzsche offers us—a world of cruelty and violence, where our joy is intrinsically related to that same cruelty and violence, springing from the same ruthless source of energy—then what *should* we do?

In this "three-cornered culture war" (*CM,* 29), the main debate is, again, not about whether there is a God, but about what moral order there is that can replenish the enormous expenditure of moral energy that the drive to Reform demands of us. All this helps us appreciate Taylor's critiques of what he judges to be the major rivals to his position, namely, a wholly immanent secularism and a recoiling from that secularism into something like the Nietzschean Übermensch. For Taylor, wholly immanent "secular" accounts of the human endeavor often are so concerned with resisting theological temptations that they fail to capture the depth and power of the moral meaningfulness that people experience in their lives every day; such accounts are finally too flat and hence unable adequately to acknowledge the transcendent power of the sources of the self. And while, for Taylor, antihumanism's "very existence . . . seems to tell against [the vision of] exclusive humanism" (*SA,* 638), exclusive humanists have not been persuaded.

Here the key disagreement seems to be one of philosophical anthropology, which surfaces in Taylor's controversial language of "fullness." For him, an ineliminable dimension of our moral orientation is properly understood as vertical—not primarily *up,* a direct appeal to some God "above" us, but more properly *down,* as a recognition of the deep-rooted nature of these convictions at the foundation of our identity, as profundity—what Taylor calls "a sense of fullness." When we act on our moral convictions, he thinks, we "function with the sense that some action, or mode of life, or mode of feeling is incomparably higher than the others which are more readily available to us."[13] Here the crucial word is *incomparably*: when we act on our moral or spiritual convictions, we are acting on goods that are, properly speaking, not only more valuable than material goods such as salary or food or promotion or sex, but in fact not measurable through whatever metrics we use to value those other, more straightforwardly material realities. They are objects of our "strong evaluation" (*SS*, 14), whose *independence* from our other "goods" we must recognize; "they command our awe, respect, or admiration" (*SS*, 20). Furthermore, these goods are the ones that really matter to us—"the goods which define our spiritual orientation are the ones by which we will measure the worth of our lives" (*SS*, 42).

This language is his attempt at expressing his conviction that humans need *moral* orientation, an orientation that is irreducible to reductionistically positivist or naturalist factors. For Taylor, "the horizons within which we live our lives and which make sense of them have to include these strong qualitative discriminations. . . . [L]iving within such strongly qualified horizons is constitutive of human agency" (*SS*, 27). That is to say, for us our moral space is "ontologically basic" (*SS*, 29). Defining our "spiritual orientation" thus, the goods we affirm express and attempt to meet our "aspiration to fullness" in a way far richer and more profound than any number of merely material goods can offer (*SS*, 43–52). Taylor is not alone in suggesting this view; many antireductionist philosophers of various persuasions, from John McDowell to Alasdair MacIntyre to Philippa Foot, would argue this as well. But it is a point worth underscoring, because this conviction underlies his insistence that the cultural resources we possess may well affect the quality of our moral lives.

This worry lies behind Taylor's long-standing complaint about the "ethics of inarticulacy" suffocating secular immanentisms, seen in his skepticism of Rawls's confidence that a theory of justice will be "self-stabilizing" over time (*SA*, 256).[14] He thinks that such efforts, though they may be sporadically successful, will not suffice to sustain human moral projects in the long term; larger resources are needed. (This is why he suggests that the immanentist's problem is how "to find a non-theistic register in which to respond" to transcendent works of art and the like [*SA*, 607].)

Nietzschean alternatives, on the other hand, are too violent, even nihilistic, in the zealotry with which they demand the overcoming of the "traditional" or received notion of the subject. Nietzschean antihumanism's zealous hostility to subjectivity, ironically enough, thus ends up acknowledging the grip of that subjectivity in a partial and slanted way. This Nietzschean critique is not driven by ressentiment, but rather is motivated by a diagnosis of a genuine problem. Taylor's response recognizes the religiously generative effects of feeling "cross-pressured" by the eclipse of the transcendent alongside the common suspicion that "something [important for human fullness] may be occluded" by a closed immanence.

For Taylor, then, the route to genuine fullness runs beyond merely this-worldly human flourishing. The *metaphysical* primacy of life is wrong and stifling, and its dominance puts in danger its *practical* primacy (*CM*, 29). That there is a source of significance that ultimately transcends the life of this world, that can lead one to sacrifice life goods for the sake of a super-self order—that can lead one to live beyond the primacy of life—is crucial for Taylor. "For Christians, God wills human flourishing, but 'Thy will be done' doesn't reduce to 'Let human beings flourish'" (*CM*, 20). The perceived flatness of a closed secularism leads some "to explore and try out new solutions, new formulae" (*SA*, 303). Thus has modernity seen a remarkable explosion in forms of religiosity and spirituality. Much of this is creative and, for Taylor, salutary. Of course, it has a darker side as well, as seen in the nihilist temptations of antihumanism. But this dynamism and turbulence attest to humans' continued need for this sense of fullness and a persistent search for some way of life that promises it.

The details of Taylor's argument for transcendence need not concern us here. Many other thinkers writing on Taylor discuss that aspect of his work. We are pursuing another line of inquiry. The problems we face as moderns are not merely due to the dominance of exclusive humanism or an insurgent antihumanism. Some of them go much deeper and are shared by everyone, regardless of their belief or unbelief. In fact, they go to the very heart of the moral order as it has developed in the West and are inherent in the drive to Reform itself, once it has, in modernity, turned prescriptive, reshaping the institutional matrix within which we live, move, and have our being with the force of a cultural imperative.

Hence, we will explore more fully the lessons of Taylor's account for modern individuals' moral lives by looking at the conditions of Christians in late modern, postindustrial societies and suggest some positive proposals that flow from Taylor's program for some such Christians. We turn to that now.

## What Should Christians Do?

Given the fact of the Reform impulse and the ambivalence of our age toward it, what does Taylor propose that Christians do? Well, Christians should be, in his words, modernity's "Loyal Opposition" (*SA*, 745), seeking appropriate ways to affirm the authentic developments of Christianity in modernity while challenging those that are not. They must not try to reduce the faith to a fixed and pre-understood *code*, a readily formulable moral algorithm, idolatrously fetishizing systemic order and form and intrinsically hostile to (by necessity supraformal) real human communities. The attractions of enlisting on one side or another of the culture wars are powerful and must be frankly acknowledged—after all, little is as comforting as the warm embrace of our fellow partisans, and picking one side over the others is an effective way of alleviating the discomfort, hesitation, and outright contradictions of life in medias res. But such strategies blind us to the full complexity of our actual lives and allure us with membership in essentially idolatrous communities, alliances that demand our total devotion. Instead, Christians should "find the center of our spiritual lives beyond the code, deeper than the code, in networks of living concern, which are not to be sacrificed to the code, which must even from time to time subvert it" (*SA*, 743). They can do this, for Taylor, when they demonstrate with real moral seriousness and thoughtfulness the terrifically challenging nature of a genuine effort to live in this world in a healthy manner. Like Mateo Ricci, the sixteenth-century Jesuit missionary to China, Christians must come to see themselves as both embedded in and distanced from their cultural worlds. That is to say, "instead of dismissing this culture altogether, or just endorsing it as it is, we ought to attempt to raise its practice by making more palpable to its participants what the ethic they subscribe to really involves" (*EA*, 72).

Crucially, such an approach must be lived out in daily life, and the living of it must take the form of agape—for the issue is what believers should *love* rather than what they should *do*. "We follow, not by walking but by loving," said St. Augustine, and Taylor's account follows this quite closely.[15] Christians should seek to engage in something that looks like the work of Reform, but is in fact committed to quite different metaphysical or axiological presuppositions; as Taylor puts it, they should learn to "collaborate with God's pedagogy" (*SA*, 674). For him, "the question becomes a maximin one: how to have the greatest degree of philanthropic action with the minimum hope in mankind" (*SA*, 699). They must be aware of how Reform has led to certain kinds of violence—whether obvious or insidious. Because of this, they must be alert to how their commitment to Reform cannot replace or eclipse their commitment to love the neighbor as a bearer of the *imago Dei*, but should always remain a contingent expression or formulation or manifestation of that love.

Taylor offers tantalizing hints in his works of how Christians ought to live. For him, Christians must always recall Jesus's lesson not to attempt to resolve all challenges by taking them at face value—on the "horizontal plane," as Taylor puts it—but rather to transform or transfigure those challenges by transcending them, redescribing them, or challenging the terms by which they define themselves in a quasi-eschatological way, as exemplary Christian actors—from Jesus Christ to Desmond Tutu—have always done (*SA*, 706). Furthermore, building on Robert Wuthnow's work, he sees the spirituality of our age as too often pitting authority against authenticity, "dwelling" against "seeking" (*SA*, 508–13), and he seeks a synthesis wherein the dimensions of both movement and stability, dynamism and rest, are captured. The truth of the gospel, on his view, is so immense that no one person, community, or civilization could know it fully in history. He describes the true Church as composed of diverse itineraries (*SA*, 772) and, quoting Jacques Maritain, says that "instead of a fortified castle erected in the middle of the land, we must think of [the Church as] an army of stars thrown into the sky" (*SA*, 744). Most obviously in *A Secular Age*, he is inspired by some of the outliers of the contemporary Christian churches, such as Taizé, which underscore the goal of unity only via a Trinitarian integrity that must be patient with our incarnated plurality, always in the service of cultivating new languages, itineraries, and practices that affirm the network of agape. All this will require that the range of the acceptable "sense of fullness" be expanded, so that Christians can come to see a wider palette of options, more commensurate with the almost bewildering diversity of choices that modernity proposes.

But Taylor offers little more than hints of how to do this. How might it work out concretely? How can North American Christians, for example, "live like Ricci"? And in what ways can they be better "carriers" of modernity's troubled logics? We turn to one group of Christians to see how their efforts are critically illuminated by Taylor's work and how they, in turn, critically illuminate his. In fact, they are themselves all of these things and more: they are a microcosm of the "galloping pluralism on the spiritual plane" that Taylor has aptly labeled a spiritual "supernova" (*SA*, 300).

## *Lex Orandi Lex Credendi:* The Evangelical "Vocation Paradigm"

Many theology-minded thinkers talk about "the church," but few look and see what churches are in fact doing. So we will consider an empirical example, a particularly powerful strand of North Atlantic Christianity, American Evangelical Protestantism.[16] We hope to show that Taylor's analysis is also and equally a powerful diagnosis of the temptations and challenges besetting real religious communities today, and that he offers helpful guidance for those communities in doing better. Furthermore, they may have insights for his account as well.

Over the past several centuries, Evangelicals have been among the most reform-minded of religious movements, central to causes such as abolitionism, the "Victorian" reformation of manners and morals, the Social Gospel, and early forms of American Progressivism. Theologically, Evangelicals combine an overriding concern with the personal authenticity of their faith with a profound sense of mission in the world—that is, an interest in influencing society at large in a way that transcends the more circumscribed concern with individual or communal purity. In practice, of course, Evangelicals have often vacillated between these two callings, cycling between periods of activism and social engagement and periods of pietistic withdrawal. Taken as a whole, however, Evangelicalism embodies an expansively reform-minded theology of vocation in one's life and society, and this theology has shaped a spiritual orientation to self and world that marks Evangelicalism out as a distinctive religious movement.

While for the middle third of the twentieth century Evangelicals were largely quiescent, since the 1970s there has been a retrieval and revitalization of "vocation" language among Evangelical elites and their institution-building, principally as a way of breaking out of the Fundamentalist model of cultural retreat and enclosure and reengaging society, culture, and politics in the face of what they saw as alarming threats to both faith and culture.[17] It sought to overcome a narrow, isolated, and generally individualistic pietism, all the while providing a robust resistance to growing influence of secular humanism in public life—reinvigorating their churches while remoralizing their cultures. So far, one might say, so admirable.

Yet, as we will see, the co-presence of Reform and the therapeutic in these movements strongly suggests that Taylor would critique as well as affirm. The Evangelical "vocation paradigm" does double duty as both a structure to act out Reform and a therapy to manage its pressures. Here we want to explore how it might also do something to resist Evangelicals' total enmeshment in the Reform paradigm and indeed perhaps to counteract it.

The strategies Evangelicals have employed are diverse. For present purposes, we can observe three ideal typical directions, though often blending into and informing each other in practice. The first aims at a renewal or restoration of individual spiritual purpose understood largely in terms of authenticity, personal growth, and fulfillment; the second is concerned with direct social, and especially political, action, by which a project of national reclamation and cultural remoralization can be pursued and accomplished; the third pursues an agenda of both personal and social regeneration and redemption through what we might call a program of "cultural renewal." We will consider each in turn.

*Type 1: Spiritual Purpose and Personal Fulfillment*

The language of "vocation" in the first type expresses the long-standing Protestant preoccupation with authenticity. In its most distilled terms, one seeks the integration of life and faith and, in turn, personal depth and fullness, by discerning one's spiritual purposes, which can only happen once one has accepted the truth of the Christian gospel. This has been articulated in numerous ways. Most stress a handful of "steps" or "spiritual laws" that must first be followed.

Beyond its place in such generic Evangelical formulas of salvation, however, the idiom of "calling" becomes a powerful tool for integrating what is commonly experienced today as a highly fragmented and anomic existence. Evangelicals often describe this late modern condition in terms of our deepest spiritual needs and hungers and the seductive but ultimately empty and false ways late modern culture promises to meet them. The process of discerning one's real, eternally enduring, and life-giving "purposes," and thus the discovery of one's most authentic self, it is promised, stems from the discovery that God has a plan for one's life. Hence, in his best-selling book, *The Purpose-Driven Life*, Evangelical pastor Rick Warren assures his readers not only that God has a plan in creating each of us, but also that "God has not left us in the dark to wonder and guess [about that plan].... [T]he Bible ... is our Owner's Manual, explaining why we are alive, how life works, what to avoid, and what to expect in the future."[18] Coming to grips with the divine purposes for one's life is heralded as the key to personal fullness and meaning, as well as to faithful witness and Christian compassion.

The goal of discovering one's true self- and life-purposes through the discernment of individual calling has become a pervasive feature of contemporary Evangelicalism through a host of institutional venues; Warren merely exemplifies this trend. A popular cottage industry of Christian counseling and expert advice has long paralleled mainstream trends in popular psychology, life-management skills, and personal growth. Books like Joel Osteen's *Your Best Life Now* sell millions of copies. Organizations such as New Life Ministries, Cross Walk, the Christian Counseling Center, and Crown Financial Ministries promote Christian equivalents through daily radio programs and the dissemination of popular small-group study guides. Evangelical colleges increasingly require students to take classes in personal and professional development employing similar language. Wherever they are located, however it is institutionalized, the goal is always the same: to bring coherence and meaning to my life by knowing God's purposes for me.

In this, Evangelicals stand in a tradition of cultural criticism as old as Christianity itself; consider Augustine on his early pagan education in *Confessions*, or Pascal's acute analysis of *divertissement* in his *Pensées* (differences between Rick Warren and St. Augustine or Joel Osteen and Blaise Pascal notwithstanding). While it would be wrong to pin each of these ministries and initiatives with the same general criticism, the net effect is worth considering. Taken together, the slippage between modes of Christian pastoral care and pop psychology, between techniques for discovering one's spiritual gifts and secular self-help, between equipping oneself for successful witness and for success in the marketplace, is hard to miss. Indeed, the affinities with developments in the culture of late capitalism are significant.[19] It is enough to point out that Rick Warren's website trumpets the following blurbs for his book and church from, of all things, *Forbes Magazine*: "The best book on entrepreneurship, management, and leadership in print," and "Were it a business, Saddleback Church would be compared with Dell, Google or Starbucks."[20] While the theological assumptions of Evangelicals ostensibly stand in some tension to the values of the wider culture, the common appeal to the therapeutic and to material success is striking. This is not a fundamental critique of the modern world, but a mode of accommodating oneself within it.

At its best, this formulation of the "Vocation Paradigm" finds its source of personal coherence and spiritual purpose outside the self, and ultimately beyond this life, in the transcendent God of historic Christianity. The knowledge of one's created purposes, moreover, has often led to the admirable acts of charity and social concern that have long been the hallmark of Evangelical activism. (The Warrens, for example, reportedly donate 90 percent of their royalties to charity through the Acts of Mercy Foundation, which they founded to fight HIV/AIDS.) But this formulation retains a highly dualistic and individualistic orientation to the world that all too often becomes a way of coping with the disenchanting and fragmenting experience of late modern life, rather than offering any genuine alternative to the instrumentalizing forces of Reform, thereby reinforcing rather than challenging the larger culture. While Warren begins his book with a very strong criticism of the secular self-help mindset ("It's not about you" is the book's first line), the irony is that by the end of the book he has returned to the criteria of worldly success. From the perspective of traditional Christianity, such an account leaves out something crucial, so to speak: attention to suffering, martyrdom, or crucifixion. This approach offers no tragic recognition that the world admits of no strategies of successful management for straightforward human flourishing. It evinces no sense of an irreducible tension between the conditions of life in this world and the calling of discipleship in Christ. Dietrich Bonhoeffer was expressing a powerful and profound Christian theme when he famously wrote,

"When Christ calls a man, he bids him come and die."[21] But no one should expect a Bonhoefferian *The Cost of the Purpose-Driven Life* in bookstores anytime soon. Somewhere, Max Weber is smiling.

*Type 2: National Reclamation and Cultural Remoralization*
*via Apologetics and Political Action*

The second ideal typical direction in which the contemporary Evangelical interest in vocation tends is to the prioritization of social and political witness over personal fullness and spiritual growth. While this approach is no less interested in evangelization, its chief concern is with a project of national reclamation and cultural remoralization—with the transformation of a secular and morally dissolute America back into the virtuous, godly nation it ostensibly was at its founding. At the center of this project is the contemporary reformation of manners and morals on the one hand, and a promotion of specific public policies on the other, both built exclusively upon Judeo-Christian moral foundations. Its mode of cultural engagement combines an emphasis on cultural apologetics with jeremiad-based critique. On this second view, vocation is a primary mechanism for spiritual warfare and cultural resistance. Faithfully discerning and living out one's calling in this way is an emphatically political act. It challenges a perceived quietism and passive inaction among the faithful, warning that a godless elite is hijacking American culture, leading it to perdition.

Here again, an entire constellation of Evangelical institutions are engaged in expressing this perspective; they include hundreds of church-based and parachurch ministries, special interest and advocacy groups, institutes specializing in Christian apologetics, religious schools and the Christian homeschool movement, not to mention scores of Evangelical media empires. On this account, what is crucial is having the right "worldview," a comprehensive cognitive schema through which one can interpret the world aright. Worldview training is essential both for apologetics (in defending the faith against rival worldviews) and for empowering and equipping Christians to witness the truth of Christ in the culture and the nation at large. Focus on the Family's Truth Project—"an in-depth worldview experience"—exemplifies the rhetorical triumvirate of "Remember, Repent, and Return" in its "Lesson on the American Experiment."[22] The ministries of Charles Colson and James Dobson, two of the most prominent

Evangelical leaders of the past three decades, have been leading advocates of worldview training, particularly for the young. Both Colson and Dobson have each publically endorsed Summit Ministries, effectively a worldview boot camp that puts on two-week intensive worldview training seminars for high school and college students. Similarly, universities such as Liberty University (started by Jerry Falwell), Regent University (founded by Pat Robertson), and Patrick Henry College (started by Michael Farris, founder of the Home School Legal Defense Association) provide representative examples of the way this perspective plays out in Christian higher education. In all these cases, faithfulness to calling—that is, to the project of defending the faith against secularism and other threatening anti-Christian philosophies, and of restoring America to its Christian roots—is only possible if Christians are trained in an authentically biblical worldview.

At its best, this approach properly challenges a sharp dualism between "private" or "personal" faith and the state of contemporary society; it seeks a robust and thoughtful engagement with the wider culture and is unafraid to take unpopular stands in the name of Christian truth. At its worst, however, this perspective succumbs to the enduring seductions and problems of Constantinianism, whether framed in terms of reclaiming America's political institutions for Christ or in terms of cultural remoralization more generally. It tends to privilege defensive and indeed reactionary "preemptory authority" over openness to multiple spiritual itineraries—it reinforces "dwelling" over "seeking." It offers too supine an acquiescence to the state model, and it embraces the code of Reform and offers a fairly narrow account of power, focusing especially on state power. (It is telling that the language of "culture war" itself derives from the architect of the nineteenth-century modern Prussian state, Otto von Bismarck.) Moreover, it fools itself that it can reinstate the moral authority of Christianity in a post-Christian and pluralistic age by apologetic and legal fiat.[23] More than the other two ideal types, this formulation is most likely to reproduce the worst and most oppressive parts of the drive to Reform.

*Type 3: Cultural Renewal for the Common Good*

Our third ideal type holds, we think, more promise. It recognizes the power of the market and the complexities of genuine political action while re-

maining ambivalent and consciously self-critical about the infiltration
of the market and politics into religious life. It finds its clearest inspira-
tion in a Dutch Reformed formulation of neo-Calvinism. At its heart is
a biblically grounded worldview (again, worldview is vital) that issues a
concern for the integrity of all "spheres" of human activity.[24] God's bless-
ing of creation and God's calling of humans to active world-building be-
stows a unique integrity and value on every sphere of human endeavor.
On this view, being a teacher, artist, engineer, journalist, accountant, or
plumber is every bit as important, theologically speaking, as being a pastor, preacher, or missionary. The shadow of the Reformation clearly
looms large.

In his popular and influential book, *The Call*, Evangelical writer Os
Guinness places this holistic version of vocation at the very center of Christian life. He does so by recounting a famous saying by nineteenth-century
Dutch prime minister Abraham Kuyper: "There is not one square inch of
the entire creation about which Jesus Christ does not cry out, 'This is mine!
This belongs to me!' "[25] For Guinness, and those who share this perspective, calling is "the premise of Christian existence itself. Calling means that
everyone, everywhere, and in everything fulfills his or her (secondary)
callings in response to God's (primary) calling."[26] Thinkers such as Guinness theorize what is now readily happening on the ground. In an enormous burst of creative energy, Evangelicals of this theological persuasion
have become involved in myriad efforts to renew their world. Moreover,
many of these efforts involve work in professional spheres in which Evangelicals have been largely absent until quite recently, at least in recent history. Alongside the long-standing work of compassion, on the one hand,
and the political activism that has marked Evangelicalism in the past few
decades on the other, one finds Evangelicals now working in urban planning and renewal, sponsoring initiatives for racial reconciliation, patron-
izing the arts, publishing books on business as a calling, founding international human rights and environmental organizations, entering into
the most elite circles of the academy, and so on.[27]

Yet again, there are a growing number of institutions promoting this
ostensibly more holistic notion of vocation. Churches such as New York
City–based Redeemer Presbyterian Church, led by Pastor Timothy Keller,
teach that the scope and direction of Christian calling in the world is

clear: Through faith in God, Christians discover their truest and deepest vocation, and through the living out of that vocation, Christians take active responsibility for the cultures in which they live.

Another relatively new endeavor that is illustrative of this third trend is the annual Q gathering. Q is a sort of Aspen Institute, or TED conference, for the Evangelical elite. At its latest gathering, Q's featured presenters included CNN reporter Soledad O'Brien, who talked about the complexities of taking care of children in a postdisaster context such as Haiti; urban geographer Richard Florida, who discussed the long-range challenges of the economic crisis for America's cities; MIT Professor Rosalind Picard, who talked about the latest developments in robotics; and Redeemer Presbyterian's Keller, who reflected on the need to reconcile the divide between those Evangelicals exclusively concerned with cultural engagement and social action and those exclusively committed to defending orthodox doctrine and evangelism. The number of presenters working in "secular" professions and discussing "secular" trends is noteworthy, as is the ubiquity of the language of the common good. Beneath it all is a vision of Christian vocation expressed in terms of a changing cultural context. "We believe that inherent in Christian faithfulness is the responsibility to create a better world, one that reflects God's original design and intention," states Q's website. Yet, the purpose of Q is to be a place where the next generation of Evangelical elites can explore fresh and innovative ways to live out that original call in what Q's founder, Gabe Lyons, characterizes as a "postmodern, pluralistic and post-Christian setting."[28] Other older and more mainstream Evangelical organizations—such as *Christianity Today*, the flagship Evangelical periodical founded by Billy Graham—are now exploring similar territory, if with more caution.

As was the case with the previous model, the formation of the next generation of Christians is a central concern for those promoting the cultural renewal model. The Harvey Fellows Program seeks "to mark, equip and encourage individuals to actively integrate their faith and vocation as leaders in strategic occupations. We understand God to be creator and sustainer, not only of human beings, but of society's disciplines and structures which make up our world. We believe God uses individuals to redeem these structures."[29] A host of similar initiatives (e.g., the Veritas Forum, university-based Christian Studies Centers, the Pew Younger Scholars initiative) target undergraduates and college grads for similar purposes. As of 2010, there were twenty of these programs across the country.

It is worth noting that a broad humanism runs through many of these movements. Despite the rhetorical emphasis on being "*counter-cultural for the common good*," they do not share the defensive and embattled tone of the previous formulation of the Vocation Paradigm. Here there is a much more sanguine view of the potential for cultural renewal and of the prospects of serving the common good that does not appear to have any explicit political overtones. At least rhetorically, these organizations seem more concerned with providing and affirming positive articulations of "the true," "the good," and "the beautiful," wherever they should be found in the culture at large, than with defending the boundaries of any specifically Christian culture.

At its best, this third type's understanding of vocation has in its scope the redemption of the entire created order, not just individual lives and not just political structures. Furthermore, its understanding of calling is robust, active, and dynamic without being apocalyptically impatient. It is also less reactionary, less preoccupied with defending Christian faith against a hostile post-Christian culture, and more interested in seeking common cause with all who care about the common good, nonbelievers and people of other religious faiths included. It takes the post-Christian and post-Constantinian realities of our historical moment as a starting point and recognizes opportunities for innovative cultural engagement within it, rather than as the last chance to save Christian America. It inspires a form of Christian activism that works for the reform of society in the interests of human flourishing, but which does not demand to see the fruit of this work in this world. Its adherents are disposed to, and chastened by, the anticipatory confidence that goes by the name of "hope." The way forward, this view holds, will not come by remoralizing culture, or from the peddling of purpose-driven lives as an antidote to the ennui of late capitalism. Instead, cultural renewal will only come through Christians working faithfully and excellently within its culture-making and -shaping institutions. Again, at its best, this third type funds a form of cultural engagement that has been aptly dubbed "faithful presence."[30]

In terms of Taylor's "loyal opposition," it is definitely "loyal." But to what degree is it in real "opposition"? Here it has some weak points, for it can all too easily fall prey to an uncritical endorsement of whatever cultural form or mode of activity best suits followers' particular interests—for example, a certain lifestyle or a specific political agenda. Furthermore, with its focus on getting Christians into leading culture-making institutions, this perspective can easily justify an elitism that is the polar opposite of Christian equality. And, in its bid to seek influence at the centers of institutional power, it can easily find itself co-opted by the standards of worldly achievement.

In the best examples of this type of Evangelical action—and perhaps exemplars of the other types as well—vocation takes the form of a quest, a process of discovery that is open and receptive to discovering fresh and even unexpected itineraries to God. At the same time, it is also an attempt to know one's place, to explore the deepest roots and the springs of the believer's own commitments and convictions in order to have a more direct, and hence richer, connection to the animating sources of one's own tradition. This type is thus capable of incarnating a style of life and faith that confirms much of Taylor's proposal. We believe this is evidence of the perspicacity of his overall vision, that it can offer so illuminating a categorical framework within which to think about the challenges of faithful life today.

Evangelicals thus have much to learn from Taylor, especially his cautions. Yet we think their examples also challenge Taylor's account in ways worth considering. Before concluding, we should briefly sketch what such an encounter between Taylor's theoretical proposal and the empirical case of Evangelicals suggests about A Secular Age.

## VOCATION AND RESPONSIBILITY

Given Taylor's picture of the modern condition, the basic question committed Christians must ask is this: how can they resist the drive to Reform while still affirming the value of the reforming impulse as theologically warranted? The Evangelicals we have looked at provide some interesting illumination here, both positive and negative.

Positively, it seems clear that the third type of Evangelical action has the right idea: Christians should affirm a commitment to the world and the common good; they should affirm the goodness of the world's being and work to respect and enhance the integrity of life, as the theological ethicist William Schweiker puts it. After all, the Christian churches exist *for* the life of the world, not against it, and are thus not fundamentally opposed to created existence; such opposition has been ruled out of bounds for Christian orthodoxy for a long time—at least since Augustine's rejection of Manicheanism and his opposition to the Donatist schismatics. For reasons related to the doctrines of both Creation and Incarnation, Christians must affirm the world as the site of God's creative and redemptive energies. Strictly speaking, radical otherworldliness is anathema.

So far, so good; this is the nice and friendly face of Christianity. But Christianity exists also as a "sign of contradiction," a critique of the received structures of the world as it exists today. So Christians, even as they affirm the goodness of the world, can understand themselves as called upon to resist the worldly terms in which the world's goodness is usually affirmed in favor of another set of terms. (This may be described as the difference between affirming Creation and affirming "the world.") Today the world's terms are, as Taylor suggests, irremediably contaminated with what the drive to Reform has wrought—exclusive humanism and the antihumanist revolt, all within the immanent frame. To be faithful to this aspect of their heritage, we suspect Christians must learn how to resist some aspects of this drive individually and institutionally; to the degree they do not, they collaborate, wittingly or no, in the perversion of their own faith. How might they engage in such resistance? We propose some strategies, in fear and trembling, below.

Institutionally, Christians can resist this drive by ordering their institutions in light of their particular intellectual commitments and not succumbing to other, sometimes radically antithetical, assumptions. Most importantly for this strategy, they must resist the perpetual, gravity-like pull toward "structural isomorphism"—the powerful tug toward ordering their communities, institutions, and social movements in ways structurally parallel to the way that the surrounding—in this case, secular—culture requires communities, institutions, and social movements to be ordered.

Here is an example of what we mean. The third type of Evangelicalism is fixated on engaging high-status figures and movements in secular culture, on terms that those figures and movements would recognize as wholly their own, for salutary reasons of hospitality and charity. But if such engagement lacks any compensatory attention to how such modes of engagement may themselves skew the character of Christian belief so engaged, this can become a potential example of such a dangerous (to those Christian communities) structural isomorphism. The fact that, in the very forms and structures of their engagement, the modes of engagement look so much like secular modes (e.g., a "Christian TED conference" or a "Christian Aspen Institute") may itself mean that the Christian engagement loses a great deal of its essential distinctiveness and may end up collaborating with the very structures of fallen human society that it set out to resist and transform, including the drive to Reform itself.

Specifying Evangelical strategies in this way highlights a danger in how Taylor may be read, or at least how he has left himself open for misreading. For example, Taylor can sometimes sound as if he presumes a kind of neutral sociocultural space in which a critical mass of "multiple itineraries" can coalesce into a "loyal opposition"—as if there are no deeply hostile forces impinging upon and attempting to foreclose that space. Such imagined spaces are probably impossible; the publics of our world are always already inflected, if not determined, by the various shaping logics of the market, the culture, and the political order, to mention only three. A loyal opposition, to be understood as such, will necessarily find its witness greeted with resistance. This is to be expected. While Taylor is clearly ready to acknowledge the reality of dilemmas and cross pressures, he associates these fundamentally with long-standing historical forces ("trajectories") almost glacial in their power (and velocity) to shape the world we have inherited. (Indeed, many of his metaphors evoke impersonal forces that, like the forces of nature, are seemingly beyond anyone's direct control; thus Taylor talks about the nova effect, the immanent frame, "spun" open or closed, the drive to Reform, the post-Axial equilibrium, and so on.) So perhaps Taylor has not sufficiently acknowledged the role of vested interest, which is to speak of the role of specific actors and institutions fighting over who gets to define the evolving terms of the modern social imaginary. This is the old political question, Cui bono? Who benefits from the hegemony of the "spinning" of the immanent frame, and how much opposition will those called to witness against its forced enclosure to the transcendent face? This is something Taylor leaves his readers to discover on their own.

Undertaking such a public witness therefore entails a serious intellectual effort dedicated to discerning how to articulate the logics of accountability and the metrics of accomplishment that Christians will use to govern, and explain, their institutional forms. Will they talk in strictly secular, typically social-scientific and quantitative terms about what they are doing? How will they resist the pressure toward purely immanent and quantifiable measures of success and accomplishment? How will they avoid the will to power when they are successful and the politics of resentment when they are not? When are they doing things right, and what does "doing things right" look like? What, also, counts as "going wrong," and what languages of social (and theological) criticism are and are not used in these diagnoses? What counts, and what does not, as exemplary?

Furthermore, though at a bit more distance, it will require Christians to consider the structures of social order and meaning making that are significantly constitutive of those logics and metrics. What counts as achievement or success for their institutions? What is the point of doing the institution's characteristic activity? For example, for Christian humanitarian movements, is the point about digging wells or inoculating children or increasing literacy or increasing material standards of living at home and abroad? To what end? Is the point something about witnessing the true story of human beings to the world? To what audience? The Gates Foundation will understandably want certain metrics front and center, and "witnessing to the true story of the world" is not likely to be among them. Christians will find, we suspect, that they must move just outside the grooves of received expectations, and often that effort will succeed only with extra intellectual (not to mention spiritual) exertion, probably at some real cost of misunderstanding and discomfort with their non-Christian colleagues.

Intellectually and spiritually, Christians should also be suspicious of the language of "fullness" that Taylor uses, but will instead talk in more particular, tradition-specific (and, we would argue, vital) dialects about living out the call of God to manifest God's judging, redeeming, and sanctifying action in the world. To be sure, Taylor intends to hold out "fullness" not as the endpoint for the Christian, but as a more common point of departure for humans in general. Christians will want to talk not just about living a rich life, but also about obeying the call of God. The highly distinctive languages to which these two approaches refer are not (and we think Taylor would agree) phenomenologically equivalent; in fact, they move in very different registers. Taylor himself points out that Christian agape requires a commitment to some good beyond fullness, where "fullness" is understood exclusively in terms of a naturalistic vision of human flourishing. Yet, while it is a commitment that will inevitably require sacrifice of one's own flourishing in the name of that higher good, it remains unclear what institutions and practices he believes to be necessary for grounding and supporting such commitment, if any at all. In the end, as some readers of *A Secular Age* have pointed out, he holds up certain religious virtuosi who have somehow managed, against all odds, to make their way through the cross pressures of belief and unbelief to God.[31] As inspiring as the lives of these exemplars are, like the stories of the saints, they are too oblique to the realities of most people's lives to provide an adequate model for living out the faith once one has "converted" to it. Taylor is best when speaking to and about "seekers" and has less to say, beyond his important cautions, to those who want to know how to "dwell" in a secular age. Again, we expect that, once one becomes a believer, the more tradition-specific languages that give belief determinate shape will better engender, sustain, and reproduce a spirituality capable of weathering the cross pressures. (Given Taylor's own recognition that there will be much lower rates of intergenerational religious continuity, this is not an insignificant matter for the transmission of the faith to the next generation; this is an ongoing worry among Evangelicals, for example, despite their not infrequent expressions of demographic smugness.[32])

Exploring the differences between these two languages is beyond our scope here, but such an exploration would raise questions, we suspect, as to the real extent to which humans' self-consciousness is "fragilized" and "reflexive" today, and indeed, how fully self-consciously subjective humans can or should be. We think that there is always a final vocabulary beyond which humans do not properly go. Reflexivity has an end somewhere; none of us is caught in a bottomless well of our own subjectivity, and all of us in the end make claims about reality that we do not question. (Perhaps, for example, they do not think about how a "fragilized" approach may not be "fragile" all the way down, but inevitably stands in intolerant (and therefore unfragile) relation to nonfragilized approaches.) Certainly there can be some virtuosi of fragilization and self-conscious reflexivity—and certainly many people, to some degree, recognize the contingency of their own convictions (and final vocabularies). But we strongly suspect that even the virtuosi have some limits to their reflexivity. While Taylor's language of "fullness" is not intended as a way of describing any such final vocabulary, we believe it is not only subject to being (inadvertently) misconstrued as such, it might also come, in fact, to function as just such an alternative final vocabulary.[33]

Now, Taylor may reasonably worry whether such an approach can be suitably pluralistic or tolerant, given the temptation of what he calls "preemptive authority." Our response is that some such final vocabulary is inevitable, and the resources for toleration and handling the reality of plurality will have to come from the content of the beliefs, not the mode in which they are held. A language that can warrant such an engagement with the energies of Reform while yet engaging in a pluralistic world is latent, we think, in many traditional religious languages, not least the traditional Christian language of the three theological virtues of faith, hope, and love. They provide one very good "grammar" of the Christian faith and offer a rich vocabulary in which to undertake a realistic and fine-grained analysis of our moral and spiritual condition.

A life lived out of these virtues may offer one way that Christians may go forward in our new moral world, one way that Christians may inhabit and affirm this moral revolution of which Taylor speaks. It is shorn of the compulsory optimism of the drive to Reform that we should find so suspicious, but retains the moral energy and purpose to which all of us are so powerfully, and reasonably, drawn. It is also an approach that we think can be inhabited by ordinary believers, not just the virtuosi; that is, it does not require a tremendous amount of perpetual self-conscious awareness of the fragile contingency of one's own beliefs. Other routes to such a stance—within the Christian faith, in other faiths, or in no faith at all—are certainly possible. But this at least is one way, and when someone asks Christian reformists why they should care about the world in this way, some of them can point to this as the answer: because in undertaking to do so, humanity participates in the fellowship of Christ and the saints who have come before, following them, as it were, at a distance.

## CONCLUSION

Charles Taylor's work has always suffered from a deficit of melodrama. Despite his engagement with some of the most profound and contested issues of our time, his work evinces little in the way of operatic apocalyptic prophecy, thundering jeremiad, or panting messianic expectation. Nor will one find there an unwarranted optimism or a plaguing pessimism (let alone a fashionable cynicism). He is neither breezy nor brooding, neither complacent nor contemptuous. If anything, his work exhibits a nondefensive sincerity—patient with those who confuse it with overearnestness, but impatient with the siren song of ironic distanciation that those so confused offer as an alternative—that is anathema to such hysterics. Perhaps it has something to do with his deep appreciation of Hegel, exposure to whom (prone as he was to such theophanic modes of pronouncement) allowed Taylor to develop antibodies to all such apocalypticisms. Perhaps it has something to do with his kind of Catholicism—mature, calm, wryly self-knowing, alert to the challenges and perils it faces, yet also unmoved by hysterical charges and countercharges of paganism and theocracy. Whatever the reason, if we are to judge intellectual eminences by their bellicosity, no one is likely to confuse Taylor with any of the other great theorists of modernity, with the possible exception of Alexis de Tocqueville—and that is not bad company with which to be associated.

Taylor's irenic spirit, however, is only partly an expression of his demeanor. It is also a quite intentional mode of living with modernity. It is an ethic stemming from a serious and evidently passionate commitment to a third way between modernity's knockers and boosters, one rooted in his own deeply held faith, and catholic in more ways than one.

We find this spirit powerful and largely right. Our aim in this paper has been to see what it can tell us about the way certain religious communities are living in the world today—both how it can helpfully offer them a better way of talking and thinking about their challenges, and also how it can perhaps help uncover their limitations more palpably than those communities could without Taylor's help. We have seen that those communities also push back on Taylor in certain ways. But even in their resistance to Taylor, the engagement helps them see more clearly what it is they want to stand for and where it is they want to be headed. And really, there is no better ground for gratitude, in intellectual engagements, than that.

NOTES

The authors thank Jeffrey Dill, Mark Storslee, and Beckett Liebendorfer for their comments on this paper.

1. To say nothing of the self itself as an object of Reform.

2. Max Weber, "Social Psychology of the World Religions," in *From Max Weber: Essays in Sociology*, trans. and ed. H. H. Gerth and C. Wright Mills (New York: Oxford University Press, 1946), 291.

3. Charles Taylor, *A Secular Age* (Cambridge, MA: Belknap Press, 2007), 510. Hereafter abbreviated as *SA*.

4. Charles Taylor, *Modern Social Imaginaries* (Durham, NC: Duke University Press, 2004), 12. Hereafter abbreviated as *MSI*.

5. Philip Rieff, *The Triumph of the Therapeutic: The Uses of Faith After Freud* (Chicago: University of Chicago Press, 1966), 22.

6. The famous case is of course the Lisbon earthquake.

7. The contemporary social theorist Peter Berger has identified this phenomenon in modernity as well and calls it "the heretical imperative": it is the condition of people who are forced to *choose* their most fundamental beliefs. See Peter Berger, *The Heretical Imperative: Contemporary Possibilities of Religious Affirmation* (New York: Doubleday, 1980).

8. Again, the connection with Berger's work is noteworthy here.

9. For a discussion of what might be called the globalization of the Reform impulse, see Joshua J. Yates, "Mapping the Good World: The New Cosmopolitans and Our Changing World Picture," *The Hedgehog Review* 12, no. 3 (Fall 2009).

10. Charles Taylor, *A Catholic Modernity? Charles Taylor's Marianist Award Lecture, with Responses by William Shea, Rosemary Luling Haughton, George Marsden, and Jean Bethke Elshtain*, ed. James L. Heft (New York: Oxford University Press, 1999), 25. Hereafter abbreviated as *CM*.

11. Charles Taylor, *The Ethics of Authenticity* (Cambridge, MA: Harvard University Press, 1991), 74.

12. David Rieff's powerful *A Bed for the Night: Humanitarianism in Crisis* (New York: Simon & Schuster, 2003) depicts the hopelessness of care providers, grimly trudging along, not daring to look up at the ever-receding moral horizon, the utopian hope of a decent life for all. For a stinging critique of one version of this, see Thomas Carothers, "The End of the Transition Paradigm," *Journal of Democracy* 13, no. 1

(January 2002): 5–21. More generally, this is but one example of what Taylor has identified as a fundamental problem of modern moral life, "the ethics of inarticulacy"—a problem vexing many modern moral undertakings.

13. Charles Taylor, *Sources of the Self: The Making of the Modern Identity* (Cambridge, MA: Harvard University Press, 1989), 19. Abbreviated hereafter as *SS*.

14. It informs his worry that no naturalism can make sense of the phenomenology of universalism, despite his recognition that some thinkers, notably Luc Ferry, have argued that some NGOs such as Médecins sans Frontières offer their workers a "horizontal" kind of transcendence (608, 677).

15. "Imus autem non ambulando, sed amando." Augustine, *Epistulae* 155.4.

16. Other contemporary groups seem to be attempting to get at these issues as well—the "emerging church," the new monasticism, etc.—and there are also certain strands within the Roman Catholic Church; but we focus on this group because of the extent of scholarship on them.

17. For one good introduction to these matters, see Joel Carpenter, *Revive Us Again: The Reawakening of American Fundamentalism* (New York: Oxford University Press, 1999).

18. Rick Warren, *The Purpose-Driven Life* (Grand Rapids, MI: Zondervan, 2013), 5.

19. We are grateful to our colleague David Franz for pointing out the clear affinities between *The Purpose-Driven Life* and a number of popular books of management theory, in which the idea of living out more fully one's vocation is equated with economic success.

20. "Rick Warren," *PurposeDriven*, http://www.purposedrivenlife.com/en-US/AboutUs/AboutTheAuthor/AboutTheAuthor.htm. Downloaded May 25, 2010. Archived site available at archive.org.

21. Dietrich Bonhoeffer, *The Cost of Discipleship*, trans. R. H. Fuller (New York: Macmillan, 1959), 89.

22. "Lesson Guide," Focus on the Family, http://www.thetruthproject.org/images/globalitems/TruthProjectLessons.pdf. Downloaded May 25, 2010. Archived site available at archive.org.

23. Christian Smith, *Christian America? What Evangelicals Really Want* (Berkeley: University of California Press, 2000).

24. It is interesting that *Time Magazine* listed "new Calvinism" as the third most powerful of ten ideas changing the world in 2009: see David van Biema, "Ten Ideas Changing the World Right Now," *Time*, March 12, 2009, http://www.time.com/time/specials/packages/article/0,28804,1884779_1884782_1884760,00.html.

25. Os Guinness, *The Call: Finding and Fulfilling the Central Purpose of Your Life* (Nashville: Thomas Nelson, 1998), 35.

26. Ibid., 34.

27. For evidence of this, see D. Michael Lindsay, *Faith in the Halls of Power: How Evangelicals Joined the American Elite* (New York: Oxford University Press, 2007). We suspect that Lindsay is too sanguine regarding these changes.

28. "Concept," *Qideas.org,* http://www.qideas.org/event/concept.aspx; and "Presentations," *Qideas.org,* http://www.qideas.org/event/presentations.aspx. Downloaded May 19, 2010. Archived site available at archive.org.

29. "Harvey Fellows Program," Mustard Seed Foundation, http://msfdn.org/harveyfellows/.

30. See James Davison Hunter, *To Change the World: The Irony, Tragedy, and Possibility of Christianity in the Late Modern World* (New York: Oxford University Press, 2010). Hunter is quite critical of a number of those we would include within this third rubric.

31. See Peter Steinfels, "Modernity and Belief: Charles Taylor's 'A Secular Age,'" *Commonweal* 135, no. 9 (May 9, 2008).

32. For an expression of this worry (not the smugness) see Christian Smith and Melina Lundquist Denton, *Soul Searching: The Religious and Spiritual Lives of American Teenagers* (New York: Oxford University Press, 2005).

33. This worry is put fairly well by Stanley Fish: "Openness to revision as a principle is itself a form of closure, not at all open to ways of thinking or acting that would bring revision to an end. 'Openness to revision' is an internal, not an absolute, measure; it is relative to whatever understood exclusions—and there will always be some—give the politically organized space its shape." Stanley Fish, *The Trouble with Principle* (Cambridge, MA: Harvard University Press, 1999), 235. For interminably more on this issue, see Charles Mathewes, *A Theology of Public Life* (New York: Cambridge University Press, 2007), esp. chapter 6, "Charitable Citizenship."

## PART IV

ETHICS AND EMBODIMENT

# CHAPTER SEVEN

# The Authentic Individual in the Network of Agape

JENNIFER A. HERDT

One of the most valuable aspects of Charles Taylor's work has been the way in which it articulates the complementary character of authentic individuality and genuine community. Throughout his career, Taylor has offered perceptive critiques of the excesses of strong social construction-ism and antimodern traditionalism, while seeking to reconcile the ideal of authenticity with both an affirmation of the social formation of the self and an openness to transcendence. The theological vision that has fueled this endeavor finally becomes transparent in *A Secular Age*. *A Secular Age* develops a vital corrective for a certain kind of bad faith to which con-temporary religious adherents are prone and offers a compelling vision of a communion of disparate itineraries toward God, linked in an ever-expanding network of agape. We see fully for the first time that Taylor's compelling appeal is rooted not in a vague Romantic aestheticism, but in an endless love of the broken neighbor who stands "among others in the stream of love which is that facet of God's life we try to grasp, very inadequately, in speaking of the Trinity."[1] Taylor seizes this postsecular moment as one opportune for his own public confession, displaying his location within the space he identifies for an open reading of the immanent frame. The appeal of this confession lies equally in its passionate conviction and in its confession of its own inadequate and tentative character. Even those suspicious of Taylor's talk of transcendence may find themselves drawn by his insistence that we recognize that our codes and institutions are not all there is. And this will in itself be a victory for Taylor, a confession, in his eyes, of the pull of transcendence, a crack in the immanent frame.

## COMMUNITARIANISM AND INDIVIDUALITY: LOOKING BACK

Taylor has often been dubbed a communitarian, though, like most other prominent so-called communitarians (the list often includes Jean Bethke Elshtain, Amitai Etzioni, Alasdair MacIntyre, Michael Sandel, and Michael Walzer), he has not claimed the name for himself. Communitarianism emerged in the context of political debates about the tasks of government and the significance of civil society and, more specifically, in response to the political theory of John Rawls.[2] The primary focus of critique was Rawls's "original position," according to which those social arrangements are just that could be agreed upon by individuals acting from behind a "veil of ignorance" with respect to their own social identity and location. Communitarians argued that the notion that individuals stripped of their concrete identities would be capable of intelligible agency was fundamentally flawed. One cannot identify a fair social arrangement, they insisted, without an understanding of what is "fair," and this is itself impossible without an encompassing induction into a comprehensive moral vocabulary, together with the practices in which that vocabulary is at home. Rawls's theory, in their view, reflected an atomistic individualism that fundamentally misrepresents the character of human moral agency. Human beings are socially constituted, coming to awareness of themselves as agents within a world of objective obligations, not individuals who pursue freely chosen life plans. This misrepresentation is particularly dangerous because it both emerges out of and threatens to feed one of the key ills of modern society—a possessive individualism that seeks simply to maximize the satisfaction of one's own desires and regards society as merely instrumental to this satisfaction. Even if Rawls was concerned with securing a meaningful equality for the most disadvantaged in society, and even if he insisted that the original position was a theoretical construct that in no way implied ethical egoism as the basic motivation of real social actors, his theory was nevertheless seen by communitarians as fostering egoism.[3] Communitarians encouraged a more robust, perfectionist understanding of the tasks of government. Laws and policies, they argued, must be carefully designed so as not to favor individual life-projects over communal enterprises. They should seek to foster the institutions of civil society, which play an important role in social formation and facilitate the pursuit of common goods.

Within this discussion, religion came to the foreground because it was seen as a vital locus for the formation of moral character and identity and an important source of non-chosen obligations. Religious bodies were among the key institutions of civil society, responsible for maintaining the social fabric in the face of the threat of possessive individualism. For some the upshot was that all those concerned to maintain a flourishing society should favor laws that nourish religious communities and make it possible for persons to fulfill their religious obligations.[4] They sought to shift the application of the Constitution to religious matters away from a focus on separation of church and state toward a focus on the free exercise clause, while at the same time arguing that the language of religious liberty misleadingly construes religious beliefs and practices as a matter of free individual expression. Religious faith and practice, they argued, are unfairly burdened when their binding character on conscience is not recognized. To remove one's yarmulke in the army is not to set aside one's preferences for the sake of the common well-being, but to place conformity to the (liberal) state over fidelity to one's deepest and most defining duties.

For others, though—notably Alasdair MacIntyre—communitarianism took on a specifically antimodern slant. The focus shifted away from the question of what present social arrangements can best secure justice to a more wholesale rejection of liberalism and modernity. Integrity of moral agency was seen as requiring a form of community fundamentally at odds with liberalism, a tradition with authoritative leaders and texts capable of cultivating the virtues required to sustain social practices directed toward the pursuit of a substantive common good. Under the conditions of modern liberalism, such a tradition could at best survive as a countercultural enclave.[5]

Within these liberal–communitarian debates of the 1980s, Taylor occupied a distinctive position.[6] While arguing for the poverty of a stance that rejects any moral sources transcending the individual, Taylor refrained from demonizing all forms of individualism, indeed, arguing in defense of an "authentic" ideal of individuality. While concerned to trace the origins of modern selfhood and identify its problematic features, Taylor did not attack modernity outright. Instead, accepting the irreversibility of the emergence of modern selfhood, he sought to identify within modernity ways of ameliorating its atomistic tendencies. And while agreeing with Sandelian-style communitarians that religious identity is rarely, if ever, a result of unconditioned free choice, he also sought to come to terms with the fact that it is also rarely in today's world, if ever, simply a taken-for-granted background.

Thus Taylor's thought has resisted a nostalgic flight to tradition and has sought a differentiated relation to modernity open to certain forms of individuality. From within Taylor's account, the path to collective reflection on the best social arrangements for the present is not barred by proscriptions on negotiating with the enemy, since modernity and liberalism are not construed as the enemy. Taylor's arguments have not simply furthered communitarianism, but have also pushed toward a transcendence of the liberal–communitarian opposition. Religion, for Taylor, is not merely social glue, a key institution of civil society, or the source of obligations that conflict with liberalism's false anthropology. Nor is it sustained only by a traditionalist retreat from modernity. For Taylor, authentic faith is, if anything, more possible today than in the past, if we free ourselves from the inhibiting grip of the secularization thesis.

SECULARIZATION AND THE DISEMBEDDING OF RELIGION

The main thrust of *A Secular Age* is to challenge this dogma of secularization, which holds that religion entered into irreversible decline with the advent of modernity and is destined to disappear. Taylor argues that this was not simply a thesis that shaped the sociology of religion, but a widespread cultural assumption that has made secularity appear as the only intellectually defensible option. Once we recognize that the secularization thesis is false, or is true only in a heavily qualified sense, we are in a position to see that in today's world, both secularity and religiosity require a leap of faith. Religiosity is not a mere remainder or aberration. While religious faith and practice continue to flourish in contemporary society, they have changed in significant ways. This is the qualified sense in which the secularization thesis is indeed true.

One of the most obvious changes has to do with the social location of religion. Where religion was once so implicated in practices at all levels of society that it could not be distinguished from politics, economics, art, family life, and so on, there now exists a wide range of autonomous social spheres within which one can function without reference to God or transcendent reality (SA, 2). Taylor does not contest the reality of this form of secularization. He does, however, argue that it is better understood not as a radical modern departure from the past, but as the culmination of very long-term trends. The first important steps toward the "disembedding" of religion took place in the shift from pre-Axial to Axial religions. In the pre-Axial archaic or early religions, the primary agency of religious action was the society as a "single undifferentiated body," the social order was understood as rooted in a sacrosanct cosmic order, and the telos of religious action was ordinary natural human flourishing (SA, 148–50). The post-Axial religions are disembedded along all three of these axes and related to a more radical sense of transcendence, a sense of some ultimate reality lying behind or beyond ordinary social reality. In post-Axial religions, God is no longer immanent within the cosmos, but transcends the cosmos; the social order is not holy, but broken and in need of fixing. It begins to be possible for individuals to conceive of themselves as potentially distinct from their social matrix, capable of creating alternative social groups relating more adequately to ultimate reality, or even of relating directly to a telos now understood as distinct from, and transcending, ordinary human flourishing (SA, 151–54). This form of religious individualism was for many centuries limited to elite minorities. Full disembedding took much longer, happening only when efforts to transform society according to the demands of a transcendent order contributed to the objectification of society and the disenchantment of the cosmos (*SA*, 155). This impulse to "Reform," argues Taylor, played a key role in bringing about a modern understanding of society as constituted by individuals and existing for their sake.

On the one hand, then, if disembedding reaches a kind of apex in modernity, it is rooted in changes initiated several thousand years ago, when religions such as Judaism and Buddhism entered the scene. If this is true, it should give communitarian critics of modernity and Christian critics of individualism pause—a point to which I will return below. On the other hand, Taylor also points out that there is another sense in which individuals remain socially embedded even in the most individualistic of eras. For it is always the case that "we learn our identities in dialogue, by being inducted into a certain language. But on the level of content, what we may learn is to be an individual, to have our own opinions, to attain to our own relation to God, our own conversion experience" (*SA*, 157). Much of the more theoretical discussion issuing out of communitarianism has focused on this formal level of embeddedness. But however true it is that individuals are socially embedded in this way and would be utterly unable to function properly apart from this socialization, Taylor rightly points out that it is beside the point for making sense of both secularization and the rise of modern individualism, since neither of these threaten embeddedness or social construction at the formal level.[7]

## RELIGIOUS POSSIBILITIES IN A SECULAR AGE

The upshot of this long process of disembedding, which Taylor associates with the emergence of a buffered rather than porous sense of the self, a homogenous experience of time, and the rise of post-Galilean natural science, is what Taylor calls "the immanent frame." We in the modern West have come to understand ourselves as living within "a self-sufficient immanent order; or better, a constellation of orders, cosmic, social and moral" (*SA*, 543). These are self-sufficient in the sense that they are intelligible apart from any origin or telos beyond themselves; they are immanent in not requiring for their intelligibility any reference to God or transcendent order. Their intelligibility and impersonality lends them to manipulation for the achievement of human ends; we, as disembedded moral agents, can take up an instrumental stance toward them.

Taylor notes on the one hand that "it is in the nature of a self-sufficient immanent order that it can be envisaged without reference to God"; the immanent order can "slough off" the transcendent (*SA*, 543). On the other hand, though, he argues that it need not necessarily do so. Even if we all (at least in the modern West) now live within the immanent frame, we can live it either "as open to something beyond" or as closed. Giving psychologically and sociologically realistic accounts of individual agency, culture, and history does not require atheism, reductive naturalism, or materialism (*SA*, 272). The immanent frame does not rule out all conceptions of God as active in history and experience; "people could and did go on sensing that they were in dialogue with God, and/or called by God, and/or comforted or strengthened by God, either as individuals, or in groups" (*SA*, 272).

Taylor's "immanent frame" and his multilayered narration of its emergence are aimed at decisively reframing the issue of religiosity in the modern world. No longer does atheism appear as the default position, with the burden of proof on anyone who would embrace a religious outlook. For atheism, too, is disclosed to be an option, one that has embraced a closed reading of the immanent frame. It is possible to identify the motivations behind closed readings as behind open readings. Both are, Taylor argues, a "leap of faith" (*SA*, 550). This language of the leap of faith can easily be misunderstood as an unconditioned act of volition, a bootstrapping operation of "the will." But this is not at all what Taylor means. His point is rather that neither an open nor a closed reading of the immanent frame is natural or logically unavoidable (*SA*, 55); in taking up one or the other position, "our over-all sense of things anticipates or leaps ahead of the reasons we can muster for it" (*SA*, 550). It is not that each individual is confronted with a naked choice between a secular and a religious option. Taylor speaks of being "pushed" or "drawn," of "attraction"; he notes that an option can seem "natural" or "unavoidable" (*SA*, 547, 550). We do not simply choose one option over another; we follow a hunch. In fact, he notes that "one or other of these takes on the immanent frame, as open or closed, has usually sunk to the level of . . . an unchallenged framework, something we have trouble often thinking ourselves outside of, even as an imaginative exercise" (*SA*, 549).

One of the central emphases of communitarian thought has been to display our most fundamental commitments not as the result of free choice, but as constitutive of our understanding of the world as a whole and of our identity as agents, so it is hardly a surprise to find Taylor offering such an account. But communitarians have often argued that it is not only difficult, but also destructive to attempt to think ourselves outside of our basic frameworks. Far from enhancing some ideal of autonomy, scrutinizing our attachments can irreparably damage identity and the capacity for coherent agency.[8] Taylor's aim here, however, is precisely to make it possible to see a closed reading of the immanent frame as an option, to bring to consciousness what would otherwise be an unchallenged framework, to see it as something one must be motivated to embrace, and to which there are alternatives. To avoid recognizing that a kind of leap of faith is involved in embracing the secular option is to suffer from "spin." Spin is "a way of convincing oneself that one's reading is obvious, compelling, allowing of no cavil or demurral" (*SA*, 551). Taylor construes this as a disability rather than as intellectual dishonesty, since he sees it as a subconscious move. Nevertheless, it is an illness that should be treated. On this point, then, Taylor's argument converges with liberal responses to communitarianism. In defending liberalism against communitarian critiques, Stephen Macedo, for instance, argues that some of our constitutive attachments may be corrupt and in need of revision. This requires not that there be some "unencumbered self" prior to all such commitments, but just that we be able to reflect critically on any particular attachment.[9] The era of embedded, unquestionable religious faith has passed. The path forward for religious faith lies through increased self-consciousness, not a denial of self-consciousness. For if unchallenged frameworks remain unscrutinized, the secular option will continue to appear to be more natural, legitimate, mature, and intellectually responsible, and even those attracted to an open reading of the immanent frame will be likely to read that attraction as a "dangerous temptation" (*SA*, 548).

We thus approach a situation in which religious faith does confront the individual as an option. One of the byproducts of the long process of disembedding was individualism: the impulse toward Reform was expressed in part in a "drive to a new form of religious life, more personal, committed, devoted; more Christocentric; one which will largely replace the older forms which centered on collective ritual; the drive moreover, to wreak this change for everyone, not just certain religious élites" (*SA*, 541; see also 532). But Taylor helpfully distinguishes among different forms of individualism: individualisms of responsibility, of self-examination, of self-development, of authenticity, and an instrumental individualism (*SA*, 541). These emerged successively, and to some extent each helped give rise to the next, but they should not simply be conflated with one another, as is often the case. Annette Baier, for instance, offers, as a definition of "the individualism of the Western tradition," "the fairly entrenched belief in the possibility and desirability of each person pursuing his own good in his own way, constrained only by a minimal formal common good, namely, a working legal apparatus that enforces contracts and protects individuals from undue interference by others."[10] Although offered as a definition of individualism as such, this is better understood as atomistic individualism or what Taylor dubs instrumental individualism, with its assumption that society exists for the good of the individuals out of which it is made up and that individuals are bound only by obligations voluntarily assumed (by the moral law they themselves impose). Often, in contemporary discourse, individualism is simply equated with possessive individualism, in which "one places oneself at the center of the moral universe, focusing on one's own entitlements to the neglect of one's obligations to others and the cultivation of those other-directed virtues that are indispensable to the flourishing of our lives together."[11]

Taylor is clearly troubled by atomistic and possessive individualism. Yet even though he recognizes that in some sense these grew out of earlier forms of individualism, he does not seek to return to a premodern collectivism. Not only does he see the shift away from embedded religions as irreversible, he is sympathetic to the drive toward more personal forms of religious life. Individualism as authenticity is an ideal to be embraced, and one that can be lived out in a way open to transcendent moral sources. It is also, Taylor argues, compatible with vibrant forms of community. In our "post-Durkheimian dispensation," privatized forms of spirituality will flourish, since religious life has been detached from political life. But social forms of religious expression will also flourish. "The new framework has a strongly individualist component, but this will not necessarily mean that the content will be individuating. Many people will find themselves joining extremely powerful religious communities. Because that's where many people's sense of the spiritual will lead them" (*SA*, 516). Note here that Taylor continues to resist describing these as "free choices" on the part of individuals. It is not that individuals will join such communities in order to engender in themselves a faith that they are otherwise devoid of but desire. Yet it is as individuals that people will "find themselves joining" religious communities. He also concedes that we should expect (as indeed we find) more movement among various religious communities and identities than in the past. So it becomes increasingly appropriate to describe these as voluntary organizations, even as we should resist equating this with a privatized religious life. Aware of other spiritual and religious options, one is drawn to this one, or finds that it feels right to remain within this one—even if none of this is experienced as or properly described as a "choice."

## Bad Faith

If one of Taylor's main aims in *A Secular Age* is to level the playing field between forms of religious belief and unbelief, a second central concern is to identify and deflect the main temptations facing religious bodies today. To claim that powerful religious communities will thrive in our secular age is not to say that it is possible to recover a world in which faith is simply an unreflective given, a background reality, or the matrix of social order. Yet, as distant as the reality of fully embedded religion is from the present, it remains for many a focus of intense longing, a longing that can give rise to a form of bad faith, just like the spin by which many secular people are affected. If exclusive humanists want to see their closing off of any transcendent reality simply as clear-sighted acceptance of reality, treating believers as ridiculous or immature, believers, too, seek a false kind of certainty. This can take the form of nostalgia for a civilizational religious order, a Constantinian revival. In the face of the vast range of ever-multiplying religious options that confronts us, some believers long to recover an embedded form of existence in which community, institution, and tradition fully define individual identity, and in which faith can be entirely secure. Church–state separation may be accepted, but Christianity may nevertheless be seen as indispensable for maintaining civilization; the decline of faith will mean a decline of order and a loss of civilization itself (*SA,* 734). Moreover, since religious belief is on the defensive in the modern West, the temptation here is to lash out against those who refuse to recognize God or who describe the transcendent differently, to seek a "false certainty of closure, and then try to shore up this certainty by projecting the chaos and evil we feel in ourselves onto some enemy" (*SA,* 769). Thus can the longing for closure take the form of religiously motivated violence.

I would add that we encounter milder forms of this longing for embedded faith, and the danger of bad faith, in other contemporary forms of Christian thought and practice that eschew violence and Constantinian aspirations. Take, for instance, postliberal narrative theology, a founding text for which was Hans Frei's *Eclipse of Biblical Narrative.* Frei's understanding of biblical narrative was inspired by Erich Auerbach's comment that scripture is not meant "merely to make us forget our own reality for a few hours, it seeks to overcome our reality: we are to fit our own life into its world, feel ourselves to be elements in its structure of universal history."[12] Our identities, our "worldviews," are then to be wholly defined by scriptural narrative—surely a form of embedded religion. In taking this as a theological prescription, though, Frei was essentially inverting Auerbach's own argument: Auerbach himself regarded the nineteenth-century novel, with its serious treatment of ordinary characters, as a latter-day *realization* of the biblical proclamation of a hero of weakness whose power is in weakness.[13] Frei, though, saw in Auerbach a way of undoing modern hermeneutic self-consciousness, of recovering an immediate relation to the objectivity of scripture.

Later narrative theology was to move away from a narrow focus on the world of the scriptural text to a broader, Wittgensteinian social constructionism.[14] Language games are embedded within forms of life; the world of Christian scripture is formed not just by the text, but by Christian practices and traditions more generally—by the form of life as a whole, even if scripture plays a central and generative role in this form of life. Fiction, in contrast, may create an imaginative world, but the world of the text is not supported in this way by extratextual practices, by a form of life, by a community. Whether the emphasis is on a text that overcomes our reality or a community that overcomes our reality, when these are taken up in an effort to get back behind reflective self-consciousness, they are doomed to fail. Frei bemoaned the fact that realistic and figural reading had given way to an "independent spiritual self-positioning."[15] Yet all the efforts over the past four decades to recover premodern modes of reading and the communal practices that sustain them have simply led to greater self-consciousness of the ways in which narratives and practices form communal and individual identity. Confining our attention to particularistic Christian practices does not overcome subjectivity any more than confining attention to scriptural narrative. This does not mean that postliberal Christians are doomed to "independent spiritual self-positioning," though, since self-consciousness about formation is also a consciousness of the limits of independence and self-positioning, a consciousness of dependency and of having been positioned, a consciousness of the limits to consciousness even if it is precisely these that cannot be identified. With this humble self-consciousness about formation—with what Taylor refers to as the awareness that "our over-all sense of things anticipates or leaps ahead of the reasons we can muster for it," comes a responsibility to form self and community well, refusing bad faith's false certainty of closure (SA, 550).

So contemporary religious life, like exclusive humanism, can fall into various forms of bad faith that reflect nostalgia for a distant form of embedded faith, for a priority of community over individual that has been irreversibly lost. Communitarianism itself, at least as it has been embraced by some Christian thinkers, is in danger of falling into just this sort of bad faith. One of the reasons that Taylor himself is free of such nostalgia is that he understands Christianity itself as one of the key forces behind the long-term push for more personal forms of religious commitment. It is not, then, just the case that the shift from embedded communal religious life to committed individual faith is in his eyes irreversible. As Taylor's own religious convictions begin to shine through his magisterial description in A Secular Age of the tectonic religious shifts in the West, it becomes apparent that he judges it to be *good* that this happened, and that religious life is no longer simply a taken-for-granted sacred canopy.

### Authenticity and Agape

In order to see this, it is important to attend to the specifically Christian contribution to the general Axial shift away from embedded religion. Taylor notes that "the New Testament is full of calls to leave or relativize solidarities of family, clan, society, and be part of the Kingdom. . . . This in turn helped to give force to a conception of society as founded on covenant, and hence as ultimately constituted by the decision of free individuals" (*SA*, 155). Embedded religion conceived of society as prior to its constituent elements and sacralized the existing social order, reinforcing loyalty to family and clan. Christianity, in contrast, called persons out of the existing social order into personal relationships with God and into forms of flourishing that transcended the natural and ordinary. The Kingdom of God, which the church prefigures, is certainly a form of community, but not one linked to a sacralized cosmos.

Taylor's characterization of the Kingdom as a "network of agape" is heavily indebted to Ivan Illich, in whose theological reflection the parable of the Good Samaritan plays a pivotal role: "If the Samaritan had followed the demands of sacred social boundaries, he would never have stopped to help the wounded Jew. It is plain that the Kingdom involves another kind of solidarity altogether, one which would bring us into a network of agape" (*SA*, 158).[16] Through Christ, God established a new personal relationship with individual disciples, and this relationship of personal love was ramified beyond the disciples through the church. The church is a "network society," but of an "unparalleled kind," transcending traditional forms of relatedness and loyalty, reaching across boundaries of us versus them. "The enfleshment of God," writes Taylor, "extends outward, through such new links as the Samaritan makes with the Jew, into a network, which we call the Church . . . a skein of relations which link particular, unique, enfleshed people to each other" (*SA*, 739). In essence, then, Taylor's claim is that Christ's coming made true community possible, a community of love capable of being initiated only by divine love (*SA*, 282). This is a community made up of personal relationships; human community is not thought of here as prior to its members, as in embedded religion.

Christianity's particular contribution to disembedding religion, then, should have resulted in a network of agape, which questions the established order of things for the sake of a new, personal relationship to God and one another. Instead, something went wrong: "What we got was not a network of agape, but rather a disciplined society in which categorial relations have primacy, and therefore norms" (SA, 158). In the place of traditional network societies, with their highly differentiated, hierarchical, and static social roles, what emerged were "categorical societies." These are conceived as made up of similar units (individuals/citizens) bound together not by personal relationships, but by impersonal rules (SA, 282). And a categorical society lends itself to instrumental individualism, in which society is understood as existing in order to allow its members to pursue their individual life-projects in maximal liberty. The governing code simply minimizes the collision of social atoms.

Why did the project of bringing about a network of agape result instead in atomistic individualism? Taylor suggests that "perhaps the contradiction lay in the very idea of a disciplined imposition of the Kingdom of God. The temptation of power was after all, too strong" (SA, 158). The network of agape grows by invitation, not by imposition; persons are freely if irresistibly attracted to it. The impulse to make over the world, to transform the existing social order, was a good one. The failure was to think that this could be achieved through a program of reform and discipline.

Whatever the explanation, what is crucial to Taylor's argument is that this development be a contingent corruption rather than a necessary progression. Instrumental individualism can be recognized as the offspring of Christianity without thereby being legitimized, and without tainting individuality as such. We are now in a position to understand the theological roots of Taylor's cautious sympathy with the individualisms of responsibility, self-examination, self-development, and authenticity. He is wary of these, insofar as they reinforce the dangerous and self-deceptive illusion of total human control over self and world—the illusion of the program of Reform. He is similarly critical of these to the degree that they feed the notion that I enter into relationships only for the sake of how these allow me to fulfill my own desires. But at the same time he recognizes that Christianity itself is "individualistic" in the sense that it conceives of the human relationship with God, with the transcendent, as an individual, personal relationship. To be sure, this relationship properly gives rise to a network of relationships and so to a community of persons in relation to God. This, though, is a community composed of individual persons in relation, not an undifferentiated social mass or collective. At the same time, it does not exist for the sake of mutual benefit, in order to enable individuals to fulfill their own desires or pursue their own projects. Rather, it exists for the sake of these relationships, this community, itself; it exists for the sake of love.

Christians, then, should not be nostalgic for embedded religion. Nor should they be nostalgic for Christendom, since this alignment of the church with civilizational order was not the realization of the network of agape but its corruption. Christians must go back in order to move forward only in the sense that they must recover a proper understanding of the kind of personal relationship with God, and the kind of community of love, initiated and made possible by Christ. The shift to personal, committed faith and the broader shift to a "secular age" do not in themselves frustrate the impulse to impose God's will on the world. They encourage the proliferation of an ever-broadening range of religious options and the destabilization of faith. But they do not rule out the possibility of the spread of the network of agape.

We are now in a position to understand more fully Taylor's distinctive form of communitarianism, together with his particular take on matters such as positive liberty and authenticity. Taylor's important essays from the late 1970s on atomism and liberty did not reject the ideal of self-realization. Rather, he argued that this ideal is finally intelligible only on a positive rather than a negative account of freedom; self-realization is possible only given a supporting social matrix and is deeply bound up with, rather than insulated from, questions about the objective worth of various capacities and the good life in which these are exercised in some holistic way.[17] In *Sources of the Self* and *The Ethics of Authenticity*, Taylor further developed this line of thought in a way that more clearly showed his own sympathy for the quest to live in a way that is true to one's own particular being. It is only degraded understandings of authenticity that dismiss all moral sources and moral demands that transcend the self: "Our normal understanding of self-realization presupposes that some things are important beyond the self, that there are some goods or purposes the furthering of which has significance for us and which hence can provide the significance a fulfilling life needs. A total and fully consistent subjectivism would tend toward emptiness: nothing would count as a fulfillment in a world in which literally nothing was important but self-fulfillment."[18] Insofar as it does not simply amount to self-preoccupation and self-indulgence, but rather recognizes a responsibility on the part of each person to be true to him- or herself, the ideal of authenticity need not result in social fragmentation. In fact, individuals who recognize their authenticity as taking shape only with reference to horizons of significance beyond the self recognize that it requires rather than precludes unconditional relationships.[19] They may not be able to take as given a sense of corporate belonging, but they will be capable of, and dedicated to, "forming a common purpose and carrying it out," rather than simply pursuing their private interests.[20]

The new element that comes into focus in A Secular Age is the way in which this ideal of authenticity is related to Taylor's theological commitments. It has been easy in the past to read Taylor as some sort of latter-day Romantic. It was clear enough in Sources of the Self that Taylor was concerned to recapture some sort of account of transcendence. But he seemed there to envision this possibility as most powerfully sustained within modernity by epiphanic art, which reveals to us a deeper and truer reality, but which does so in a way always "indexed to a personal vision."[21] This interest in art as an opening to transcendence persists in A Secular Age. Here, though, Taylor highlights the ontological indeterminacy of poetic language, which constitutes a great part of its appeal in a context in which many waver between open and closed readings of the immanent frame (SA, 356–57; 757). Taylor himself, though, is finally attracted to epiphanic art and to the ideal of authenticity because he sees these, with their ontic uncertainty and their insistence on the personal, as at least holding the door open for something further, for a recognition of the kind of personal relationship with God that lies at the heart of Christianity.

## CRITIQUING CODES

Another, closely related aspect of Romanticism that resonates with Taylor's take on Christianity is its critique of moralism, to which he sees Schiller as having given a "wonderfully clear, convincing and influential formulation" (SA, 358). The imposition of the moral law on our desires (à la Kant) divides us against ourselves; only the aesthetic realm can bring about a harmonious unity of the self and a harmony between desire and morality. It is not that the moral law or its demands are canceled or set aside, but rather that human fulfillment is completed by something that includes but transcends morality. Romanticism is often read as substituting the art object or the artist for God as site of transcendence. Taylor, though, argues that Romantic aestheticism was not a strict "alternative to the love of God as a way of transcending moralism. . . . God is not excluded. Nothing has ruled out an understanding of beauty as reflecting God's work in creating and redeeming the world" (*SA*, 359). Schiller may give way to a Nietzschean opposition of the aesthetic and the moral—or he may reinforce a Christian vision of the irreducibly personal quality of communion with God.

Taylor's own version of Schiller's critique of Kantian moralism takes the shape of an insistence on a tension between Christianity and the impersonal, disciplined modern moral order of fixed modern codes. Taylor writes that "Christian faith can never be decanted into a fixed code" (*SA*, 706). Thinking in terms of fairness and justice leaves us in a "two-dimensional" moral space; Christianity induces us to seek to transcend the code, to move vertically, to seek a solution that is not merely fair, but which instills trust and brings about reconciliation (*SA*, 706). There is, moreover, a strong eschatological dimension to this vertical thrust; Desmond Tutu had the charismatic power to help shift a whole society into the vertical dimension, but overall we cannot expect this-worldly societies to embody any more than a hint of the agapic community into which we are invited by Christ. To identify Christ's body with any particular civilizational order is to blind ourselves to the way in which we are always summoned to transcend any present moral order: it is to "lose sight of the further, greater transformation which Christian faith holds out, the raising of human life to the divine (theiosis)" (*SA*, 737).

Here again, Taylor's theological stance is heavily influenced by Illich. Illich sees a "profound betrayal" of the Christian faith in the attempt to embody agapic community in "a code of rules enforced by organizations erected for this purpose" (*SA*, 737). A set of universal rules is substituted for the immediate response of one particular person to another. The network of agape is institutionalized, and in the process, "the spirit is strangled" and communion is lost (*SA*, 739). Our relationships are determined by the categories into which we fall, rather than by our idiosyncratic particularity. Codes, disciplines, and institutions take over. These are not simply depersonalizing, but also, at least at times, ruthless and cruel in their discipline and disengagement.

In the end, Taylor distances himself somewhat from Illich's radicalism. Like Schiller, Taylor wants to transcend moralism without denying it a certain legitimacy. He concedes the necessity of both legal and moral codes, but insists on the importance of recognizing that "that is not all there is"; "we should find the center of our spiritual lives beyond the code, deeper than the code, in networks of living concern, which are not to be sacrificed to the code, which must even from time to time subvert it" (*SA*, 743). Ultimately, Taylor offers the Communion of Saints as a primary image for making sense of the network of agape. This, he suggests, should be understood as "a communion of whole lives, of whole itineraries towards God" (*SA*, 754). It is crucial that we understand these itineraries as including moments of falling away as these are taken up into a broader movement toward communion with God. It is also vital that we accept the Communion of Saints as consisting of a myriad of distinct ways to God, that we "respect the integrity of different ways of life" (*SA*, 772). The summons to transcend the present order in search of communion with God should not be understood as a license to assume that I have grasped more than the tail or ear or foot of the elephant, that I know the only way to love and be loved by God. The church, writes Taylor, was "meant to be the place in which human beings, in all their difference and disparate itineraries, come together, and in this regard, we are obviously falling short" (*SA*, 772).

## DISENGAGEMENT AND SCAPEGOATING

What are we to make, finally, of this combined emphasis on vertical transcendence, personal communion, and suspicion of codes and institutions? Might it not end up providing an excuse for a kind of high-minded social withdrawal that turns a blind eye to injustice and suffering? For if the neighbor is the one I stumble across, and I am convinced that social institutions can only betray the communion I seek with that neighbor, I might seem to be licensed to ignore the suffering of those across whom I do not stumble, whose claim on my attention is less concrete, less gut-wrenching, to whom I can respond only in an institutionally mediated way. I might easily slide from being modern civilization's "loyal opposition," prophetically critiquing present institutions for their failures, to being wrapped up in my own personal pursuit of transcendence and my own cozy community of the likeminded. It is not enough merely to acknowledge that institutions and codes are indispensable, if my primary impulse is to keep my hands as clean as possible of them. We must be equally attuned to the dangers of idolatry and violence on the one hand and passivity and withdrawal on the other.

Our awareness of all the suffering and evil in the world can begin to overwhelm us, Taylor notes. One response to this is to try to shut it out. Another, of course, is to try to respond positively; to do something "to heal the world," to be "part of the solution" (*SA*, 681). He suggests that the impersonal order of modernity and the disengaged stance it fosters tend to push us in the former direction. The modern moral agent faces the facts without letting them get to her; "the liberal self, benevolent towards all mankind, but within the limits of the reasonable and possible, is capable of facing the facts of unavoidable suffering and evil, and writing them off inwardly" (*SA*, 682). What this "writing off" seems to mean is that the self identifies the limits of practical efficacy and feels excused from worrying about what exceeds these limits. Taylor wonders whether this tendency may not be inherent in any merely humanistic view: "Perhaps only God, and to some extent those who connect themselves to God, can love human beings when they are utterly abject" (*SA*, 684). While he recognizes that both humanists and Christians may be tempted to disengage, he is hopeful that Christians might be capable of learning "to dwell in the suffering and evil without recoil, sure of the power of God to transcend it" (*SA*, 685). There might also be parallel "unbelieving solutions," though Taylor's hope here is considerably more muted. So Christians are exhorted both to practice solidarity with the suffering and to work actively to heal suffering. Connection with God is not a sanction for withdrawal from the world, but rather the source of the power to dwell with its weakest and most repulsive elements.

The challenge here is to attend to the pitfalls on either side of the way—the temptation to withdrawal and detachment on the one hand and the temptation to violent eradication of evil on the other. It is no easy feat to keep both of these in focus simultaneously. The modern disengaged stance must be held responsible not just for distancing itself from suffering, but also for rationalizing and thereby legitimizing the use of violence. Before the Axial Age, the gods were the source of both blessings and curses; the holy was a site of deep ambiguity. The Axial transformation identified God solely with the good; evil is something to be wholly eliminated. But Taylor argues that new legitimations for violence continued to be invented. Essentially, violence is seen as justified when employed in the service of God and the good, for the purpose of eliminating evil. The movements of Reform and the rise of modernity only further refine this logic; modern moral codes rationalize violence, that is, they seek to ensure that it is "directed against targets that really deserve it" (*SA*, 687). If the good is cleanly separated from the evil, there is hope of exterminating the latter once and for all. Both religious and secular thinking are subject to this basic logic, and Taylor is pessimistic that anything short of divine grace can preclude the descent into endemic violence that it feeds: "It would appear that any conception of purity can suffer the subversion of the scapegoating move, whereby our own righteousness is guaranteed by our violent combat against those projected as evil; even the 'purity' defined in terms of human rights and democracy" (*SA*, 692).

Taylor is, to my mind, quite right that only the "divine pedagogy" can ultimately heal humanity of this demonizing tendency. Given the dangers of sliding into a triumphalist imposition of solutions or a totalitarian extermination of those who resist the truth, the passion to heal the world should be chastened and modest: this is the force of his argument. But to chasten this passion for Reform is not license to abandon the political for the poetic. Reviewing the seemingly inexhaustible fund of legitimations for demonizing and exterminating others, it might seem that the only post-Axial options are the refusal of the use of all force (rightly recognizing, in his eyes, the "spirit of Christianity" and the fact that "violence has no more place at all in the sanctified life" [*SA*, 689]) or the subversion of this logic in scapegoating and holy war. This would suggest that we have no resources at our disposal for ethically disciplining the use of force. But the modern West is heir as well to just war thinking, to which Christian thinkers from Augustine onward have made key contributions.[22] This tradition has developed and refined principles for acting justly in the context of war.[23] At its heart lies Augustine's conviction that while justice may require the use of force to protect the innocent against aggressive force, it never exempts those who use force from loving those it targets. The created goodness of the aggressor can thus never be cleanly separated from the evil of their violent aggression; persons are never an evil to be simply "eliminated" or "exterminated." It would, of course, be the height of naiveté to suggest that wars in the West are now conducted in accordance with the principles of just war thinking, but it is not insignificant that governments now at the very least commonly feel the need to justify their conduct by appeal to these principles, and that public debate over warfare is carried out in its terms. Moreover, while they can and have been invoked as mere rationalizations for the use of violence, these rationalizations can in turn be critiqued according to just war criteria.[24]

Taylor rightly argues that human violence differs from animal violence in that it has meaning for us, meaning that opens it up to transformation (*SA*, 660). But while it is important to inquire, as Taylor does, into the ways in which a descent into violence can stabilize our identities and shore up our sense of identification with purity and goodness, it is equally important that such analyses not obscure the more differentiated ethical judgments and distinctions we constantly need to make about the use of force. This is true not only in the case of war, but also in the case of other uses of force and coercion, ranging from police forces to parental discipline. The critique of moral codes and principles that sounds a dominant note here makes it easy to elide the fine-grained distinctions in these areas that are crucial to critiquing the abuses of violence that so rightly worry Taylor. If we lose our grasp on these conceptual resources, it will become difficult to articulate what is wrong about scapegoating and sacred killing and thus also difficult to sustain our opposition to such practices. We must be able to articulate how such practices assume that the means can be justified by the end or (in a more Thomistic vein) that evil may be done for the sake of good, and we need to be able to say more than this: to be able to point, for instance, to the evil of the means in terms of the principles of just cause, last resort, proportionality, noncombatant immunity, and so forth. That it requires practical wisdom in order to descend to particulars and discern whether a particular action is acceptable or not does not make the principles meaningless. Taylor worries that impersonal codes tend to homogenize and deny particularity, that they become dehumanizing and cruel to enfleshed human beings. But we must avoid conflating the rules themselves, which are of course in some sense impersonal and abstract, with their concrete application, which is all about attending to the particularities of persons and circumstances. The indispensability of practical wisdom has been one of Taylor's long-standing themes, one to which he here again adverts: "Situations, events are unforeseeably various; no set of formulae will ever capture all of them. Any pre-fixed code will have to be adjusted to new situations. That is why the good person with phronesis really operates on a deep sense of the goods concerned, plus a flexible ability to discern what the new situation requires" (*SA*, 704). This is a key insight: rules and codes do not apply themselves. We need not be hostile to the codes themselves, but rather to an idolatry of codes that treats them as substituting for concrete practical wisdom. As Eric Gregory writes, "to romantically privilege an ethics of personal encounter or an institutional politics of structural analysis" is in either case to commit an "error of false opposition."[25] This side of the eschaton, Illich's vision of an expanding network of agape offers not an *alternative* to codes and institutions, but a way of *humanizing* these, of keeping them responsive to the just claims and needs of real persons and communities, especially those who are least visible and least powerful.[26]

One of the most important sites of such efforts today is the broad-based organizational activity associated with grassroots democracy, in which faith-based organizations play a leading role.[27] Broad-based organizing works through one-on-one conversations and house meetings to identify common needs and concerns, link institutions together on the basis of these needs and concerns, and cultivate leaders who are able to hold accountable those possessing economic and political power. This is one of the ways in which we can work to ensure, for instance, that the use of force is made responsible to the principles of just war theory. Christians are engaged in this activity not because they regard faith-based institutions as the most effective *means* of reweaving the social fabric (although some, perhaps even most, might *also* think this), but because they feel called *as Christians* to do this work, to take responsibility in this way for the world. They find Christlike love incarnate here. A natural next step for one concerned with the ways in which codes can become dehumanized would be a recommitment to practical wisdom's cultivations of traditions of moral reflection, situated within the task of cultivating networks of mutual accountability.

I have argued that Taylor's transcendence of the liberal–communit-arian opposition, his challenge to the secularization thesis, and his nu-anced appreciation of authenticity and personal, committed faith allow him to articulate insightfully both the ongoing possibilities for vital reli-gious commitment and community today and the main temptations these must resist, notably a bad faith that arises out of a longing to recreate em-beddedness, a temptation to poetic withdrawal, and the invitation to de-monize and exterminate the other. While he intends these arguments to apply beyond confessional boundaries, Taylor's argument becomes more intelligible when its own religious presuppositions become evident, as they do in *A Secular Age*. From its inception, argues Taylor, Christianity has called persons out of embedded social orders into a network of personal relationships, giving Christians particular reason to resist both their own temptations to embeddedness and the tendency to drift into instrumental individualism. Taylor's contributions to our efforts to think well about au-thentic community in relationship to authentic individuality have been in-valuable. So is his account of our secular age, its complex genealogy, and the particular opportunities and dangers confronting religious life today. We need to appreciate the fact that codes and institutions are "not all there is" while nevertheless retaining a commitment to applying and extending these. We need to dwell in suffering, as Taylor urges, rather than writing it off, in part as a simple expression of love and solidarity, but also because it is only by doing so that we can descend from principle to particulars in a truly wise and attentive way. Here is one of the sites at which agape be-comes embodied. Divine pedagogy, beyond and within the immanent frame, can work through the development and application of moral prin-ciples, as well as through poetic ascent. And the process by which we hold ourselves and others responsible to them is necessarily both individual and communal.

## Notes

1. Charles Taylor, *A Secular Age* (Cambridge, MA: Belknap Press, 2007), 701. Hereafter abbreviated as *SA*.

2. For an overview of the evolution of the debates surrounding communitar-ianism from the 1980s to the 2000s, see Daniel Bell, "Communitarianism," *The Stan-ford Encyclopedia of Philosophy (Spring 2009 Ed.)*, ed. Edward N. Zalta, available at http://plato.stanford.edu/archives/spr2009/entries/communitarianism/.

3. John Rawls, *Theory of Justice* (Cambridge, MA: Belknap Press, 1971), 129.

4. See, e.g., Michael Sandel, "Freedom of Conscience or Freedom of Choice?," in *Articles of Faith, Articles of Peace: The Religious Liberty Clauses and the American Public Philosophy*, ed. James Davison Hunter and Os Guinness (Washington, D.C.: Brookings Institution, 1990), 74–92.

5. Alasdair MacIntyre, *After Virtue* (Notre Dame, IN: University of Notre Dame Press, 1981), 263.

6. See in particular Taylor's "Cross-Purposes: The Liberal-Communitarian Debate," in *Philosophical Arguments* (Cambridge, MA: Harvard University Press, 1995), 181–203.

7. What I am calling a formal level of embeddedness is closely related to what Ruth Abbey identifies as ontological communitarianism, as opposed to communitarianism at the advocacy level: see her *Charles Taylor* (Princeton: Princeton University Press, 2000), 124.

8. Bell, in "Communitarianism," sees Taylor himself as making such an argument in *Sources of the Self: The Making of the Modern Identity* (Cambridge, MA: Harvard University Press, 1989), 26–27.

9. Stephen Macedo, *Liberal Virtues: Citizenship, Virtue, and Community in Liberal Constitutionalism* (Oxford: Clarendon Press, 1990), 246–47. See also Will Kymlicka, *Liberalism, Community, and Culture* (Oxford: Clarendon Press, 1989), 52–53.

10. Annette Baier, "The Need for More than Justice," in *Justice and Care: Essential Readings in Feminist Ethics*, ed. Virginia Held (Boulder, CO: Westview Press, 1995), 52.

11. Nicholas Wolterstorff, *Justice: Rights and Wrongs* (Princeton: Princeton University Press, 2008), 3. Wolterstorff's focus is on redeeming rights-talk from the charge of fostering atomistic and possessive individualism; he offers a kind of communitarian redescription of rights: "Rights are normative bonds between oneself and the other. And for the most part, those normative bonds of oneself to the other are not generated by any exercise of will on one's part. The bond is there already, antecedent to one's will, binding oneself and the other" (4).

12. Hans Frei, *Eclipse of Biblical Narrative* (New Haven, CT: Yale University Press, 1974); Erich Auerbach, *Mimesis: The Representation of Reality in Western Literature*, trans. Willard Trask (Garden City, NJ: Doubleday, 1957), 48.

13. Auerbach, *Mimesis*, 42. The Bible represents one of the historical high points of realistic narrative—Dante and the nineteenth-century novel (particularly in France) being the other two. In realistic narrative, characters are set firmly within a specific historical period, and character and circumstances are mutually rendered through action. Realistic narrative does not merely illustrate a theme that could be otherwise expressed; it develops governing themes only in the course of unfolding a particular, temporally connected world of interpersonal experience.

14. See, in particular, George Lindbeck, *Nature of Doctrine: Religion and Theology in a Postliberal Age* (Philadelphia: Westminster Press, 1984).

15. Frei, *Eclipse of Biblical Narrative*, 199.

16. Taylor explicitly acknowledges Illich's influence on his thought (737). In his preface to *The Rivers North of the Future*, Taylor writes of having discovered Illich's

work after having worked for some years on the problem of the rise of secular civilization, of feeling a profound resonance with Illich's thought, and of finding it "more than useful, even inspiring." David Cayley, *The Rivers North of the Future: The Testament of Ivan Illich* (Toronto: Anansi Press, 2005), xiii.

17. See, for instance, Charles Taylor, "Atomism" and "What's Wrong with Negative Liberty," in *Philosophy and the Human Sciences: Philosophical Papers 2* (Cambridge: Cambridge University Press, 1985). Both essays were originally published in 1979.

18. Taylor, *Sources of the Self*, 507.

19. Taylor, *Ethics of Authenticity* (Cambridge, MA: Harvard University Press, 1991), 72.

20. Ibid., 112.

21. Taylor, *Sources of the Self*, 428.

22. The literature is vast. Paul Ramsey played a key role in placing the just war tradition on the table for contemporary Christian ethics, starting with *War and the Christian Conscience: How Shall Modern War Be Conducted Justly?* (Durham, NC: Duke University Press, 1961). James Turner Johnson shows that much of the contribution usually attributed to Augustine may be traced back to Ambrose; see his "Historical Roots and Sources of the Just War Tradition in Western Culture," in *Just War and Jihad*, ed. John Kelsay and James Turner Johnson (New York: Greenwood Press, 1991), 9.

23. I am intentionally echoing Oliver O'Donovan's cautionary note about so-called just war theory, that "this tradition is in fact neither a 'theory,' nor about 'just wars' but a *proposal for doing justice in the theatre of war.*" Oliver O'Donovan, *Just War Revisited* (Cambridge: Cambridge University Press, 2003), vii.

24. Ruth Abbey offers a brief summary of Taylor's political activity in *Charles Taylor*, 6. A noteworthy recent example is Taylor's work on the Consultation Commission on Accommodation Practices Related to Cultural Differences in Quebec, the final report of which was delivered in May 2008: "Mandate," Government of Quebec, http://www.accommodements.qc.ca/commission/mandat-en.html. Accessed 19 November 2009; available at archive.org.

25. Eric Gregory, *Politics and the Order of Love: An Augustinian Ethic of Democratic Citizenship* (Chicago: Chicago University Press, 2008), 359.

26. John Milbank gestures in a similar direction, noting that "Perhaps the really big question which remains is this: How do we acknowledge the truth of Illich's insights while still saluting the uniquely practical bent of Latin Christianity? How do we allow that some procedure and institutionalization is required, without destroying the interpersonal?" John Milbank, "A Closer Walk on the Wild Side: Some Comments on Charles Taylor's Secular Age," *Studies in Christian Ethics* 22, no. 1 (2009): 103. Milbank's primary worry about *A Secular Age* lies elsewhere, however; he worries that Taylor is insufficiently attentive to the dangers of disenchantment (94). It is crucial, I believe, to see that Taylor places disenchantment within the broader context of a disembedding about which he is fundamentally positive. Whether the two thinkers are ultimately on the same page with regard to enchantment rests, I suspect, on how Milbank chooses to situate himself with respect to the Great Disembedding and the asso-

ciated "liberal" aspects of Taylor's thought. Intriguingly, though, Milbank has nothing to say about these matters here.

27. I am indebted here to Jeffrey Stout's *Blessed Are the Organized: Grassroots Democracy in America* (Princeton: Princeton University Press, 2010). The critique Stout develops of Sheldon Wolin's "fugitive democracy" might also serve to highlight the dangers of Taylor's Illichian agapism (as articulated in *A Secular Age*, not as lived out in Taylor's political engagement): "The fugitive democrat's distaste for assuming the responsibilities of governance spills over into distaste for earned representative authority within democratic organizations. No wonder democracy strikes Wolin as ephemeral. It is hard to imagine groups formed on this basis accomplishing anything but Romantic expressivity" (254). Luke Bretherton's *Christianity and Contemporary Politics: The Conditions and Possibilities of Faithful Witness* (Oxford: Wiley-Blackwell, 2010) also promises to help us think concretely about Christian involvement in grassroots political activity.

# CHAPTER EIGHT

# Enfleshment and the Time of Ethics

*Taylor and Illich on the Parable of the Good Samaritan*

ERIC GREGORY AND LEAH HUNT-HENDRIX

*The law is like a ponderous speaker who cannot say everything in spite of all his efforts, but love is the fulfillment.*

— Søren Kierkegaard, *Works of Love*

Charles Taylor is a gifted storyteller. His elegant master narratives both thrill and frustrate scholars, sometimes at the same time. Provocative tales of disenchantment as a predicament of modern secularity are important examples of philosophical history that—alongside canonical texts in sociological theory—have been massively influential in the academic study of religion. Consider, for example, the influence of figures as diverse as Weber, Durkheim, Nietzsche, Heidegger, Foucault, Habermas, MacIntyre, and Milbank. Taylor's stories are capacious, implicating all readers in "cross pressure" rather than winner-take-all tournaments. Tacking between the analytical and historical, they reach deep into pre-articulate horizons that give shape to multiple cultures. Taylor describes the "background" against which certain questions can arise and others rest forever silent, the space in which particular experiences become possible and others remain inconceivable. His narratives trade in imaginaries more than theories, practices more than doctrines, conditions of belief rather than beliefs themselves. He adopts a kind of existential genealogy that narrates "how our sense of things, our cosmic imaginary, in other words, our whole background understanding and feel of the world has been transformed."[1] Taylor's ambitious scope invites skepticism from wary historians, anthropologists, and theologians, who look on as he races through specialist territory with (often admitted) speed and generality. Rejoinders are also heard from those who find themselves too simply caricatured or feel absent from Taylor's narrative. Nevertheless, his contested reception seems to speak to a recurring desire for such stories.

No longer naïve theists or atheists, modern Westerners, Taylor confesses, "can't help understanding ourselves in these terms."[2] Our context breeds stories of origins, transformations, and possible futures. Of course, religious traditions have their own stories to tell, and at least one interpreter has invoked the parable of the prodigal son to describe Taylor's ambivalent account of modernity. In response to *A Catholic Modernity?*, historian George Marsden suggests that "Taylor's main argument can be seen as a proposal for Christianity to reach out to its prodigal offspring (recognizing, of course, that Christianity was not modernity's only progenitor)."[3] He praises Taylor's balanced approach between extremes, especially in "recognizing the valuable achievements of modernity and using them as the points of contact for presenting the gospel."[4] In this evenhandedness, however, one can detect an ambivalence that is a prominent disposition in Taylor's philosophy. Despite the presence of a theological undertow, his vagueness encourages speculation and appropriation by different theological movements seeking a new recruit. Taylor's ambivalence is closely related to his irenic and conversational style, but also flows from his substantive commitment to dialogical pluralism as antidote to polarization. It fuels his rejection of "the straight path account of modern secularity" in favor of "a zig-zag account, one full of unintended consequences" (*SA*, 95). This posture of gains and losses sets him apart from many other story-tellers, especially within religious ethics, where heated disputes about rights, virtues, and moral ontology are prominent. His theological humanism resists more familiar narratives of progress or decline, ones that roughly end up compelling a choice between religion and modernity.

In contrast to these linear and decisive narratives, Taylor's *Sources of the Self* set out to diagnose the "unique combination of greatness and danger, of *grandeur et misère*, which characterizes the modern age."[5] A *Catholic Modernity?* found that "in modern, secularist culture there are mingled together both authentic developments of the gospel, of an incarnational mode of life, and also a closing off to God that negates the gospel."[6] Now, in *A Secular Age*, Taylor continues his effort to complicate secularization stories by describing how the West was transformed from a "society in which it was virtually impossible not to believe in God, to one in which faith, even for the staunchest believer, is one human possibility among others" (*SA*, 3). But, again, this is no story of doom and gloom. In fact, by praising the "practical primacy of life" in secular humanism, Taylor suggests that "there is some truth in the self-narrative of the Enlightenment.... [W]e might even be tempted to say that modern unbelief is providential, but that might be too provocative a way of putting it" (*SA*, 637). Throughout his career, and in each of these writings, Taylor has aimed not to "score points" but to identify the "range of questions around the moral sources which must sustain our rather massive professed commitments in benevolence and justice."[7] Here we find a Dialectic of Christianity as much as a Dialectic of Enlightenment. It is these commitments, and the way they operate in Taylor's story, that will be the focus of this essay.

## Stories and Parables

Before turning to our specific interests, it is important to recognize the ambivalence some critics have had about Taylor's ambivalence. When Marsden writes that Taylor's narrative resembles the parable of the prodigal son, he illuminates the complexity of the relationship between Christianity and modernity, and the uncertain possibilities for reconciliation. The story of the prodigal, which depicts a moment of charitable reunion, a welcoming embrace on the son's return home, necessarily involves critique of the son who strayed away: "The prodigal's principles are deeply flawed and dangerous, not least of all to the prodigal, who has been living high on borrowed moral and intellectual capital much longer than anyone has a right to expect."[8] To be sure, Taylor's rebuke of nostalgia rejects any presumption that the son can simply return to the hearth and the family can once again be whole. And yet, Calvinist Marsden expresses anxiety that the Catholic Taylor "tiptoes" around particular Christian commitments in his professional work.[9] If modernity criticism tends to employ a "rhetoric of excess," Taylor's genre tends toward a rhetoric of qualification.[10] He is apologetic for his apologetic. For Marsden, modernity is the prodigal. One might push Taylor in this direction by using his admission that modernity "needs to be saved from its most unconditional supporters."[11] But, if the image is apt, suspicious readers may rightly wonder which characters or traditions are implicitly cast by Taylor as the prodigal, the elder brother, or indeed, the merciful father. He is promiscuous in his criticism of different spiritual visions as much as exclusive humanism, and his open-ended vision of reconciliation perpetuates this ambiguity. But this rhetoric and his critique of dogmatism can obscure the underlying claim that a sense of fullness requires something like a theistic construal of transcendence. By our lights, Taylor's lament about a cramped moral universe and stifled spirit becomes more palpable as his writings develop, and this may be connected to his greater willingness to engage constructive religious thought as he recounts "the world we have lost, one in which spiritual forces impinge on porous agents" (SA, 61).[12]

This essay focuses on another famous parable as a route into tracing Taylor's religious conception of "fullness" beyond human flourishing. It is a rare biblical passage that Taylor explicitly interprets: the parable of the Good Samaritan (Luke 10: 25–37). Recall the power of the parable's surprising message of a Samaritan—a representative enemy of the Jewish people—showing mercy on a wounded man who had fallen among robbers. In addition to the story's emphasis on the fundamental relation between the love of God and the love of neighbor, early Christians often interpreted the parable as an allegory of Christ's gracious healing of wounded (sinful) humanity. But, like the prodigal son, the story has fraught moral dimensions of its own, given a long history of Christian anti-Judaism. Christian exegetes and preachers, confident in their generosity, also have

employed the parable in stereotyping Jews as prideful "lawyers" or hypo-
critical "priests and Levites." Both explicitly and implicitly, the parable
became a convenient story for Christian "supersessionism," which pits
a New Covenant (of love) with a universal Church over against an Old
Covenant (of law) with a particular Israel. This history also shapes the
experience of modernity, especially this side of Luther's reading of Paul
and Protestant constructions of the concept of religion. It is predicated
on readings of a love "beyond the law" and a universal community that
replaces the narrow particularity of Jewish election. Scholars continue
to debate the actual practices of Christian care for strangers in light of the
parable's apparent impartiality as well as the scrambling of notions of identity in response to the radical teachings of Jesus. Disputes remain within the
Christian tradition about charity's relation to justice, the scope of Christian beneficence, and the bearing of works of mercy on salvation. But for
those who welcome the parable's implications about who counts as "neighbor" and its emphasis on a compassion that transcends boundaries, this
complicated heritage often goes unrecognized.

   We do not claim Taylor's exegesis as the hidden key to unlock the
mysteries of his theology, his story of moral sources, or even as a single
hermeneutical guide to his manifold writings. Given the prolific commentary on Taylor and religion, however, it is striking that little has been said
about his reading of the parable as a window into persistent themes in his
work. We focus on his long-standing concern with the rise of benevolence
in relation to the eclipse of transcendence within the immanent frame. According to Taylor, modern practical charity arises within Enlightenment
moralities, which suppress their roots in Christianity and the strong moral
sources that were once lodged in the "old enchanted cosmos" (*SA*, 63). In
*Sources of the Self*, Taylor described this "moral earnestness of benevolent
determination" as "one of the central beliefs of modern Western culture: we
all should work to improve the human condition, relieve suffering, overcome poverty, increase prosperity, augment human welfare."[13] He returns
to and expands upon this theme in *A Secular Age*. The "Reform Master Narrative" describes its continued acceleration and intensification. Taylor's
gloss on the parable of the Good Samaritan illuminates reasons for his
ambivalence in relation to this aspect of modernity and also reveals more
constructive content than has been previously recognized. To accomplish

these goals, this essay reads Taylor with and against the iconoclastic Catholic philosopher Ivan Illich (1926–2002). Taylor has claimed Illich as a compatriot and attests to his influence in reading modern secularity as "neither the fulfillment nor the antithesis of Christianity, but its *perversion*."[14] Illich and Taylor agree that modern ethics has distorted the message of the Good Samaritan by reducing its prescriptions to a code. They assert that the parable must be understood as an event, an occurrence in time, in flesh, and in love. This essay focuses on the spatial and temporal dimensions of ethics and the roles of contingency and spontaneity, as well as proximity and place, which are transformed in the modern reception of the parable. The examination bears upon both the interpretation of Taylor and his interpretation of modernity.

## TAYLOR WITH AND AGAINST ILLICH ON THE GOOD SAMARITAN

A common assumption of recent American "culture wars" is that theists pride themselves on the basis of morality, while atheism justifies itself on account of its rationality. But a major thesis in Taylor's recent tome is that the disenchantment of modern secularism actually justifies itself, in large part, on its ethical status. Indeed, the status and conception of morality in modern secularity is a significant result of changes within the long history of reform in Latin Christendom. Unlike stories that highlight the emergence of natural sciences as an epistemic challenge to religious traditions, *A Secular Age* displays the continuity between Christianity and secularism, tracing the transformation of the Christian church's proselytizing work to save the world into the secular project of civilizing the world. The mission to lead populations to salvation was transfigured into the attempt to spread prosperity and progress around the globe. In the secularization of this effort, the ends and means of this "civilizing" have been altered, and while in certain ways this has resulted in greater tolerance and openness, Taylor asks whether in some ways this might have involved certain losses and given rise to new dangers. To explore this question, Taylor turns to Illich.

Taylor and Illich share the perspective that modernity can be understood, to a great extent, as the remolding of strenuous Christian efforts to cultivate religious and moral purity. Both draw on the parable of the Good Samaritan as an example of the appropriation of Christian ethics into secular moral thought and political practice. This parable has been known for its expansion of the realm of love and is frequently used as a way to think about forms of benevolence, charity, and duties toward strangers. As a story originally involving a transcendent orientation becomes incorporated into the immanent frame, however, significant changes take place. For Illich, these changes are neither beneficial nor even benign. Despite its parade as an expansive ethic, the disciplined and organized character of the modern moral order has ended up as a parody of the parable.

For Illich and Taylor, the charity of the Good Samaritan, like the Incarnation, is a moment of a radical in-breaking of God into the human order.[15] It inaugurates the possibility for new relationships and new opportunities to experience God. Agape is "the love which God has for us, and which we can partake of through his power" (SA, 20), and the parable shows how "the enfleshment of God extends outward, through such new links as the Samaritan makes with the Jew, into a network, which we call the Church" (SA, 739). But in each case, this "network of agape" happens at a particular place and time and in the interaction of particular felt bodies (SA, 158). It signals a "way of being," not a "set of universal rules" (SA, 738). For Illich, and presumably for Taylor, the fleshly action of the Samaritan "prolongs the Incarnation" as participation in the life of the Trinity through the Son (RNF, 207).

Here, without denying ethical import, Taylor and Illich revive a daring spiritual reading of the parable at some distance from the historical-critical method of modern biblical scholarship and the exclusively moralistic interpretation of secularists. But their spiritual reading does not take its cue from the creative fascination of patristic theology with finding the whole of salvation history in a single pericope.[16] Early church fathers typically read the parable back into the drama of Jesus as the Samaritan healing the wounds of sin by being closer to humanity than the law or the prophets; Taylor and Illich read the parable as a continuing speech-act for the lives of its hearers. Their target, it seems, is not the abstraction of Christological allegory per se. It is the familiar reading of the story as moral example in the contemporary world. In the effort to garner lessons from the parable, to adopt its message and generalize it for universal action guidance, spatial aspects of the parable are privileged to the exclusion of its temporal performance. The notion that all people should be helped when in need, that our duties are not confined to our family, community, or ethnicity, has been attractive to modern thinkers seeking to widen the realm of justice.[17] Modernity clings to this expansive aspect of the parable. But without transcendence or something like biblical eschatology, salvation is transformed into a theodicy of a technocratic regime of progress. Illich will argue, with Taylor in accord, that the message of the parable cannot be understood in isolation from its spatial and temporal coordinates, which make it a spontaneous and enfleshed occurrence, an event that cannot be codified or generalized into a rule. Many have noted that the celebrated status of this adaptable parable speaks to its relevance for the modern world in its supposed promotion of individual virtue for a society of strangers, bare humanity.[18] But Taylor and Illich note something more pernicious in the modern affinity for the lawyer's question. With codification, the specter of modern anxiety emerges. The freedom of love becomes the conscience of obligation, the criminalization of sin, and the institutionalization of hospitality as service.

A secularized version presents the parable as if it were a response to a question such as "To whom do I have duties?" But the conversation leading up to Jesus's telling of the story initially had quite a different concern in mind. A man came to Jesus and asked, "What must I do to have eternal life?" This man was concerned not about his civic duties, but about salvation and the "abundant life" (John 10:10) that interests Taylor. For many modern readers, Jesus starts with a stock answer and turns the question back to him: "What does the law say?" The man answered, "Love the Lord your God with all your heart and with all your soul and with all your strength, and love your neighbor as yourself." But this man, in a moment of insight, realized the vagueness of that prescription. So he pressed Jesus further: "But who is my neighbor?"

The surprising parable was not the expected answer to this man's question. It makes a desire for God embodied in relationships on Earth; it expands the sphere of neighborhood beyond the borders of one's community; and it reemphasizes the Hebrew Bible's indication that at the heart of ethics is a commandment to love.[19] Given that the parable was offered, however, not in relation to questions about the welfare state or utility, but in regards to eternal beatitude, extrapolating its meaning for a social or political ethic involves a decontextualization that significantly affects its interpretation.[20] Severing the fleshly response from the celestial aspiration of the question results in a divide between the immanent and the transcendent, the chasm the parable promises to bridge.

But eternity, divinity, love, and bodies have always been complicated terms for ethical thought. Interpreting the commandment to love one's neighbor as oneself, to love the stranger lying on the side of the road, has particularly made the question of love an issue of ongoing contestation. In cutting agape off from its transcendent source and bringing it into the immanent frame, this interpretation transforms the love of God in a drive to make the world into a kinder and more civilized place. On one hand, this had led to a radical expansion of benevolence. As Taylor writes, "Our age makes higher demands of solidarity and benevolence on people today than ever before. Never before have people been asked to stretch out so far, and so consistently, so systematically, so as a matter of course, to the stranger outside the gates" (*SA*, 695). But on the other hand, that benevolence has taken on a distorted character as it has sought stability in the establishment of laws and codes: it has been "excarnated," yet another manifestation of disengaged reason.

Throughout *A Secular Age* Taylor acknowledges the temptation to conceive of modern secularization as a kind of subtraction story—that, in freeing ourselves from previous metaphysical and religious notions, we can finally encounter the truth of nature and humanity. Indeed, this was the way in which many Enlightenment thinkers conceived of their project. Taking themselves to be uncovering natural drives and motivations, they developed naturalistic and psychological explanations for a notion of universal benevolence. Altruism, they claimed, was a human drive that had little to do with God or grace. The moral psychological explanation asserted that "we are motivated to act for the good of our fellow human beings. We are endowed with a specific bent in this direction" (*SA*, 246). Taylor makes the point, however, that in the changing notions of love, time, bodies, and space, modernity does not reveal a substratum of truths that had been obscured by religion, but rather gives birth to significantly new content, constructing a whole new conception of humanity and the world. The rise of modern benevolence did not come from the subtraction of God, but rather indicates the trace of grace in a whole new form.

In the immanent frame, the dignity of all human life becomes a spur for the modern notion of obligation to strangers, a kind of human solidarity that should take precedence over community affiliations. But according to Taylor and Illich, the Christian idea takes its starting place elsewhere. The assertion that any stranger might be your neighbor does not arise out of recognition of universal solidarity, uncovering a primal unity. Rather, agape can exist because God exists; agape can become a force in social contexts because of the free act of human beings who choose to recognize the presence of God. Without this transcendent source, however, the modern imperative to work toward the good of one's fellow human beings begins to change in character. In the secularized, codified version of charity toward the neighbor, both the ends toward which the aid of the Good Samaritan was originally intended and the means by which that aid is dispensed are reconfigured. A fetishized duty emerges to promote human flourishing, a flourishing marked by a secular and material character, with "no reference to something higher which humans should reverence or love or acknowledge" (*SA,* 245).

What is illuminating in the story Illich and Taylor tell is that the rise of secularism does not lead to a diminished concern for the poor and those in need. Contemporary atheism claims to be more tolerant, more efficient, and more successful in promoting the general welfare, as it strives to eliminate violence and establish a perpetual peace. Concern for the helpless becomes the responsibility of the community at large, and institutions are built to deal with the poor and homeless. However, a new, more immanent and diffuse, crusade emerges: the "rage for order." In this order, the orientation toward poverty and pain shifts. Whereas, in the Middle Ages, the poor were an unapologetic opportunity for sanctification, for to help a stranger was to help Christ, in the modern period, the poor become problems to manage. According to Illich and Taylor, the rise of poor laws and later developments in the reform of charity link the process of providing work and aid to confinement in institutions, judgments about who is worthy, and the evaluation of the poor as morally inferior.[21] For Illich, this is a detrimental occurrence. With the "institutionalization of neighborliness," Christians lose habituation in the practice of loving their neighbor, and hospitality is degraded to caregiving institutions (*RNF,* 57). When a homeless shelter is built down the road, Christians put away the candle and extra mattress that they had always kept ready for the stranger who might appear, in need of a bed for the night. Now, when the Christian opens her door to a knock, she gestures in the direction of the hostel down the street and washes her hands of the need to engage personally with the visitor in need.

For Taylor and Illich, the broadening and secularizing of the imperative to help the stranger has led to at least two disfigurations of the parable. The first is the equation of ethics with norms. The parable is a story about freedom: the fact that one can establish a personal relationship with a wounded "stranger" because one desires to do so, because of God's love and goodness. It relies on a "skein of relations which link particular, unique, enfleshed people to each other, rather than a grouping of people together on the grounds of their sharing some important property" (*SA*, 739). An ethical system that resorts only to "oughts" and rules for behavior fundamentally overlooks this freedom, which is at the heart of the Samaritan's approach to the man on the road. But in an attempt to ensure that all desires are met and needs succored, modern secular humanism begins to administer aid in cold and depersonalized ways. Indeed, Taylor notes, modern ethics is obsessed with creating prescriptions for behavior, codes of conduct, whether moral or legal, in the bureaucratic world of humanitarianism, business, or politics.

When helping one's neighbor turns into a requirement that is ordered by a particular code, agape recedes from view. Taylor turns to Illich for the insight that "the code can rapidly become a crutch for our feelings of moral superiority" (*SA*, 743). Illich goes a step beyond Taylor in his articulation of the development of a sense of "responsibility" as cover for something that is actually insidious. According to Illich, offering a Christian variant on Nietzsche and Foucault, modern attention to the neighbor and stranger is inextricable from a drive to fashion the world in our own image. The sense of responsibility, motivated by pity or duty, becomes the flip side of a coin whose reverse is a will to power. The obligation-driven will assumes a right to take control of the lives of others, to construct the world according to its own wishes.

How, exactly, is this modern expression of responsibility and benevolence different from the Samaritan's love of his neighbor? The transformation can be identified in the shift from narrative to principle. Stories are generally characterized by the fact that they take place at a particular place and time. They involve specific people in determinate situations. The reception of the parable, however, has involved uprooting and shuffling its temporal and spatial components. Certain elements have been adopted, others forgotten. Secular humanism has rallied around one aspect of the parable, which we can define as a spatial orientation: its expansive momentum, which breaks through a narrow ethics confined to one's own ethnos, group, or community, and broadens the scope of possible ethical relationships. However, this appropriation overlooks other elements of the parable that are critical in preserving its meaning in a Christian context, a meaning that Taylor and Illich agree may need to be restored if we are to find a way out of the currently reigning depersonalized systems of help/power.

If the universal reach of the new ethical command is one spatial aspect of the parable, another spatial component is its carnal, enfleshed occurrence, as a relationship that emerges between specific bodies in a specific place. In Christian theology, the parable of the Good Samaritan is inextricable from the Incarnation and the Eucharist, and in each of these three moments, what is emphasized is the enfleshment of God, the fact that God takes on a human body, a physical form. The Christian conception of the body, as Taylor writes, marks a departure from a Greek dualism between physical and spiritual. The Incarnation fundamentally baptizes the body. If the body/spirit dualism remains present at all, Taylor notes, it is subordinate to a more central concern that, drawing on Peter Brown, he calls "the direction of the heart" (*SA*, 276). The good life is no longer about getting beyond the physical, for God himself has entered into it. Ascetic practices are meant not to transcend the body, but to help reorient the loves and purify the thoughts. Christianity, therefore, offers an ethic that seeks not to shun the physicality of our world, but rather to embrace it. Thus, for Illich and Taylor, the story of the Samaritan is not simply the story of the *expansion* of love; it is also a story about the tangibility of love, real bodies taking up real space.

In the attempt to secularize agape in the modern institutions of benevolence, care has been disembodied. The poor and sick are pushed away, out of sight, to be attended to by professional, paid caretakers with plastic-gloved hands. The body becomes an object, a site upon which to work, whose operations must be calculated and measured. Illich laments the disconnection we feel from our own bodies, how we look to experts and doctors for knowledge of ourselves. But this is not solely the fault of secu-larism. Illich marks out several significant moments when Christianity began its departure from the embodied ethic that was inaugurated in the life of Christ. They fit Taylor's story about shifts in background that create opportunities for new spaces of questions and, in this case, a new orienta-tion to the body. This movement can be exemplified, Illich writes, in the story of the medieval monk, Berengarius, who became skeptical about the relationship between the Eucharist and the Body of Christ. For almost a thousand years, believers had accepted the notion that the bread and wine were body and blood, when suddenly this became a scandal. How could this be so? The church then turned to Aristotle and developed explana-tions regarding categories, substances, and accidents, to explain away the body that Christ asked his church to share in.

The relationship to the body expressed in the parable, in the Incarna-tion, and in the Eucharist has thus been transformed to obscure the ways in which the body can be the *source of love*, and the ways in which it can be the *object of care*. The institutionalization and rationalization of aid have displaced the role of affect, feeling, and empathy as sources of care. Experts analyze how to distribute aid most efficiently as medical students study their textbooks, and meanwhile the sense is lost in which one can be "moved in the bowels by compassion" (*SA*, 115; cf. *SA*, 741). Care becomes excarnated work and aid established as an industry. But the way in which the body is the object of care has also been transformed. In the realm of im-manence, with no other end in sight, material well-being signifies the en-tirety of human flourishing, making pain and suffering the primary evils to avoid. But, for Illich, this is a distortion of what it means to be mortal. Suffering is a part of human life, one that Christ chooses to share in with us in the Passion.

Talal Asad has devoted attention to this aspect of modernity, which makes its goal the abolishment of pain and the augmentation of pleasure. In his work on the topic, he points toward the relationship between pain and agency.[22] A modern agent is one who is capable of avoiding pain; only someone passive would endure discomfort. But as Asad emphasizes, suffer-ing has played an important role in many religious traditions. The embrace of pain has been an important source of agency. Going a step further, we can say that the story of the Samaritan sheds another ray of light on the topic of suffering. The frailty of our bodies and the occasions of our suffering are opportunities for others to show concern. They are the moments at which a relationship is created between two passersby who would otherwise never connect. Suffering, though never to be courted or desired, can nevertheless enable community.

Illich displayed this personally in his lifetime. As David Cayley tells it, Illich chose to live with the great pain of a tumor rather than be seen by a doctor and treated for possible cancer. He preferred to bear his pain rather than enter into the game of risk calculation that modern medicine recommends, a calculation he saw as central in the disembodiment of modern society. Instead, Illich recommended an "art of suffering" and treated his pain as a gift that enabled him to be constantly aware of the vulnerability and neediness of our bodily state. In fact, according to Illich, to overlook the bodily aspect of the parable is the greatest perversion: "Take away the fleshy, bodily, carnal, dense, humoral experience of the self, and therefore of the Thou, from the story of the Samaritan and you have a nice liberal fantasy, which is something horrible. You have the basis on which one might feel responsible for bombing the neighbor for his own good. This use of power is what I call the *corruptio optimi quae est pessima* [the corruption of the best is the worst]" (*RNF*, 207).

While Taylor accords with the critique of disembodiment, he does not follow Illich to his conclusions about suffering. In *Sources of the Self*, Taylor highlights the fact that the Enlightenment and the Romantic era have left us with a moral framework in which we seek to reduce poverty, promote prosperity, and relieve suffering.[23] And if these aims have been problematized by their divorce from fuller accounts of the human good, they are still the better legacies of this heritage. Taylor acknowledges, in *A Secular Age*, that that meaning of suffering remains a dilemma, and that it may be particularly important for Christians to hold onto the transformative meaning that Christ's passion gives to suffering: "Crucifixion cannot be sidelined as merely a regrettable by-product of a valuable career of teaching" (*SA*, 651). But he demarcates his perspective on the issue when he writes, "Perhaps there is something deeply wrong with all hermeneutics of suffering as divine. Perhaps we are wrong to seek meaning here" (*SA*, 653). In his divergence from Illich and a more traditional Christian perspective on the sanctity of suffering, we can see an example of Taylor's hope for a kind of bricolage of modern ethics. There can be no wholesale return to a premodern form of life. But neither is the character of modernity inevitably determined. As Taylor repeatedly emphasizes, modern secularism is not a subtraction story: it is the product of a dialectical process that involves collective innovation. The rejection of suffering may be a positive remnant of Enlightenment thought that should remain constitutive of our modern ethical orientation. But its consolidation into a code-based institutionalization may need to be reinvigorated by the transcendent source of agape. He articulates his hope that this divine love may still be available to us, "but only to the extent that we open ourselves to God, which means in fact, overstepping the limits set in theory by exclusive humanisms. If one does believe that, then one has something very important to say to modern times, something that addresses the fragility of what all of us, believer and unbeliever alike, most value in these times" (*SA*, 703).

## The Good Samaritan and the Time of Ethics

Taylor differs from Illich, then, in his greater ambivalence about and openness to modernity. He seeks to create an account of Western modernity that acknowledges what is "good, even great, in it, and of what is less good, even dangerous and destructive" (*RNF*, xiii). He is more willing than Illich to admire the achievement of an exclusive humanism as its own original spiritual vision that "can be inspired and empowered to beneficence by an impartial view of things" (*SA*, 255; cf. 572). But he agrees with Illich that important aspects of Christian ethics, depicted in the parable of the Good Samaritan, have been overshadowed. At this point, we have looked at some of the spatial and embodied aspects of a Christian ethic. But, as Taylor notes, it was not until Newtonian science that space and time were separated into distinct entities. The enfleshment of Christ, the incarnation and the birth of the body of the church, also give history and narrative a central place in Christianity. Earthly time is oriented by its relation to God's time, a God who enters in and orders that time toward himself, who begins a new calendar that takes the Incarnation as its starting point. An understanding of time is therefore inextricably bound up with humanity's experience of itself. Taylor's thoughts on time develop in his previous works as he lingers with Heidegger on Dasein's temporality and MacIntyre on the importance of narrative. In *A Secular Age*, we get another treatment of the topic. And, when paired with the parable of the Good Samaritan, and particularly Illich's emphasis on contingency, we have an illuminating explication of the ethics of time.

According to Taylor, prior to the Enlightenment, ordinary time could not be understood without reference to higher times. Higher times structure a community's orientation to the things it holds important, draw its focus onto certain moments and periods, and in some cases, direct the community teleologically toward a set of ends. Taylor writes that, for our medieval predecessors, secular time was a kind of horizontal dimension that was shaped and "warped" by vertical dimensions: "The flow of secular time occurs in a multiplex vertical context, so that everything relates to more than one kind of time" (*SA*, 57).

In the ancient and medieval world, these higher times came in several kinds, including multiple notions of eternity. The Platonic conception imagined the eternal as the realm of the forms, the fixed and unchanging. What existed in time was less real, in a sense, than that which was eternal. In Christianity, however, a new notion of eternity develops. "Secular," worldly time is validated by God's entry into it. But there remains a higher time toward which secular time is oriented. Taylor draws on Augustine for this articulation of a *gathered* time in which all creation and eternity, past, present, and future, comes together in an instant in which we can participate in the life of God (*SA*, 57).

The modern emphasis on science has opened up a gap between space and time and their transformation into mathematical quantities to be dissected and calculated. Once again, this is not a subtraction story. Time has not been shorn of its false significance and exposed for what it truly is. Rather, this process, bound up with the rigorous spirit of Reform, has created a very new experience of time. With the introduction of modern science, time can become a tool of measurement, where each second is identical and exchangeable for any other second.

In *Modern Social Imaginaries*, Taylor makes the point that this notion of time was crucial for the development of modern secularism. But in *A Secular Age*, resisting temptations to oversimplify, Taylor displays ambivalence about a narrative that depicts modernity as characterized entirely by the "homogenous, empty time" Walter Benjamin so artfully describes.

Modernity is still marked by kairotic time—we still have festivals and celebrations that remind us of our origins, and we still tell ourselves stories and narratives that shape our identities. Indeed, on Benjamin's account as well, empty time is characteristic of bourgeois temporality. Bourgeois time contrasts with the time of revolutions, which "blast open the continuum of history," as well as the present of the historical materialist, which is "not a transition, but in which time stands still and has come to a stop," and is "shot through with chips of messianic time."[24] Foucault's notions of "heterotopias" and "heterochronies" have also emphasized the fact that modernity continues to be inflected by diverse notions of time. Nevertheless, for Taylor, there is the overwhelming sense that even these different speeds and experiences of time are cut off from an outside, from a transcendent source. They circulate purely within the immanent frame. And despite some degree of heterogeneity, one particular kind of time has, indeed, become hegemonic.

While refraining from the assertion that naturalized scientific time is the *only* form of time that characterizes modernity, it is nevertheless a highly influential one. Taylor writes that more than any other aspect of modernity, this new notion of time makes up much of the "iron cage" in which we live. As Philip Goodchild argues, time and money have come to share a similar structure; each began as a neutral instrument to measure other values, but slowly took on value in itself. Time has become a resource to be saved or spent, an abstract unit to be counted and calculated. It becomes interchangeable with money where the two values are measured against each other. And ultimately, time *is* money and should not be wasted.

As time takes on a life of its own, it inflects all other situations as a tool of evaluation, an oppressive ticking clock against which everything else is forcibly measured. Any given experience becomes subject to a cost-benefit analysis, judged according to the amount of time it will take. While time is at first something we measure and control, it increasingly becomes something that measures and controls us. As Goodchild notes, "If God is dead, *he is replaced by time and money,* not man."[25]

This has vast importance for ethics. As time takes on a totalizing character, other modes of experience are eclipsed. The multiple notions of time in premodern periods enabled the rupturing of experience, a kind of complementarity to the everyday. A significant part of modernity, according to Taylor, is a loss of this contrast, the notion that everyday life needs to be balanced by "the principle that contradicts it" (*SA*, 51). Premodern periods retained room for an "anti-structure": carnivals, celebrations, and fantastical festivities that temporarily suspended the dominant structure, allowing for moments of transgression and release. These did not necessarily challenge the overarching structure, but rather provided respite from its strictures, for an evening, some hours, the duration of a dream. Social hierarchies and the bounds of what is acceptable would be temporarily suspended, conveying a subtle reminder of their transient and arbitrary nature. The relationships of master and slave that characterized daily life were revealed to be temporary and temporal relationships, limited to a specific moment in earthly time, not necessarily congruent with a divine perspective.

In a modernity severed from transcendence and higher times, however, what exists in time is all that is real. Modern morality must be equally totalizing. Given the absence of recourse to a complementary existence, perfection must be sought in a code here and now, which will be dependable, certain, and authorized to reign without limits. The flattening of time into a single register corresponds with the reduction of ethics to a code, for in such an ordered world, each moment can be evaluated, each second judged. This calculated and measured world leaves no room for relationships that do not fit the prescribed specifications. In contrast, the parable of the Good Samaritan slices through this notion of a timely ethics. Suddenly, the code is called into question with the chance arrival of God or the neighbor, the Event.

When ethics becomes a system to follow and time its encasement, "the ideal is to master it, to extend the web of control so that contingency is reduced to a minimum" (*SA*, 742). But as Taylor notes, there can be no planning around that man lying on the side of the road. There can be no calculation about the time required to provide help. Central to this event is its contingency. Taylor writes that the answer to the question, "Who is my neighbor?" is simply "the one you happen across, stumble across, who is wounded there in the road" (*SA*, 742). Accident and contingency are the venue of love. In a world that is planned to the minute, where busy people rush down the sidewalks or speed by in their cars, there is little time to notice a stranger in need, except perhaps to stare.

As Illich tells it, contingency is a concept of specifically Christian origin. While Aristotle acknowledged the fact of luck, of fortune or misfortune, which applied in the world under the moon, the Greeks had no sense that the very existence of the world was a contingent occurrence. With Christianity, however, the world is suddenly and simply gift, entirely dependent on the grace of God. Illich writes, "contingency expresses the state of being of a world which has been created from nothing, is destined to disappear and is upheld in its existence by one thing, and one thing only: divine will" (*RNF*, 65). For Illich, in contrast to a more modern sense that provides each of us with a raison d'être or, alternatively, leaves us wondering about our purpose and sliding into nihilistic, existential angst, a sense of our contingent existence entirely transforms the set of concepts, feelings, intuitions, and actions that characterize our relationships to ourselves and others. Illich writes that to linger over the fact of our creation and dependence upon God, "to contemplate such a universe was to cultivate a sense of contingency, a sense of having received as a free gift one's own existence and the existence of everything which God has invented and brought forth" (*RNF*, 74). Not only the creation of the world, but even the relationship between man and God is a contingent act. Everything about the Incarnation, God's generous approach to humanity, rings with surprising and seemingly inappropriate elements. God becomes man, is born in a stable, and laid for his first night of sleep in a manger. As Dostoyevsky asks so poignantly in the story of the Grand Inquisitor, who would notice such a God today? Similarly, the neighbor, the stranger, the man on the road are reminders that our lives are enveloped by grace, that love, even salvation, is an event that appears unexpectedly.

Not until modernity, however, does contingency take on the meaning of chance. What is contingent in Christianity is still replete with meaning and pregnant with possibility. But in modernity, the contingency that once signified gift is now a burden. It is increasingly understood simply as an arbitrary event, pointless and purposeless. Time becomes empty units, and contingency becomes chance. But Taylor and Illich remind us that the parable offers a different notion of time and of our participation in its unfolding. In the parable, God's time breaks into the present. When God becomes man, the eternal appears in the temporal, and the stranger becomes neighbor. And in this rupturing of time, the suffering of the body is shared in the breaking of the bread, and agape pours out with the wine become blood. For Taylor and Illich, the secular surrogates of benevolence and progress mask this central import of the parable as a story of communion: "Communion has to integrate persons in their true identities, as bodily beings who establish their identities in their histories, in which contingency has a place. In this way, the central concept which makes sense of the whole is communion, or love, defining both the nature of God, and our relation to him" (*SA*, 279).

As with *Sources of the Self*, Taylor concludes *A Secular Age* with a provocative theological intervention by expressing sympathy for John Milbank's stress upon developments in late medieval theology as central to the rise of modern secularity. According to Taylor, his emphasis upon Reform is a complement to the "Intellectual Deviation" story offered by Radical Orthodoxy. They are "exploring different sides of the same mountain, or the same winding river of history" (*SA*, 775). Milbank's Protestantism that does not drive out the "magic" of an erotic cosmos might be the sort of Protestantism that Taylor counterfactually imagined would have led to a different modernity (*SA*, 75).[26] But Taylor's remarks are instructive in light of our reading of his relationship to Illich, a relationship that shares the same ambivalence that characterizes his account of modernity.

Taylor says he does not want to blunt Illich's radical message, but he does seem to soften its blow when he reads it in terms of political correctness and a reminder not "to become totally invested in the code, even the best code of a peace-loving, egalitarian, liberalism" (*SA*, 743). It is a helpful reminder, but presumably one that any Christian would have resources to affirm. What is less evident in Taylor's story is Illich's concern that the projects of the secular state, itself an expression of the immanent order, are bound up with exclusive humanism. For Illich, the political institutionalization of charity is a sinful witness to a modern "brutal form of earnestness" (*RNF*, 58). Illich tells a story from best to worst; Taylor's ambivalence is reflected in his perplexity at "the century both of Auschwitz and Hiroshima and of Amnesty International and Médecins sans Frontières."[27] It would be too strong to suggest that Illich would not here see a difference, but it would be hard to imagine him serving on the Consultation Commission on Accommodation Practices Related to Cultural Differences.

Reading Illich in this way might allow further dialogue between Taylor's concluding remarks about Radical Orthodoxy and his own political commitments to rights culture, democracy, and the rule of law. In his reading of Taylor and Illich, Milbank asks a very helpful question: "How do we acknowledge the truth of Illich's insights, while still saluting the uniquely practical bent of Latin Christianity? How do we allow that some procedure and institutionalization is required without destroying the interpersonal?"[28] If Taylor were to take up this question, he would contribute to ongoing debates within Catholic social thought, including arguments about the political implications of Catholic personalism between followers of Jacques Maritain and Dorothy Day. In the spirit of the parable, addressing this problem would put flesh on Taylor's resistance to hypertranscendence and hyperimmanence.

Taylor appears to agree with Milbank that we need to find ways to get beyond a stark choice between the spontaneity of immediate encounter and practices of charity in complex social wholes. Like Taylor and Illich, Catholic encyclicals of the early twenty-first century invoke agape as the heart of the Church's social doctrine and offer extensive remarks on the parable of the Good Samaritan as both universal and concrete. But they offer a more positive account of what Pope Benedict XVI calls the "institutional path of charity" that is "no less excellent and effective than the kind of charity which encounters the neighbor directly outside the institutional mediation of the polis."[29] Sounding more like Milbank than Taylor, however, Benedict writes that "*only in charity, illumined by the light of reason and faith*, is it possible to pursue development goals that possess a more humane and humanizing value."[30] Perhaps, in the end, rather than evidence of a lack of theological courage, Taylor's ambivalence is an expression of courage to hope, beyond these dichotomous options, for a possibility not yet imaginable.

# Notes

This essay is a contribution to an interdisciplinary project on The Pursuit of Happiness, supported by the Center for Study of Law and Religion at Emory University and by the John Templeton Foundation.

1. Charles Taylor, *A Secular Age* (Cambridge: Belknap Press, 2007), 325. Hereafter abbreviated as *SA*.

2. Charles Taylor, "Afterword Apologia pro Libro suo," in *Varieties of Secularism in a Secular Age*, eds. Michael Warner, Jonathan VanAntwerpen, and Craig Calhoun (Cambridge, MA: Harvard University Press, 2010), 300.

3. George Marsden, "Matteo Ricci and Prodigal Culture," in Charles Taylor, *A Catholic Modernity? Charles Taylor's Marianist Award Lecture, with Responses by William Shea, Rosemary Luling Haughton, George Marsden, and Jean Bethke Elshtain*, ed. James L. Heft (Oxford: Oxford University Press, 1999), 85. For a systematic theological reading of modernity as prodigal, see Oliver O'Donovan, *The Desire of the Nations: Rediscovering the Roots of Political Theology* (Cambridge: Cambridge University Press, 1996), especially 275–88.

4. Marsden, "Matteo Ricci," 84.

5. Charles Taylor, *Sources of the Self: The Making of the Modern Identity* (Cambridge, MA: Harvard University Press, 1989), x.

6. Taylor, *Catholic Modernity?*, 16.

7. Taylor, *Sources of the Self*, 518.

8. Marsden, "Matteo Ricci," 85.

9. Ibid., 88. For similar criticism from a nontheological perspective, see Quentin Skinner, "Modernity and Disenchantment: Some Reflections on Charles Taylor's Diagnosis," in *The Politics of Postmodernity*, ed. James Good and Irving Velody (Cambridge: Cambridge University Press, 1998), 49–60.

10. On the usefulness and danger of rhetorical excess, see Jeffrey Stout, "The Spirit of Democracy and the Rhetoric of Excess," *Journal of Religious Ethics* 35, no. 1 (2007): 3–21. Taylor's rhetoric of qualification is connected to, but can be distinguished from, what Stephen K. White describes as Taylor's "weak ontology." See Stephen K. White, *Sustaining Affirmation: The Strengths of Weak Ontology in Political Theory* (Princeton: Princeton University Press, 2000).

11. Taylor, *Sources of the Self*, xi.

12. For a helpful account of Taylor's "religious turn," see Ruth Abbey, "Turning or Spinning? Charles Taylor's Catholicism: A Reply to Ian Fraser," *Contemporary Political Theory* 5 (2006): 163–75.

13. Taylor, *Sources of the Self*, 85.

14. See Taylor's preface to David Cayley, *The Rivers North of the Future: The Testament of Ivan Illich as Told to David Cayley* (Toronto: Anansi Press, 2005), ix. Hereafter abbreviated as *RNF*.

15. Taylor's soteriology is radically incarnational: "Redemption happens through Incarnation, the weaving of God's life into human lives, but these human lives are different, plural, irreducible to each other. Redemption-Incarnation brings reconciliation, a kind of oneness . . . the oneness of diverse beings who come to see that they cannot attain wholeness alone" (Taylor, *Catholic Modernity?*, 14). It seems, for Taylor, the Incarnation is the significant content of atonement rather than the crucifixion.

16. On patristic readings, see Riemer Roukema, "The Good Samaritan in Ancient Christianity," *Vigilae Christianae* 58 (2004): 56–74.

17. References to the parable as an illustration of universal concern abound in secular moral and political philosophy. For a recent example, see Amartya Sen, *The Idea of Justice* (Cambridge, MA: Harvard University Press, 2009), 170–73. Sen retains the modern preoccupation with the "classificatory question" but argues that universalism is secondary to the primary point that "the story as told by Jesus is a reasoned rejection of the idea of a fixed neighborhood" (171). Notable contemporary invocations of the parable in debates about obligation and supererogation can be found in the writings of R. M. Hare, John Rawls, and Judith Jarvis Thomson. For classical and modern readings in relation to contemporary debates about global poverty, see Eric Gregory, "Agape and Special Relations in a Global Economy: Theological Sources," in *Global Neighbors: Christian Faith and Moral Obligation in Today's Economy*, ed. Douglas A. Hicks and Mark Valeri (Grand Rapids, MI: Eerdmans, 2008), 16–42.

18. See Robert Wuthnow, *Acts of Compassion: Caring for Others and Helping Ourselves* (Princeton: Princeton University Press, 1991), esp. 157–87.

19. On the connections between the parable of the Good Samaritan and the Hebrew Bible (especially 2 Chron. 28: 5–15), see Craig A. Evans, "Luke's Good Samaritan and the Chronicler's Good Samaritans," in *Biblical Interpretation in Early Christian Gospels, Volume 3: The Gospel of Luke*, ed. Thomas Hatina (Edinburgh: T & T Clark, 2010), 32–42.

20. For political readings of the parable, see Richard Owen Griffiths, "The Politics of the Good Samaritan," *Political Theology* 1 (November 1999): 85–114.

21. For an alternative interpretation of these developments, see Jennifer A. Herdt, "The Endless Construction of Charity: On Milbank's Critique of Political Economy," *Journal of Religious Ethics* 32, no. 2 (Summer 2004): 301–24. Herdt's criticisms of Milbank apply to Taylor to the extent that he adopts parts of Milbank's story.

22. Talal Asad, *Formations of the Secular* (Stanford, CA: Stanford University Press, 2003), especially 67–99.

23. Taylor, *Sources of the Self*, 394–95.

24. Walter Benjamin, *Illuminations*, trans. Harry Zohn (New York: Schocken Books, 1968), 263.

25. Philip Goodchild, *Capitalism and Religion: The Price of Piety* (New York: Routledge, 2002), 133.

26. For Milbank's vision of an ecumenical Protestantism that develops key themes in patristic and medieval theology, see John Milbank, "Alternative Protestantism: Radical Orthodoxy and the Reformed Tradition," in *Radical Orthodoxy and the Reformed Tradition*, ed. James K. A. Smith and James H. Olthius (Grand Rapids, MI: Brazos Press, 2005), 25–41.

27. Taylor, *Catholic Modernity?*, 37.

28. John Milbank, "A Closer Walk on the Wild Side," in *Varieties of Secularism in a Secular Age*, ed. Michael Warner, Jonathan VanAntwerpen, and Craig Calhoun (Cambridge, MA: Harvard University Press, 2010), 80.

29. Pope Benedict XVI, *Charity in Truth: Caritas in Veritate* (San Francisco: Ignatius Press, 2009), 7; emphasis added.

30. Ibid., 9.

PART V

OUTLIERS

# CHAPTER NINE

# Recovery of Meaning?

*A Critique of Charles Taylor's Account of Modernity*

IAN ANGUS

Modernity—its nature, critique, and possibility—is Charles Taylor's abiding theme. Modernity has altered the basic relation of religion to society and therefore the experience of meaning in modern society. In Taylor's version of the secularization thesis, the contrast is between "the world that we have lost, one in which the social was grounded in the sacred and secular time in higher times, a society moreover in which the play of structure and anti-structure was held in equilibrium; and this human drama unfolded within the cosmos. All this has been dismantled and replaced by something quite different in the transformation we often roughly call disenchantment."[1] But, unlike Weber's melancholy acceptance of life within the iron cage, Taylor has persistently sought a recovery of meaning without rejecting the modern age. Modern society produces both a crisis of meaning and the possibility for its recovery, but the condition for this recovery is that "the link with God passes more through our endorsing contested interpretations—for instance, of our political identity as religiously defined, or of God as the authority and moral source underpinning our ethical life."[2] Religion in modernity is thus oriented toward the recovery of meaning in ordinary life. Recovery of meaning is a central task of the critique of modernity.

## THE RELIGIOUS SIGNIFICANCE OF SOCIAL PHILOSOPHY

Taylor's thinking on modernity finds its beginning in the philosophy of G. W. F. Hegel, not least because modernity was the central organizing idea of Hegel's philosophy. The principle of particular subjectivity, manifested in different ways by the figures of Socrates and Jesus, becomes the foundation of modern society. "Secular life is the positive and definite embodiment of the spiritual kingdom—the kingdom of the will manifesting itself in outward existence."[3] Spirit, *Geist*, comes into its own in the modern world by ceasing to occupy a heaven, or a world of ideas separate from ordinary reality, and by becoming the principle or organization of that reality itself.

Philosophy, in Hegel's view, is centered on the concept, which is the foundation for speculative reason. Unlike ancient philosophy, which had to create the very basis of conceptual knowledge through abstraction, modern philosophy must bring reason from abstraction to concrete reality. "Hence the task nowadays consists not so much in purging the individual of an immediate, sensuous mode of apprehension, and making him into a substance, that is an object of thought and that thinks, but rather in just the opposite, in freeing determinate thoughts from their fixity so as to give actuality to the universal, and impart it to spiritual life."[4] The meaning of the modern world is precisely a reconciliation of reason and reality. As Hegel pointed out in his *Aesthetics*, the ideal of chivalry, of righting wrong through the action of a noble knight, is gone, and we are left with "the prose of life" in which "art is mastery in the portrayal of all the secrets of this ever profounder pure appearance of external realities."[5] Taylor has similarly affirmed that the modern moral order consists in "the affirmation of ordinary life" where "the full human life is now defined in terms of labor and production, on the one hand, and marriage and family life, on the other. At the same time, the previous 'higher' activities come under vigorous criticism."[6] For Taylor as for Hegel, the affirmation of ordinary life is rooted in the Reformation, in which the externality of the Church institution and its corruption is overcome by belief, which is referred back to the individual spiritual will.[7] Philosophy completes itself in modern reality insofar as modern reality completes itself in philosophy.

While this project of reconciliation of reason with reality permeates all the differentiated spheres of modern existence, it pertains most centrally to political philosophy, where the social existence of humans demands a rational form that recognizes each subject's autonomy. "Plato in his *Republic* makes everything depend on the government, and makes disposition the principle of the state; on which account he lays the chief stress on education. The modern theory is diametrically opposed to this, referring everything to the individual will. But here we have no guarantee that the will in question has that right disposition which is essential to the state."[8] The problem of modern political philosophy is thus to find the forms through which individual wills can be reconciled into a free, egalitarian, and rational order. Thus, it is a key concern of Hegel's political philosophy to identify mediating institutions within civil society that combine individual wills voluntarily, so that the individual would not have to confront the state alone. It is through such mediating institutions that the modern polity can avoid ancient authority, on the one hand, and arbitrary modern subjective will, on the other. Philosophy should thus attend to the formation of individual wills into institutions that is the concrete form of reason.

Social reality is thus the realm for resolution of philosophico-theological reason, and social philosophy is the form in which philosophical reason is shown to permeate the mediating institutions and activities of ordinary life.

## THE IMPOSSIBILITY OF HEGELIAN RECONCILIATION

The central theme of the reconciliation of philosophy and social reality in Hegel accounts for its persistence as a point of reference in addressing contemporary issues, even though the reconciliation itself, despite its centrality to Hegelian philosophy, has tried the credulity of most readers. Particularly remarkable is the case of Jean Hyppolite, who rejected the idea of Hegel's system[9] while simultaneously taking his work as a model of philosophic discourse, in the sense that we are compelled to interrogate the positive, specialized sciences "to translate for mankind the meaning that they hold for us."[10] This position is predominant no less than it is remarkable in that it rejects the standpoint of the reconciliation of reason and reality in which the task that it articulates was grounded and rendered possible. If reason and reality are not reconciled, then the telos of philosophy in the prose of life cannot be founded in reason; it becomes a goal, an argument, a *polemos*—which is to say, no longer a Hegelian conception of philosophy.[11] A similar acceptance of Hegel, but not on Hegelian terms, characterizes the final word of Charles Taylor's *Hegel*. If, as he says, "this magnificent Hegelian synthesis has dissolved," then the reconciliation of Enlightenment reason and Romantic expressivism has either to be abandoned or become a project, a goal, so that the failure to have reached the goal can be diagnosed precisely as a failure requiring remedy.[12] "Modern civilization has thus seen the proliferation of Romantic views of private life and fulfillment, along with a growing rationalization and bureaucratization of collective structures, and a frankly exploitative stance towards nature."[13] First the diagnosis, then the failure: the Hegelian ontology remains a live option because "the opposition . . . continues in different forms to our day. It seems ineradicable from modern civilization, which as heir to the Enlightenment constantly re-awakens expressivist protest, and along with this, the claim of absolute freedom. The very urgency with which the claims are pressed makes the search for a situated subjectivity all the more vital."[14] Hegel survives not as reason but as protest, as countercurrent to bureaucratic reason, as a Romantic promise of reconciliation. Hegel's problem survives, but not Hegel's solution. Such a formulation should already give us pause: Does not the system define the terms of diagnosis? And if the system is no longer viable, how can the terms of diagnosis survive? Or, if they survive, then they do so in a different form that would require a different justification, and imply, one suspects, that the diagnosis cannot remain the same.

One suggestion made by Taylor in this context does shift the grounds of both systemic understanding and diagnosis. He turned to Herder to probe "deeper, unreflective levels of experience" against Hegel's "complete self-clarity of *Geist*."[15] This turn opened up a line of inquiry that culminated in his defense of a politics of recognition based in Quebec nationalism such that "a society can be organized around a definition of the good life, without this being seen as a depreciation of those who do not personally share this definition."[16] Such a definition of the good life, insofar as it appropriates the influence of Herder, cannot be a thoroughly rational definition. Or, more exactly, it cannot be expected to be subjected to rational definition prior to the belonging that sustains it. In other words, prerational belonging to human collectivities and reflective acceptance of that belonging cannot be made to coincide. This is just another way of saying that the Hegelian synthesis does not obtain: history contains an unerasable, experiential "prior" in excess of its rational kernel. Such prerational belonging to that which "one is and must be" has been investigated by Taylor under the heading of identity, especially in its specifically modern form of authenticity.

I want to turn now to Taylor's social philosophy, which I understand in the non-Hegelian Hegelian terms sketched above as a search for mediating institutions that can recover authenticity within a society committed to bureaucratic reason. I will argue that Taylor's understanding of the *polemical* drive for reconciliation fails on two counts: with respect to its account of instrumental reason, or technology, as "particularity" in the Hegelian sense and with respect to the notion of the "direct-access society" that he uses to describe contemporary society. If these arguments might be thought viable, then it would require us to rethink the philosophical project of retaining Hegel for diagnosis and telos but rejecting him for ground and thus systematic philosophy.

## TECHNOLOGY AS HEGELIAN PARTICULARITY

In *The Malaise of Modernity* Taylor distinguishes three endemic issues of modernity: the loss of meaning or, more exactly, the loss of moral horizons; the loss of final ends, or purposes, due to the instrumentalization of reason; and a loss of freedom.[17] He argues that the basic issue is authenticity, a concept that he derives from Herder and which refers to the idea that "each person has his or her own 'measure' . . . [or that] there is a certain

way of being that is *my* way."[18] Since modern individuals strive to define
their own identities, it is extremely difficult to recognize any moral horizons, such as were traditionally found in religion, to that search. Moreover, social institutions, communities, and organizations are seen as merely
instrumental to the single individual. Such instrumental, bureaucratic,
social institutions thereby come to restrain the freedom of the individual.
The main burden of Taylor's argument is thus to develop a concept of
authenticity that does not eclipse the horizons of significance that can
ground a meaningful identity.

I will not address this argument itself, but rather the aspect of modernity that Taylor refers to variously and without distinction as "instrumental reason," "technological civilization," and "technology." *Instrumental
reason* refers to the rationality that emerged from modern physical science and also underlies the bureaucratic form of modern social organization. In general terms, Taylor seems to accept Max Weber's account of instrumental reason in which "in principle a system of rationally debatable
'reasons' stands behind every act of bureaucratic administration, that is,
either subsumption under norms or a weighing of ends and means," while
he argues against Weber that technology can be put into a different, non-
instrumental framework through authentically modern horizons of meaning.[19] The core of the argument is that technology was developed in the
first place for the moral goal of subduing the destructive forces of nature
in illness, scarcity, or natural catastrophe in order to improve the conditions for humanity. Thus, "if we come to understand why technology is
important here in the first place, then it will of itself be limited and en-
framed by an ethic of caring."[20]

But why should this be so? Why should the fact that a moral ideal got
instrumental reason going in the first place be sufficient reason to believe
that instrumental reason still operates within such a framework? Taylor
admits that there are many forces in contemporary society that push in
the direction of instrumental reason, and even that "left to themselves they
have a tendency to push us in that direction."[21] Without stopping to ask
why this should be the case, his argument for authenticity within horizons of significance leads him to deny the necessity of this tendency and
to end with a plea for citizen participation. "The effective re-enframing
of technology requires common political action to reverse the drift that

market and bureaucratic state engender toward greater atomism and instrumentalism."[22] I do not want to argue with this plea on a political level, but rather to notice how diagnosis has slipped into exhortation. In Hegelian terms, instrumental reason, or technology, is characterized as "particularity," the isolated individual in retreat from community, so that the solution is seen as the return to community on a higher level. This is exactly the problem as Hegel saw it in *Philosophy of Right*: the atomism of civil society is to be overcome by the reconciled community and individual of the state, though the Hegelian reconciliation is of course not actual for Taylor. It remains to be done and thus expressed as a *polemos*. Something is missing here.

What is missing is, first, a more thorough analysis of instrumental reason that might show why it tends to dominate our thinking and possibilities for action, and second, an analysis of where-how-why resistance to it arises and how it can be addressed.[23] I am suggesting that the understanding of instrumental reason, which is the space of these two questions, has been occluded due to a Hegelian rendering of the problem of technology. The genuine contemporary problem of technology has been undercut by fitting it into the Hegelian dialectic as the second term of the triad: 1) unmediated, hierarchical community; 2) isolated, atomistic, particular individuals; and 3) genuine, reconciled, egalitarian community-of-individuals. Without *Aufhebung* between parts two and three, the reconciliation of reason and reality degenerates into exhortation. It is important to note that, on this model, the proposed site of reconciliation is at the level of the society as a whole. If specific technologies provoke resistance, the resolution is at the level of government, not in redesigning the technology so that it has different local effects. While the "state" in Hegelian terms does not mean simply the existing nation-state, it does refer to the whole, the totality of social organization: so while disruption and resistance is local (due to its association with particularity), reconciliation must be holistic, at the level of the highest social organization.[24]

What is it about technology, instrumental reason, that militates against this understanding? A lot could be said here, but there is only room for a little. While modern science indeed got started through recourse to the Christian virtue of charity, as Taylor asserts—which can be confirmed through reference to Bacon's and Descartes's connection of the domination of nature to the virtue of charity[25]—it has not been held within that horizon of meaning.[26] Anyone these days could name a technology that has "progressed" beyond any sensible relation to human need.

It would be too far from the present critical purpose to argue for an alternative understanding of technology that could explain why it transgresses horizons of meaning, but we can discern the lines of such an understanding by suggesting that it is because the new physical science was at once mathematical and experimental. Its mathematical aspect involved abstraction from experienced objects toward a teleology of formal systematicity that cannot be held within the merely instrumental understanding of technology that Taylor proposes.[27] The experimental aspect reestablished the pertinence of a formal-mathematical system of knowledge to a material domain of objects through a correlative abstracting, and therefore standardizing, of experimental conditions from ordinary experience. The new science was at once formally systematic and inherently tied to technological development through its experimental dimension. As a consequence, it could be applied to an increasing number of new domains. This "infinite task" of progressive scientific development projected the unprecedented idea of "the idea of a rational infinite totality of being with a rational science systematically mastering it."[28] It is thus no accident that technology has burst the confines of the nation-state through its immersion in a global economy. In short, modern science contained a theoretical structure of unprecedented universality inherently tied to continuous practical innovation that has made it a force in modern society that explodes, rather than remaining within, horizons of meaning.

There is, no doubt, a Hegelian reason for the return of Hegel as *polemos* that occludes these explosive features of instrumental reason. Taylor remarks that "whether we leave our society to 'invisible hand' mechanisms like the market or try to manage it collectively, we are forced to operate to some degree according to the demands of modern rationality, whether or not it suits our own moral outlook. The only alternative seems to be a kind of inner exile, a self-marginalization."[29] But is there never a time for inner exile? How do we know that now is not such a time? We may hear speaking here the Hegelian confidence that nothing important is lost by giving oneself, and one's thinking, over to the direction of history. But once reconciliation has become *polemos*, surely such confidence is no longer warranted or, at the very least, has become one of several possible decisions. Why is remaining in touch with the larger stream better than attending to the rivulets of poetry, friendship, or local attachment?[30] What hooks the task of philosophy to such a decision?

## The "Direct-Access" Society

The upshot of Taylor's narrative of modernity is the final replacement in our own time of the residues of premodern moral order by what he calls the "direct-access society." The completed modern moral order is constituted in secular time, that is, a time shorn of any public reference to the transcendental time of God, cosmos, or Being. Such a society is simultaneous and horizontal such that each member is "immediate to the whole," in clear distinction from premodern moral orders that were hierarchical and rooted in sacred time, and in which the relation of each to the whole was mediated by personal dependence on others.[31] For this reason, premodern moral orders can be described as relations of "hierarchical complementarity," whereas the modern moral order is one of "impersonal equality."

Disenchantment implies that the three modern institutions of economy, the public sphere, and popular sovereignty become separated from the social order as a whole. In Habermas's terms, they become "subsystems" differentiated from the lifeworld. "These systemic interconnections, detached from normative contexts and rendered independent as subsystems, challenge the assimilative powers of an all-encompassing lifeworld. They congeal into the 'second nature' of a norm-free sociality that can appear as something in the objective world, as an *objectified* context of life."[32] But it is not clear in what sense the public sphere and popular sovereignty can be considered "self-regulating (sub)systems" comparable to the economy. Their arguable separation, or differentiation, from the social system as a whole does not necessarily imply that they are "self-regulating." A subsystem may have sufficient autonomy to run according to its internal rules and not be directly subservient to those of the whole social order and yet require occasional, or even continuous, intervention from that order to remain viable. It is arguable that the exemplary case for a "self-regulating subsystem" is the economy, even though it is certainly not the only one.

This is, of course, the classic dispute between Marxists and Weberians. Both Taylor and Habermas are Weberians in the sense that they do
not regard the economy as especially significant in the differentiation of
modernity. Be this as it may, there is a specific point at which I want to
argue that Taylor's account can be found inadequate. In the first place,
Taylor's narrative of extension of an egalitarian moral order does not enter
the economic sphere itself. Indeed, the condition for the notion of a self-
regulating economy is that labor (in Marxist terms, labor power) is considered as one economic cost among others. This being so, the worker cedes
autonomy to those who control the labor process. The conditions of wage
labor remain those of command, not egalitarian morality. Taylor admits
that there is neither common decision nor a public domain in economic
transaction, but that still "it is a 'sphere' because the agents in an economy
are seen as being linked in a single society, in which their actions reciprocally affect each other in some systematic way."[33] But, surely, this criterion
is too thin: agents are often reciprocally linked in hierarchical and complementary relations of command; such was the case, as Taylor points
out, in pre-Revolutionary French rule.[34] Taylor seems blind, not only to
the persistence of command relations, but also to the extent to which they
are rooted in the notion of a "self-regulating economy" and thus produced
in new forms by modern differentiation. This is, of course, a key question
raised by Marxism, especially that variety that emphasizes the production
process (rather than the "anarchy of the market") as the central element
of capitalism.[35] Whatever one wants to make of it, here is a pervasive fact
that his own analysis cannot logically avoid: the worker and the capitalist
are not "immediate to the whole" in the same sense at all. The modern
moral order stops at the factory gates. For all the contemporary reasons
to revise or abandon Marxism, this basic fact should not be lost. The general point here is that it is simplistic to associate hierarchical social relationships with premodern societies and egalitarian ones with modernity.
Egalitarian relationships between specific social bodies are perfectly compatible with hierarchical relationships within those bodies themselves.
This is true not only in the case of the market. Professors in universities
may treat each other as equals, with inviolable spheres of influence, such
that each gains the freedom to order one's own office, students, and staff
in a hierarchical fashion. Equality and hierarchy interweave within moder-

nity, as Weber no less than Marx was able to see through the proliferation of bureaucratic organization organized "rationally," that is to say, in a top-down structure of the military sort. It may well be this conflict, not that between agency and objectification, that motivates resistance to objectified processes.

## POLEMOS FOR THE MIDDLE WAY

The modern moral order, according to Taylor, produces a society that is dually constituted by objectified processes—such as the self-regulating mechanism of the market, the bureaucratic features of government, or the techniques of mass marketing—and moral agency. "Active and objective categories play complementary roles in our lives. It is inconceivable that we could dispense with the second."[36] This claim is characteristic of his approach to critiques of modernity. "The trouble with most of the views that I consider inadequate, and that I want to define mine in contrast to here, is that their sympathies are too narrow. They find their way through the dilemmas of modernity by invalidating some of the crucial goods in contest."[37] The two contending forces in modernity are such that, Taylor asserts, the best approach is to steer a middle way between them. "Governing a contemporary society is continually recreating a balance between requirements that tend to undercut each other, constantly finding new creative solutions as the old equilibria become stultifying."[38] Since the critiques of modernity are made possible by modernity and depend on some of the same basic postulates as what they are criticizing, the critiques are internal critiques of modernity. They should thus aim at improving modernity, not at abandoning it for something else. Such a "something else" is always conceived by Taylor as an *in principle* impossible attempt to return to features of premodern society that has the practical effect of succumbing to the "totalitarian temptation" within modernity.[39] The narrative thus mutes its Hegelian triumphalism only slightly.

The tension between collective agency and objectifying processes is thus understood by Taylor as an ineradicable feature of the fully modern society due to its origin in the morality of the social contract. The identical view appears in *A Secular Age* while discussing Ivan Illich's critique of the Church as having succumbed to evil by identifying Christian faith and civilizational order. Taylor renders this radical critique, which implies a risk of social and institutional marginalization, as simply a lukewarm reminder of the danger of triumphalism.[40] The perennial conclusion when Taylor confronts moments of decision such as this is that political action, social analysis, and one supposes philosophy also, should recognize that modernity and the critics of modernity belong together and that the task is to balance them, to find some equilibrium that will always be temporary. This effort defines the pervasive Hegelianism of Taylor's oeuvre: he seeks the mediation whereby the similarity in the two conflicting tendencies can be recognized and the tension thus drawn toward a balance rather than escalating toward a rupture. Like most contemporary Hegelians, he refuses a final *Aufhebung* in which the tension is resolved by being taken to a higher level and contents himself with a perpetual balancing act. Taylor is a philosopher of the middle way.

## EGALITARIAN COMPLEMENTARITY

"What else is there?" one may ask. Can technology be understood in terms other than Hegelian particularity? Can not only the persistence, but re-creation, of command structures within modernity be addressed? Is there a better path than the middle way? Full answers to these questions would require extensive reflection and probably several books as long as Taylor's often tend to be. But at least a suggestion is in order, a suggestion that speaks to the description of modernity as egalitarian and premodernity as hierarchical, because the limits of this dichotomous description imply the limits of Taylor's account of current possibilities.

One way in which this issue can be raised is to observe that the relation of humans to nature is a nonreciprocal relation. While we may have moral obligations to preserve other natural beings, it is unlikely that they have such obligations to us. Hans Jonas described this as the general problem of ethics in our time. He began his analysis in the nonreciprocal obligation of parents for their children and argued for a consequent obligation to future generations.[41] While modernity has certainly changed the moral ideal toward which we attempt to educate our children, it is not the case that they can be treated as already the free and equal individuals that the social contract requires. "For it is the future of the whole existence, beyond the direct efficacy of the responsible agent and thus beyond his concrete calculation, which is the invisible co-object of such a responsibility in each of its single, defined occasions."[42] Nonreciprocal relations of responsibility to children will not disappear even in the realized modernity of the direct-access society. Children will not have direct access, and responsibility must be taken for bringing them to the stage of partaking in the moral ideal. In short, children and parents are not "immediate to the whole" in the same way.

But apart from this example, Jonas suggests that nonreciprocal relations are precisely those that need thinking about in realized modernity because they are concealed by the assumptions of the modern moral ideal. Perhaps it is relations of complementarity that need to be considered now. Modern morality tends to regard all complementary relations, because they are nonreciprocal, as hierarchical. Consider the relation of husband and wife in a family. It is commonplace to argue that the previous hierarchical relation between husband ("man") and wife was oppressive in the name of modern equality. But is equality sameness? Can the relations of male and female be thoroughly just the relation of two "individuals"? Contemporary sensitivity to difference suggests that equality and difference may be compatible and, if so, would be the basis for a new ethic that is both in a certain sense modern (because egalitarian) and in a certain sense premodern (because complementary). Indeed, perhaps the same issue of what we might call "complementary egalitarianism" is at the ground of the ecology movement also. It is certainly at the basis of a genuine ethic of teaching. To go back to the example of command relations in work, democracy in the workplace would have to reckon with the complementary relations of the division of labor alongside egalitarian relations of self-management.

Obviously, such an ethics of egalitarian complementarity would not displace all simply egalitarian relations, and perhaps not all simply hierarchical ones either. The suggestion is not that all social relations might become of this type, but rather that the ethics of such relations may bear an important relationship to the issues of our time, precisely because modern egalitarianism has produced objectified structures and command relations from within itself through the repression of what was true about hierarchy and could be recaptured as complementarity.

Such a possibility would be the source of a recovery of meaning, of a new twist to the relation between identity and difference. The difference inherent in a complementary relationship implies that the meaning of the other cannot be fully instantiated by the one and thus that the one needs what cannot be understood in the other. Such an understanding would necessarily involve a return of some sense of enchantment, of beguilement by the otherness of the other. Insofar as such an encounter with otherness defines the basic experience of contemporary social movements, they contain a possibility going well beyond a corrective to instrumental systems. They foster a recovery of meaning that modern society deeply repels and which requires a more radical risk to preserve.

## RELIGION AND MEANING

Taylor has consistently argued that individualism is not the whole of modernity and that new forms of collective action are generated that can balance the tendency of individual self-interest. Such collective action requires "horizons of significance," but such horizons cannot be generated by individual self-interest alone. What, then, can generate them? One constant of Taylor's defense of modernity is his refusal to consider atheism as an outcome of the realized modern ethic. He argues that the secularity of the modern moral ideal is a displacement of religion from its public role in connecting society to sacred time and not a rejection of religion as such. "God can seem the inescapable source for our power to impart order to our lives, both individually and socially."[43] Religion can survive as personal religion and also as an important aspect of political identity. *Sources of the Self* ended with the "promise of a divine affirmation of the human."[44] In *Varieties of Religion Today: William James Revisited* he said that "a thoroughly post-Durkheimian society would be one in which our religious belonging would be unconnected to our national identity" and then proceeded to find three ways in which this is not likely to come to pass: the persistence of churches, the role of religion in some national identities, and the personal spiritual quest.[45] Religion remains in the picture for Taylor because it is the only way he can explain the flip from objectifying processes to collective action. "It is not just a matter of my own experience of the good, but something which is woven into a cherished and crucial collective identity, whether it be that of a nation, or an ethnic group, or religious movement. Here is a crucial collective good which seems 'consubstantial' with God, or in some essential relation to transcendence."[46] While he maintains that modernity pushes religion out of the public realm, it nevertheless seems that it is the persistence of cosmic, natural, and spiritual experiences in individuals and the possibility, though difficult, of their entering the public domain that provides the recovery of meaning that motivates collective action.

My suggestion would indicate, in contrast, that it is the social experiences of egalitarian complementarity in which the recovery of meaning is experienced and which motivate social movements and the critique of modernity because there is some enchantment in complementarity due to its partiality. Since such experiences are in conflict with modern disenchantment, an ethic built on them would have to depart from Hegelian confidence in the direction of the future, risk exile, and embrace the *polemos* of its enchantment.

## Notes

1. Charles Taylor, *A Secular Age* (Cambridge, MA: Belknap Press, 2007), 61. See also Charles Taylor, *Modern Social Imaginaries* (Durham, NC: Duke University Press, 2004), 49.

2. Taylor, *Secular Age,* 554.

3. G.W. F. Hegel, *The Philosophy of History,* trans. J. Sibree (New York: Dover, 1956), 442. All of my references to this text remove the arbitrary capitalizations of nouns.

4. G.W. F. Hegel, *Phenomenology of Spirit,* trans. A.V. Miller (Oxford: Oxford University Press, 1979), 19–20.

5. G.W. F. Hegel, *Aesthetics, Vol. 1,* trans. T. M. Knox (Oxford: Oxford University Press, 1975), 196.

6. Taylor, *Modern Social Imaginaries,* 102; and Charles Taylor, *Sources of the Self: The Making of the Modern Identity* (Cambridge, MA: Harvard University Press, 1989), 213.

7. Taylor, *Secular Age,* 144, 370–73; Hegel, *Philosophy of History,* 416–18; Hegel, *Philosophy of History,* 146–55.

8. Hegel, *Philosophy of History*, 449.

9. Jean Hyppolite, "The Structure of Philosophic Language According to the 'Preface' to Hegel's *Phenomenology of Mind*," in *The Structuralist Controversy: The Languages of Criticism and the Sciences of Man*, ed. Richard Macksey and Eugenio Donato (Baltimore: Johns Hopkins University Press, 1972), 158. See also his more explicit statement that "there is little doubt that in general Kierkegaard is right against Hegel" in Jean Hyppolite, *Studies on Marx and Hegel*, trans. John O'Neill (New York: Basic, 1969), 22.

10. Jean Hyppolite, "Structure of Philosophic Language," 160. Taylor similarly comments that "the results of the empirical sciences should reveal the structure of the Concept, with the degree of approximation and inexactness appropriate to the level of reality concerned. But the sciences had already in his own day broken the bounds of the synthesis which Hegel's commentary imposed on them," in Charles Taylor, *Hegel* (Cambridge: Cambridge University Press, 1975), 543.

11. My non-Hegelian, phenomenological conception of the relationship of philosophy to *polemos* has been expressed in Ian Angus, "In Praise of Fire: Responsibility, Manifestation, Polemos, Circumspection," *The New Yearbook for Phenomenology and Phenomenological Philosophy* 4 (2004).

12. Taylor, *Hegel*, 537.

13. Ibid., 541.

14. Ibid., 571.

15. Ibid., 569.

16. Charles Taylor, *Multiculturalism and "The Politics of Recognition"* (Princeton: Princeton University Press, 1992), 59. I have criticized this understanding of multiculturalism in Ian Angus, *A Border Within: National Identity, Cultural Plurality and Wilderness* (Montreal: McGill-Queen's University Press, 1997), 147–54.

17. Charles Taylor, *The Malaise of Modernity* (Toronto: Anansi Press, 1991), 10.

18. Ibid., 28–29.

19. Max Weber, *From Max Weber: Essays in Sociology*, trans. H. H. Gerth and C. Wright Mills (New York: Oxford University Press, 1976), 220.

20. Taylor, *Malaise of Modernity*, 106.

21. Ibid., 109.

22. Ibid., 120.

23. I am not going to pursue here the question of the origin of social movements attempting to limit instrumental reason in contemporary society. I have attempted such an analysis in Ian Angus, *Primal Scenes of Communication: Communication, Consumerism, Social Movements* (Albany: State University of New York Press, 2000); and Ian Angus, *Emergent Publics: An Essay on Social Movements and Democracy* (Winnipeg: Arbeiter Ring, 2001).

24. I have made a similar argument in criticism of another Hegelian, James Doull, who understood very clearly the problem posed by contemporary global economy and technology to the Hegelian formulae, in Ian Angus, "James Doull and the Philosophical Task of Our Time," *Animus* 10 (2005). (Supplement to *Animus* 5, 2000.)

25. See, for example, Francis Bacon, *Novum Organum*, aphorism lxxiii, in Edwin A. Burtt, *The English Philosophers from Bacon to Mill* (New York: Random House, 1939), 51–52; and René Descartes, *Discourse on Method*, trans. Laurence J. Lafleur (New York: Bobbs-Merrill, 1956), 39–40.

26. This phrasing of the issue derives from a critique of Taylor's analysis of instrumental reason and therefore does not mention other pertinent aspects of Christian doctrine that influenced the development of modern science and that are not mentioned by Taylor—notably the doctrine of Creation that implies that the empirical world can be known exactly and not merely approximately (in form but not in substance), as the Greeks thought. On this issue, see the three marvelous classic articles by M. B. Foster: "The Christian Doctrine of Creation and the Rise of Modern Natural Science," *Mind* 43 (October 1934); "Christian Theology and Modern Science of Nature I," *Mind* 44 (1935); and "Christian Theology and Modern Science of Nature II," *Mind* 45 (January 1936).

27. Before one jumps to the common conclusion that the new physics was Platonic, in distinction from the Aristotelian science of the Middle Ages, it must be noted that mathematics had undergone a significant reformation since late antiquity such that it was based on a "symbol-generating abstraction" without direct reference to experienced objects. Unlike the ancient *arithmos*, which referred to "a definite number of definite things," the mathematics taken over by Galileo "intends another *concept* and not a *being*." Jacob Klein, *Greek Mathematical Thought and the Origin of Algebra*, trans. Eva Brann (New York: Dover, 1968), 46, 174. The severing of concept from intention of experienced objects grounds the two other major characteristics of this form of knowledge. It is only the symbol-system *as a whole* that can be brought to refer to a domain of objects and that, by virtue of its abstraction from experience, becomes *systematic* in the sense of postulating an internally consistent and transparent relation between concepts. I have explored the significance of Klein's thesis for the relations between formal systematicity and concrete experience in "Jacob Klein's Revision of Husserl's *Crisis*: A Contribution to the Transcendental History of Reification," *Philosophy Today* 49, no. 5 (2005).

28. Edmund Husserl, *The Crisis of European Sciences and Transcendental Phenomenology*, trans. David Carr (Evanston, IL: Northwestern University Press, 1970), 21–22.

29. Taylor, *Malaise of Modernity*, 97.

30. Taylor appears to reconsider the possibility of attending to the rivulets instead of the larger stream in his discussion of Ivan Illich at the end of *A Secular Age*. He agrees with Illich's argument that reifying modern bureaucratic organizations and their "fetishism of rules and norms" (742) is based in the Christian attempt to step beyond tribal belonging and into a pure human universality. He is therefore sympathetic to Illich's reinterpretation of the parable of the Good Samaritan, not as the establishment of a new universal code, but as a reminder that we "should find the center of our spiritual lives beyond the code, deeper than the code, in networks of living concern, which are not to be sacrificed to the code, which must even from time to

time subvert it" (743). If this sympathy were definitive for the argument of *A Secular Age*, it would demonstrate that Taylor had shifted his understanding of philosophy as a *polemos* for the middle way in his later work. Taylor accurately comments that we can see imbalance between larger (spiritual) order and established order in two ways. "This lack of fit could be seen as a fact just about the present order, something that could be overcome by establishing a new order, a real Christendom . . . [o]r we could see this gap as endemic in the human condition itself" (744). However, in the same manner as in his earlier work, Taylor then proceeds to mitigate this alternative: he interprets Illich as adding something different into the bureaucratic world (743), as balancing it rather than rejecting it; he argues that the difference between these two, "far from allowing these modes to be neatly ranked, . . . is the difference which enables them to give something to each other" (745). So, we are back to a balancing act between two opposing principles, just as in the earlier work. There is no real consideration of a radical departure from the principle of good order, which necessarily commits one to "the larger stream." My point is not that this is wrong, but rather that it functions as an unproven assumption in Taylor's work.

31. Taylor, *Modern Social Imaginaries*, 157.

32. Jürgen Habermas, *The Theory of Communicative Action. Vol. 2. Lifeworld and System: A Critique of Functionalist Reason*, trans. T. McCarthy (Boston: Beacon Press, 1987), 173.

33. Taylor, *Modern Social Imaginaries*, 104.

34. Ibid., 71.

35. Taylor's critique of Marxism refers to the form of Marxism that diagnoses capitalism through the "anarchy of the market," which is why he often refers to Lenin in his discussions. He refers in several places to the lesson that is to be learned from the failure of Marxism and Communism—between which he sees no meaningful distinction precisely because Lenin's Marxism is the only one for him. In contrast, my point is about the command relations of the factory, which were extended, not eliminated (even in principle), by the subsumption of the economy under the state that characterized Communism. In *Modern Social Imaginaries*, Taylor's remarks about Marxism refer primarily to the base-superstructure model, in order to reject "materialist" determination of the social imaginary (32–33, 72–73), and to ill-fated attempts to subsume the economy to state control (171). In *The Malaise of Modernity* he claims that both the idea of the economy being run by the "associated producers" and that of doing away with the bureaucratic state are illusory because we have learned that the market is necessary to industrial society (109–10). In *Hegel*, Taylor interprets Marx and Marxism as an attempted synthesis of expressivism and Enlightenment science, and thus as an inheritor of Hegel's philosophy, but argues that the transition from quantity to quality assumed by a revolutionary change cannot be understood by Marx (as in Hegel) because the boundary between these two would shift. This is what accounts for the self-contradictory conception of revolutionary change in Marxism as both an act of will and a historical necessity. The basic issue, according to Taylor, is that the immanentization of spirit by Marxism produces a radical concept of freedom

that corresponds to Hegel's absolute freedom in that it is situationless and therefore empty (551–58). My point is not that there are no lessons to be learned from Communism, but rather that one of the lessons is that Communism occluded, no less than capitalism, the persistence and renovation of hierarchy within modernity, especially within the sphere of work, despite its commitment to egalitarian relations. How to respond to this fact remains a difficult and important problem. However, it is a fact, even though one has to be less than confident of the direction of history to register it.

36. Ibid., 165.

37. Taylor, *Sources of the Self*, 502–3.

38. Taylor, *Malaise of Modernity*, 111.

39. Taylor, *Modern Social Imaginaries*, 171.

40. Taylor, *Secular Age*, 743–44.

41. Hans Jonas, *The Imperative of Responsibility* (Chicago: University of Chicago Press, 1984), 108–22.

42. Ibid., 107.

43. Taylor, *Modern Social Imaginaries*, 193.

44. Taylor, *Sources of the Self*, 521.

45. Taylor, *Varieties of Religion Today: William James Revisited* (Cambridge, MA: Harvard University Press, 2002), 111–16; the same point is made in *A Secular Age*, 516.

46. Taylor, *Secular Age*, 545.

# CHAPTER TEN

# Transcendence and Immanence
# in a Subtler Language

### The Presence of Dostoevsky in
### Charles Taylor's Account of Secularity

BRUCE K. WARD

Why speak of Fyodor Dostoevsky in relation to Charles Taylor's magisterial analysis of modern secularity? At first sight there might seem little in common between the irenic, carefully measured, scholarly argumentation of the Canadian philosopher and the sometimes wild, often unnerving visionary genius of the Russian novelist. But this first impression underestimates the profoundly existential nature of Taylor's account of our secularity, as it also underestimates the argumentative care and philosophical insight with which Dostoevsky composed his great novels. I will now outline the case for bringing Taylor and Dostoevsky together.

I begin with three significant correspondences, which are closely related, between Dostoevsky's work and Taylor's account of secularity. The first has to do with what Taylor finds most important in modern secularity.

In his introduction to *A Secular Age,* he defines secularity in three senses, noting that his account will focus on secularity not as the privatization of religion, nor as a decline in religious belief and practice (the first two secularities), but as the modern situation of doubt, or "fragilization," characterizing all forms of belief *and also* unbelief. This "Secularity 3" is the inescapable awareness of religious believers and unbelievers alike that our views are not held by other intelligent people of reasonably good will in our midst—the inescapable sense of looking sideways, which casts doubt on our own construal of reality. This condition of reflexive doubt as a modern destiny is prime Dostoevskian territory. As Kirilov says of Stavrogin in the novel *Demons,* "If Stavrogin believes, he does not believe he believes. And if he does not believe, he does not believe he does not believe." Indeed, Dostoevsky said of himself that his own faith was "tried in the crucible of doubt" and that for him, as a child of the modern age, the doubt would always be there, right up to "the moment they close the lid of my coffin."[1]

The second correspondence has to do with Taylor's mapping of the fragilized ideological terrain of modern secularity as a three-cornered struggle involving not only Enlightenment secular humanists and religious believers, but also neo-Nietzschean antihumanists (whom he identifies, for instance, with Foucault and Derrida). Such a three-way struggle for the heart and mind of modernity constitutes the basic argumentative pattern of Dostoevsky's great dialogic novels of faith and atheism, in which the dialogue between secular liberal and Christian voices is always shadowed by the presence of a third, the nihilist. To be specific, one might say that while Dostoevsky always had Rousseau and Hegel in his sights, from *Notes from Underground* through *The Brothers Karamazov,* he also anticipated Nietzsche—and, moreover, saw clearly the extent to which progressive humanism provokes and also anticipates Nietzschean nihilism.[2]

The third correspondence between Taylor and Dostoevsky involves the development and deployment of "subtler languages." Taylor is concerned with creating a space for meaningful dialogue between secularists and believers instead of the usual fruitless polemic, and in furthering this possibility he places the onus particularly on people of religious faith, whom he divides between those who are merely nostalgic for the past and those who are willing to defend transcendence in a "subtler language." He includes himself among the latter. Here the correspondence with

Dostoevsky needs no justification, since Taylor himself, in response to the question—What is it to speak transcendence in a subtler language?—points directly to Dostoevsky as among the foremost pioneers in Western modernity of "new itineraries" or "paradigm shifts" out of the immanent frame toward God.[3] It is worth noting that these pioneers are often literary artists; one of the chief characteristics of Taylor's philosophical writing is the impressive range and depth of reference to literature, not merely as a source of concrete illustration for philosophical or theological concepts, but also as an independent source of new cognitive insight.

A more direct case can also be made for discussing the relationship between Taylor and Dostoevsky. There is, for instance, Taylor's remarkable but little-known essay on Dostoevsky published several years ago in a small Canadian journal.[4] Much of Taylor's reading of Dostoevsky in this piece finds its way into the two major works that have propelled him into the forefront of English-speaking philosophy: *Sources of the Self* and *A Secular Age*. In both there are frequent references to Dostoevsky—above all, strategically crucial references.[5] Apparently Taylor sometimes spoke of his desire to write a large-scale work on Dostoevsky; in its own way, *A Secular Age* might be regarded as that work.[6]

In what follows, my concern is not to demonstrate a direct line of intellectual influence from Dostoevsky to Taylor (even though this might be arguable). My concern, rather, is with the question of intellectual *affinity*, which I think is ultimately more instructive. It is instructive for our understanding of the role that Christianity plays in Taylor's philosophical program. He has understandably been reticent about this subject, and at a decisive moment toward the end of *Sources of the Self*, when the affirmation of a theistic perspective appears imminent, he declines the move, appealing instead to Dostoevsky, who "has framed this perspective better than I ever could here."[7] This affinity is also instructive for our understanding of the philosophical dimension of Dostoevsky's art. Reading Dostoevsky through the lens of Taylor's account of modernity can vastly enhance one's appreciation of the prophetic force of a writing such as "The Grand Inquisitor."

My focus on affinity rather than direct influence allows latitude for *divergence* as well as *convergence* of views. And it is at the points where Taylor and Dostoevsky diverge that things can become especially interesting.

Two principal (and, as I shall try to show, related) areas of convergence-leading-to-divergence are Taylor's *historical* thesis that modern secularity and the exclusive humanism inseparable from it arise from a mutation of Latin Christianity, and his *philosophical-theological* critique of the moral sources (or absence thereof) of modern secular order.

THE HISTORICAL THESIS: MODERNITY AS
A DEFORMATION OF WESTERN CHRISTIANITY

At the heart of Taylor's secularization thesis is a general reading of Western history that is not unprecedented; it belongs to the camp of those few but powerful voices—Dostoevsky, Nietzsche, René Girard, and most recently, Ivan Illich—who interpret modern secularity as a deformation or "mutation" of Christianity.[8] Taylor's particular thesis can be stated succinctly: secularization is the final outcome of Western Christianity's self-undoing through its effort to reform the lives of Christians and their social order to the end of forcing them into conformity with the demands of the Gospel. To put it more precisely: modern secularity has come about through the institutionalization, and therefore perversion, of Gospel compassion (agape) in the name of Reform. Put like this, Taylor's thesis sounds as "radically daring" as John Milbank claims it is.[9] A remarkable feature of Taylor's book is the manner in which the radical thesis tends to be subsumed, almost forgotten, within a persuasive historical narrative of such assured detail and reassuring chronological conventionality, as we are taken through the expected stages of Protestant Reformation, Renaissance, Enlightenment, Romantic Counter-Enlightenment, and so on. Yet the eye-opening unexpected remains. To cite two instances: his account of the rage for Reform that has gradually brought us to where we are now begins not with the Protestant Reformation, but with Latin Christendom, specifically with the reforms of Pope Gregory VII (Hildebrand) in the eleventh century; and the chronology is not a straight line but a series of zigs and zags—the Romantic counter to the Enlightenment Deist counter to the Calvinist counter to the scholasticism of the latter Middle Ages—each appearing to take Western history in a new direction while actually confirming the general tendency. Taylor's nuanced historical narrative is able to confirm the experience of those who find that modern secular space is not religiously neutral because it is somehow Christian, while at the same time confirming the experience of those who find that secular space is not religiously neutral because it is *anti*-Christian, indeed, antireligious.

This brings me to the principal feature of Taylor's historical account that I want to emphasize—his focus on the rise of "exclusive humanism" as the key explanatory feature of modern secularity. By *exclusive humanism* Taylor means a stance affirming that the fullness of human life toward which we should direct ourselves is to be found within and only within life itself, whether within human reason, nature, our inner depths, or a combination of these. In other terms, it is an affirmation of immanence that excludes transcendence—not only in theory, but also as lived experience. In Taylor's words, "The coming of modern secularity has been coterminous with the rise of a society in which for the first time in history a purely self-sufficient humanism came to be a widely available option. I mean by this a humanism accepting no final goals beyond human flourishing. Of no previous society is this true."[10]

For Taylor, if modern secularity is the child of Christianity, this is above all because exclusive humanism is the child of Christianity. Taylor's story of how exclusive humanism arose first as an intellectual vision among the elite during the Enlightenment and then, through political-cultural developments, became a livable option for many ordinary people, and of how all this is linked to the obsession with Reform originating in Latin Christendom, is dauntingly complex. It begins with the mission to lay people of the mendicant friars in the Middle Ages as the first stage in an ongoing Christian Reform of society that culminates in the Protestant Reformation. With the crucial mediation of the "Providential Deism" of the Enlightenment, the Christian Reform is eventually given secularized expression in the "modern moral order" of mutual benefit envisaged by liberal political thought. From there it is but a short step to the exclusive humanism that has come to characterize the metaphysics of the liberal project. The story is one of an ever-decreasing need for the presence of God in the developing modern moral-political order of mutual benefit, hastened by a justified reaction against bad Christian theology and authoritarian Christian institutions. If in 1500 in the West it was almost impossible not to believe in God, whereas now it is relatively easy and in some milieus even the default position, this is not, according to Taylor, primarily due to the famous disenchantment of the world brought about by modern science, nor to the exclusion of religion from the public sphere, but to the rise of exclusive humanism, with its alternative vision of human flourishing, as an attractive option on a mass scale. Religious belief is now inevitably beset by the uncertainty raised not only by the presence of other religious faiths, but also by the assertive presence of an attractive unbelief. That secular moral, political, and cultural space within which diverse religions now coexist, shaped as it is by three centuries of exclusive humanism, constitutes, in Taylor's phrase, an "immanent frame" profoundly tending toward closure against transcendence.

One of the key early moments in the long development of Taylor's story occurs in the context of his discussion of Hildebrand's successful resistance to the political powers of medieval Europe in the Investiture Controversy:

> It might have seemed obvious that one should build on this defensive victory with an attempt to change and purify the power field of the "world," make it more and more consonant with the demands of Christian spirituality. But this naturally didn't happen all at once. The changes were incremental, but the project was somehow continually re-ignited in more radical form, through the various Reformations, and down to the present age. The irony is that it somehow turned into something quite different; in another, rather different sense, the "world" won after all. Perhaps the contradiction lay in the very idea of a disciplined imposition of the Kingdom of God. The temptation of power was after all, too strong, as Dostoevsky saw in the Legend of the Grand Inquisitor. Here lay the corruption.[11]

Here Taylor's own words confirm the decisive convergence with Dostoevsky. Indeed, the first half of A Secular Age can be read as a detailed historical elaboration and confirmation of Dostoevsky's original insight, in the famous "Grand Inquisitor," that Western modernity has its ultimate origins in the Roman Church's acceptance of Satan's offer to Christ of the "kingdoms of the world." There is, however, one intriguing and, I believe, ultimately very significant difference: while Taylor implies that the "disciplined imposition of the Kingdom of God" aimed too high, Dostoevsky's Grand Inquisitor claims just the opposite—that his disciplined control of the masses is a concession to human weakness. As he says to Christ, "I swear, man is created weaker and baser than you thought him! How, how can he ever accomplish the same thing as you?"[12] It seems to be Dostoevsky's view that the world did not win "somehow," imperceptibly, in the long course of time, but at the very moment that power was taken up as an instrument of the Gospel, an employment of power that came from aiming not too high, but too low, indicating a lack of faith in the efficacy of agapic love in the face of the "power field" of the real world.

Why this turn to worldly power to realize the Kingdom of God? Taylor modestly disclaims having the answer to this question.[13] Dostoevsky does not answer it directly either, but he does point to where the beginning of an answer might be found when he has the Inquisitor declare to Christ that the Church's betrayal of the Gospel started "exactly eight centuries" earlier.[14] Since the conversation is set in the mid-sixteenth century, this would place us in the mid-eighth century, when the secular power of the papacy was initiated through Pope Stephen II's acquisition of certain Italian territories. This historical detail does not answer the question, but it does suggest an important link—between the temptation of power and the question of the meaning and status of the papacy. This, in turn, was linked to a yet more profound theological issue that was beginning to divide Latin and Greek Christianity at this time: the most proper way to articulate the delicate balance between "oneness" and "threeness" in the Trinitarian God (with the Latins favoring the inclusion of the *filioque* clause in the Nicene Creed). Dostoevsky's Inquisitor, then, is making, at least indirectly, a connection between the acceptance of worldly power and an issue in Trinitarian theology. Where Taylor would locate the key historical moment in the fourteenth century, with the rise of the Reforming mendicant movements, or possibly earlier in the eleventh-century Hildebrandine Reform, Dostoevsky would push the moment back yet further again, to the Latin West's revision of the Nicene Trinitarian formulation, which had become widespread in Western churches by the eighth century.[15]

Just where one locates the historical origin of the Christian deformation that precipitates the eventual turn toward modernity is a highly contested and quite possibly insoluble question, since there are always exceptions in the face of attempts at generalization. Yet the enterprise remains vital to our civilizational self-understanding. What, then, is significant about the divergence between Taylor and Dostoevsky on the precise whys and wherefores of the historical corruption of the Latin Church by the temptation of worldly power? I think we can come to a clearer view of this significance by considering first Taylor's engagement with another influential contemporary account of the Christian-historical roots of modernity, that of Radical Orthodoxy.

Radical Orthodoxy has focused on the theological voluntarism of late medieval scholasticism as the matrix for the "bad turn" in Christianity that provoked the Enlightenment reaction that brought about modernity. According to this theological-historical account, the nominalist theology of Duns Scotus and William of Ockham, in its overriding emphasis on the sovereignty of God, made all goodness derivative of acts of divine will; the divine will determines what is good, rather than willing according to what is good. An emphasis that might well have been intended to protect the divine mystery against human efforts to define and control it according to human conceptions of what is good for God to be and do had far-reaching implications for the Western understanding of the world, God, and human beings. The diverse beings of the world were no longer seen as participating in an order of goodness in which each being found the fulfillment proper to its nature, as in the realist (Thomist-Aristotelian) vision; rather, the world came increasingly to be seen as a self-contained mechanism of things, connected only by God's sovereign willing. This vision of all things, or entities, as existing in the same way (*univocity,* in Milbank's term) comes to include God, increasingly conceived as a sort of super-entity, who stands over against the world. There is a disconnection between transcendence and immanence, a disconnection that will lead finally to the self-enclosed "immanent frame" of which Taylor speaks.

Taylor considers his account (the "Reform Master Narrative," or RMN) of the origins of modernity and the Radical Orthodox account (the "Intellectual Deviation" story, or ID) to be complementary, "exploring different sides of the same mountain." While the former gives more weight to the social-cultural dimension (practice) of the turn in Christianity, the latter lays more emphasis on the theological dimension (theory). If we now return to Dostoevsky's historical cue, pushing the "intellectual deviation" back to the Trinitarian debates between the Greek East and the Latin West, then we arrive at a historical juncture in which the theoretical—the *filioque* question—and the practical—the papal claims, symptomatic of the Church's entanglement in the "power field" of the "world"—are not merely complementary, but intrinsically joined. As Philip Sherrard has insisted in his remarkable account of the controversy that eventuated in the Great Schism of 1054, the theological question of how to *think* (or not) the Trinity was inseparable from the social-political question of how to *enact* the agapic Kingdom of God. He argues persuasively that the concern of Latin theology with rationalizing the Trinity in order to emphasize the unity of the three Persons (due to concerns with the Arian heresy) has demonstrable connections with the effort to rationalize and centralize ecclesiastical organization on the basis of the papacy—and both were in turn connected with a tendency to conceive of God as utterly transcendent of the world, as in effect "absent" from the world, rather than also immanently and transfiguratively present in the world, which thereby becomes nothing but a field of power relations.[16] Dostoevsky's Grand Inquisitor might reflect to some degree an anti–Roman Catholic bias on the Russian Orthodox author's part, but that does not diminish its significance as a reminder that any historical account of the decisive turn within Christianity should attend to differences in the Latin and Greek understandings of the Trinity (without resurrecting those differences!).

Taylor himself invokes Dostoevsky's Grand Inquisitor when speaking of the way in which Latin Christianity was "somehow" corrupted by power. I would submit that the Grand Inquisitor also points to the possibility of clarifying that "somehow" in a way that acknowledges Dostoevsky's serious engagement with the Orthodox theological critique of Western Christianity. This is a step, moreover, that would seem mandated by Taylor's own deepest conceptual concern in *A Secular Age*. Somewhere near the heart of the Trinitarian theological controversy between Greek East and Latin West lay the question of how to relate divine transcendence and immanence. This is the very question according to which Taylor frames conceptually the whole problem of exclusive humanism; as he notes in his introduction, "the distinction immanent/transcendent is tailor-made for our culture."[17] His ensuing account of secularization might, indeed, be regarded as the definitive laying out in detail of the truth of Hegel's insight in *The Phenomenology of Spirit* (in the section entitled "The Struggle of Enlightenment with Superstition") that the crux of the Enlightenment, and therefore of modernity, has to do with a fundamental confusion in Western thought about how to relate, while distinguishing, immanence and transcendence, the here-below and the beyond, the finite and the infinite.[18] For Hegel, modernity is best interpreted as a theological development, albeit one that is best comprehended by philosophy, just as the truth of how transcendence and immanence ought to be related *is* its rational comprehension in his philosophical system. This is not to say that Taylor is with Hegel in the claim that the immanent/transcendent problem is better understood by philosophy than theology. It is noteworthy, however, that despite the crucial role that the "cut" between transcendence and immanence plays in *A Secular Age*, one does not finally find there an indication of how the two *ought* to be related. This absence, as we shall see, looms large when we come to the issue of moral sources, the next major area of convergence-divergence between Taylor and Dostoevsky that I want to explore.

## THE PROBLEM OF MORAL SOURCES: CONVERGENCE ON THE QUESTION OF TRANSCENDENCE

Taylor's exhaustive historical genealogy of modern secularity (in the first half of *A Secular Age*) prepares the way for a philosophical critique aimed at the instability of those "moral sources" that "inspire us to embrace" the modern moral order and the evoking of which "strengthens our commitment to it."[19] Taylor is certainly not the first to discern the theoretical shakiness of the modern liberal virtues—respect for equal human dignity, tolerance, and compassion—as they are currently articulated. Much of the best liberal thought is well aware of its own lack of coherent theoretical foundation but prefers, in the style of Richard Rorty, to dismiss the problem; after all, the hegemony of the modern moral order is assured in practice.[20] Taylor, however, is not willing to ignore the theoretical incoherence, preferring to affirm the ancient philosophical insight that there is ultimately a connection between what we think and how we act. Speaking, for instance, of our modern international philanthropy, our concern for the suffering of human beings on the other side of the globe whom we shall never meet, he asks: Does our reason for embracing it effectively motivate us to carry out what it calls for?[21] This is almost identical to the question posed by Dostoevsky to modern humanism: "Do you love or despise humanity, you, its coming saviors?"[22] Here, in this sort of question and where it leads, we have the convergence between Taylor and Dostoevsky on which I want to reflect.

I start with Taylor. His critical questioning of the moral shibboleths of secular humanism aims not at destruction, but at retrieval and renewal. The argumentative strategy he employs in this aim is closely tied to that three-cornered struggle that he thinks defines the ideological terrain of modernity: the struggle among the Enlightenment secular humanists, the neo-Nietzscheans, and the theists; as he puts it, "any pair can gang up against the third on some important issue."[23] Let us take the important issue of *compassion* and see how the sides line up. 1) Theism and secular humanism against neo-Nietzscheanism: compassion is a value crucial to human flourishing, to be affirmed rather than rejected. 2) Neo-Nietzscheanism and theism against secular humanism: liberal compassion is some kind of "Christianity without Christ," and without a transcendent basis it cannot stand; indeed, compassion insufficiently supported by empowering moral sources morphs into something else—for instance, the self-satisfaction and desire for power of an imperialism of do-goodery. 3) Neo-Nietzscheanism and secular humanism against theism: the biblical God of transcendent command cannot in any case be the basis for genuine compassion, since authentic compassion cannot and should not be commanded from on high.

One might generate further rounds of argument and counterargument, but we have enough here to draw a conclusion. Theism can be both strongest and weakest where it draws on the Nietzschean critique of secular humanism as an inconsistent attempt to retain biblical morality without the biblical faith on which it is based. Playing the neo-Nietzschean card against secular humanism is a temptation for religious believers, but it can also be a trap if defenders of a God-based humanism accept Nietzsche's interpretation of the *manner* in which belief in God constitutes the justification of, for instance, compassion. According to Nietzsche, the obligation of compassion for the suffering other can *only* be presented as transcendent command, enforceable by transcendent reward and punishment.[24] We exercise compassion because this is good for something else—in this case, our *own* relationship with God as "father," as "judge" and "rewarder" (however we might finesse the emphasis in these images). Acceptance of this point entails acceptance of Nietzsche's model of the biblical God and of the divine–human relationship. Such an acceptance forecloses further attention to what is really the most important and potentially fruitful question posed to religious faith by Nietzsche's announcement of the death of God: *Which* God has died? Simple reaffirmation of the religious tradition in the space opened up by Nietzsche's exposure of the shaky foundations of secular liberalism is not enough; what is needed is a critical retrieval of the more profound strata of the tradition's teachings about God—and the divine–human relationship.

There is a second and closely related problem with the strategy of arguing to God by invoking the neo-Nietzschean critique of Enlightenment humanism. As Nietzsche asks and answers: "Why atheism today?—'The Father' in God has been thoroughly refuted; ditto 'the judge,' the 'rewarder.'"[25] Simply to resurrect the "God" who has died would require forgetting that the Enlightenment took place, or at least supposing that the Enlightenment critique of revealed religion had no significant validity for religious faith itself. So long as the religious foundation without which the virtue of compassion cannot stand is identified with the "rewarder" or "judge" of transcendent moral command, its uncritical reaffirmation would only lead to a repetition of the Enlightenment, in the wake of a repetition of religious dogmatism and conflict.[26] Faced with this possibility, why would the thoughtful liberal humanist not move in the other direction, with Nietzsche, toward the revaluation of all values, including the value of compassion? While Nietzsche looked ultimately to the overcoming of modern nihilism, he anticipated that it would first have to become more widespread. A major growth source could well be among disenchanted liberal humanists.

Taylor himself does not fall into the trap of affirming the model of God that Nietzsche claims to be the basis of Christian morality. Au contraire, he makes it clear that he is an acknowledger of transcendence who nevertheless thinks there is "some truth in . . . the Enlightenment."[27] How, then, does one affirm a transcendent basis for compassion without invoking the God of transcendent command?

Here the need to speak transcendence in a subtler language is pressing, and for Taylor the need has been met above all by literary geniuses such as William Blake, Charles Péguy, Gerard Manley Hopkins, and Dostoevsky, who offer us models of "how to recover a new way of expressing and validating" the transcendent dimension of human life.[28] Of all these, Taylor seems to point to Dostoevsky as the one who does so most explicitly in relation to the problem of moral sources.[29] Dostoevsky self-consciously took up the challenge of articulating a transcendent basis for the ethical. His most famous articulation of it is in the formula of Ivan Karamazov: "If there is no God, then everything is permitted." A common misconstrual of this formula is to think that Dostoevsky *did* fall into the trap of claiming that morality stands or falls with the God of transcendent command—so that the difference between him and Nietzsche is simply that he chose in a leap of faith to affirm the actual existence of this God. This misconstrual overlooks the obvious—that it is one of Dostoevsky's great *atheist* characters who expresses the formula. Dostoevsky's *own* understanding of the relationship between God and human virtue is closer to this formulation by Dmitri Karamazov: "How is man going to be virtuous without God? A good question! Because whom will he love then—man, I mean?"[30] Here we have an understanding of virtue as the outcome of love, rather than desire for reward or fear of punishment. As the Eastern Orthodox theologian Georges Florovsky says, "Dostoevsky believed from love, not from fear."[31]

Dostoevsky's response to the challenge of articulating a transcendent basis for the ethical lies in his development of what I would call a poetics of agapic love. This poetics of love—at least in its negative dimension—is reflected with marvelous clarity in Taylor's analysis of what is perhaps *the* paradox of modernity: "Before the reality of human shortcomings, philanthropy—the love of the human—can gradually come to be invested with contempt, hatred, aggression. . . . The history of despotic socialism, i.e., twentieth-century communism, is replete with this tragic turn, brilliantly foreseen by Dostoevsky over 100 years ago . . . and then repeated again and again with a fatal regularity, through one-party régimes on a macro level, to a host of 'helping' institutions on a micro level from orphanages to boarding schools for aboriginals."[32] It is clear from the context that Taylor's identification and analysis of this paradox draws heavily from a close reading of Dostoevsky, who is likely unparalleled in his revelation of the psychospiritual dynamics of the strange dialectic whereby philanthropy slides into misanthropy. The dialectic reaches its culminating point in the compassion of Ivan Karamazov, who is emblematic of what Dostoevsky takes to be the fatal contradiction of exclusive humanism. Ivan affirms compassion for suffering humanity to the point of rejecting God and immortality in its name, in those famous words of "Rebellion": "I don't want harmony, for love of humankind I don't want it. . . . And therefore I hasten to return my ticket." Indeed, Ivan claims that his compassion is *more* compassionate than that of Christianity—of *Christ himself*.[33] Here he is emblematic of modern humanism too, in its claim that its compassion is more comprehensive and more efficacious than Christian compassion. To this claim, Dostoevsky responds with the contradiction-evoking question that might be formulated as follows: You reject God in the name of compassion; but can compassion be enacted, or even understood, without the idea of God? True to his commitment to a dialogic approach, respectful of the freedom even of his fictional characters, Dostoevsky shows how the insight into the unsustainability of compassion within a purely immanent humanism gradually becomes accessible to Ivan's *own* consciousness. Not only the reader, but Ivan himself, becomes aware of an ineluctable slide from compassion into contempt for suffering human beings, a slide most dramatically noticeable in a careful reading of the Grand Inquisitor's argument (of which Ivan is the ostensible author) for a "compassionate" tyranny over the weak.[34]

The slide within exclusive humanism from compassion into contempt and even hatred for those who suffer is not merely asserted, but traced in psychological detail by Dostoevsky. In a fascinating meditation in *A Writer's Diary*, for instance, he attempts to place the reader within the consciousness of a thoughtful and sensitive person who honestly embraces the vision of human existence as entirely without any transcendent meaning or purpose, destined to end in annihilation. In the course of this meditation he shows how the compassion aroused by the spectacle of pointless human suffering within an indifferent universe can be subtly transformed into an actual hatred of the sufferer: "In just the same fashion, it more than once has been noted how, in a family dying of starvation the father or mother, toward the end when the sufferings of the children have become unbearable, will begin to hate those same children whom they had previously loved so much, precisely because their suffering has become *unbearable*."[35] For

Dostoevsky, the exclusion of transcendence is the exclusion also of any possibility that suffering can have spiritual meaning or significance; it can always only be "useless" suffering. This is not to say he thought that suffering could be "justified" according to a providential theodicy of one kind or another. Dostoevsky was at one with his character, Ivan Karamazov, in rejecting any theodicy, whether Christian-providential or humanist-progressive (in the style of Hegel), that justified the necessity of innocent human suffering as "manure for someone's future harmony." As Taylor points out in *A Secular Age*, the rejection of theodicy is not tantamount to a rejection of Christian faith, since theodicy is very much a modern apologetic response to the problem of suffering, which already has accepted the central notion of Providential Deism that the universe is a scrutable immanent order.[36] A theodicy within this context, such as that of Leibniz, actually invites rejection; and it is noteworthy in this regard that Dostoevsky once set himself the task, undoubtedly fulfilled in Ivan's "Rebellion," of writing the Russian *Candide*.

The rejection of transcendence provoked by the God of modern Deistic theodicy, however, leaves the modern rebel face-to-face with a useless human suffering that cries out for remedy through a ceaseless struggle. It is somewhere at this point that the Dostoevskian phenomenon of the parents' "hatred" for those "same children whom they had previously loved so much" emerges. Taylor is most interested in tracing out this phenomenon on the more comprehensive level of the political. Hence his reading especially of Dostoevsky's *Demons* ("one of the great documents of modern times"), in which he offers at once an insightful interpretation of Dostoevsky's novel and of the spiritual dynamics of modern terrorism.[37] The key concept developed by Taylor in this reading is that of the "noble schismatic"—and potential terrorist—who is so very acutely sensitive to suffering and injustice that he is led not only to reject God but also to separate himself radically from God's world, thereby affirming his own purity: "We are utterly other than those who inflict harm. We have no part with them. . . . There are no reasons to stay your hand when the target encompasses only evil, filth, the negative. As Stalin put it: 'Who's going to remember all this riff-raff in ten or twenty years' time?' "[38] Yet our distancing from the perpetrators of evil and injustice also has the effect of distancing us from the victims. Why is this? Taylor's explanation, developed at greatest length in his discussion of Dostoevsky in *Sources of the Self*, gets at one of the most central notions in Dostoevsky's religious thought. In cutting ourselves off from the world, we also cut ourselves off from the "grace" that flows like a current throughout the world; Dostoevsky's own term for what Taylor calls grace is "living life" (*zhivaya zhizn'*).[39]

So much for the negative face of Dostoevsky's poetics of love. I will now consider the positive face: that "unconditional love of the recipients of compassion" (flowing from "grace") which Taylor claims can alone overcome the ugly dialectic of philanthropy/misanthropy.[40]

There is a popular image of Dostoevsky as someone tormented by the question of the existence of God. But this image gets things backwards. Dostoevsky's effort to articulate a religious basis for the ethical begins not with the question of the reality of God, but with the question of the reality of agapic *love*. Does the unconditional love that can overcome the slide from compassion into contempt actually exist? And if it does, how can this be experienced in life and shown convincingly in art? *These* are the questions that preoccupied Dostoevsky. As an artist at the center of whose aesthetic is the image of Christ, his whole concern was to show the transcendent ideal as incarnate in reality and transformative of reality, without falsifying reality, which is radically resistant to the ideal. The outcome of this testing of the efficacy of agapic love against the cycle of power and violence inherent in unredeemed reality is never certain, never equally persuasive for all readers. It is perhaps drawn in its starkest terms in the famous confrontation between the silent Christ and the "Grand Inquisitor" in *The Brothers Karamazov*. The silence of Christ is broken elsewhere in the novel in two characters, who can be taken to embody agapic love in theory and in practice.

In regard to *theory*, there is the Russian monk Zosima's advice to the woman who finds herself unable to believe in God, advice striking precisely in the manner in which it *reverses* the connection between God and compassion presupposed in the formulations of Nietzsche and Ivan Karamazov: "Try to love your neighbors actively and tirelessly. The more you succeed in loving, the more you'll be convinced of the existence of God."[41] Zosima's words make sense only if it is possible to love the other one sees without the support of a consciously acknowledged divine command; that is, such love must have a real presence in the world *already,* not reducible,

278 BRUCE K. WARD

as it is for Nietzsche, to lower egoistic drives or psychic forces. This independent reality of compassionate love is guaranteed by its rootedness in the higher reality of divine love. Through Zosima, Dostoevsky expresses the notion of a compassion that is neither exclusively this-worldly (it has its roots in a higher reality), nor otherworldly (it is enacted in this world, directed toward living, suffering human beings). Transcendence *and* immanence are held together.

In regard to the *practice* of what Zosima calls "active love," there is Alyosha Karamazov's founding of the tiny community of children (twelve in all) in the last pages of the novel. This is a concrete showing of a community held together in agapic love; a community characterized by a unity that does not diminish but enhances the unique personhood of each child, a merging in which particular *names* (Ilyushechka, Kolya, Kartashov), *voices*, and *faces* are all retained. One might well regard it as the literary prototype, or I would say the *icon* in words, of an idea of human order invoked by Taylor in the last chapter of *A Secular Age*. As an alternative to our common categorial groupings, based on abstract criteria such as citizenship or, more universally, human rights, Taylor speaks of a "network of agape," a network of "relations which link particular, unique, enfleshed people to each other."[42] This is, in effect, the Gospel idea of the Church before it was deformed by its historical entry into the power field of the world. In Dostoevsky's art the ancient vision is rediscovered and creatively reapplied.

For Taylor, I suspect, there is a literal sense in which Dostoevsky discovered a subtler language for validating the transcendent dimension of human life. The agapic community founded by Alyosha is founded above all *by dialogic language*, expressing a harmony or unity that is literally a "joining of voices" (*soglasimsia*, translated as "Let us agree" in the opening phrase of Alyosha's speech to the boys).[43] In an earlier exploration of the idea of authenticity, Taylor argued that the original moral force of the idea could be recovered by emphasizing the relatedness-to-others that is actually inseparable from finding our own identity. Taylor's strategy was to revise Rousseauean authenticity to recognize that the authentic self is inherently "dialogic" rather than "monologic," a revision that should foster a strong sense of our moral obligation to treat others with respect and compassion. In this discussion he acknowledged his indebtedness to Mikhail Bakhtin's insight into the fundamentally dialogical nature of human identity, an insight that Bakhtin first developed in his classic study, *Problems of Dostoevsky's Poetics*.[44] In this early work Bakhtin credited Dostoevsky with opening up a new dimension of human life, the "dialogic sphere of existence," with his discovery of the polyphonic (multivoiced) novel, in which the author renounces the power to impose any meaning on characters that is not accessible to their own consciousness, to subject them to "artistic assimilation from monologic positions." By *monologism* he meant the tendency to locate truth in the unity of a single, self-sufficient consciousness, with its concomitant refusal really to accept the legitimacy of other consciousnesses. According to Bakhtin, Dostoevskian "dialogism" signifies the coexistence of spiritual diversity, of a plurality of perspectives that is yet, somehow, an ultimately harmonious whole.[45] There is an optimism here that Bakhtin did not justify by explicating the source of this wholeness in which the free interaction of diverse selves inheres, whether in Dostoevsky's artistic world or in human life itself. This same optimism is reflected in Taylor's notion that an identity that is both authentic and morally responsible is something "I negotiate through dialogue, partly overt, partly internalized, with others."[46]

Bakhtin's insight could well bring us to the culminating point of the convergence between Dostoevsky and Charles Taylor. The open-ended dialogicality of *A Secular Age,* with its generous, even indulgent acknowledgment of a polyphony of perspectives, accomplishes for philosophy what Dostoevsky accomplished for literature.

## The Problem of Moral Sources: Divergence on the Apocalyptic Question

It should be emphasized, however, that Taylor does have his own voice, just as some characters in Dostoevsky's novels—for instance, Zosima—speak more for the author than others. Taylor's own voice, like Dostoevsky's, might best be called theological, even in an apologetic vein, and more pronouncedly so toward the end of *A Secular Age.*[47] Having focused on the convergence between Taylor and Dostoevsky in regard to the problem of "moral sources," I am now going to point to a telling divergence, and just where theology appears most explicitly on the horizon. It is this: while Taylor endorses and appropriates Dostoevsky's poetics of love, he appears to ignore, if not reject outright, Dostoevsky's poetics of apocalypse. The two novels that Taylor cites most often, *Demons* and *The Brothers Karamazov*, are filled with foreboding about the apocalyptic situation of Western modernity, with many allusions, both direct and indirect, to biblical apocalyptic (especially the Book of Revelation). The complete disintegration of the modern order of mutual benefit into anarchic violence is one scenario found in Dostoevsky's art (for instance, in Raskolnikov's dream at the end of *Crime and Punishment*), but he was most preoccupied with the possibility evoked in "The Grand Inquisitor" of a global tyranny based on philanthropy, totalitarianism with a compassionate face — so smoothly disguised that we are hardly aware of living within it. "The Grand Inquisitor" is Dostoevsky's poetic elaboration of the apocalyptic symbol of the Antichrist.

Other contemporary thinkers have taken Dostoevsky's cue; for instance, Jean Baudrillard refers to the fate of the Grand Inquisitor's domesticated masses as our possible fate; René Girard warns of the "objectively apocalyptic" situation of our times, which he sometimes identifies with the "other totalitarianism" that outflanks Christianity on its left wing; and Ivan Illich claims that we live not in a post-Christian but in an apocalyptic age, evoking the *mysterium iniquitatis* of Thessalonians 2, which the early Church came to call the Antichrist.[48] Taylor, however, despite his close affinity with Dostoevsky, seems unwilling to venture into apocalyptic territory, especially where liberal humanism is at issue. His stance is illustrated in the following statement: "A race of humans has arisen which has managed to experience its world entirely as immanent. In some respects, we may judge this achievement as a victory for darkness, but it is a remarkable achievement nonetheless."[49]

In taking seriously the achievement and the appeal of modern humanism, Taylor does show himself an astute reader of Dostoevsky, for whom this is a special theme. Take, for instance, this passage from *The Adolescent*, in which the liberal humanist Versilov shares his vision of a future without any human connection to transcendence whatsoever:

> "I imagine to myself, my dear," he began with a pensive smile, "that the battle is over and the fighting has subsided. After the curses, the mudslinging and whistling, a calm has come, and people are left *alone,*

as they wished: the great former idea has left them; the great source of strength that had nourished and warmed them till then is departing, like that majestic, inviting sun in Claude Lorrain's painting. . . . And people suddenly realized that they remained quite alone, and at once felt a great orphancy. My dear boy, I've never been able to imagine people ungrateful and grown stupid. The orphaned people would at once begin pressing together more closely and lovingly; they would hold hands, understanding that they alone were now everything for each other. The great idea of immortality would disappear and would have to be replaced; and all the great abundance of the former love for the one who was himself immortality, would be turned in all of them to nature, to the world, to people, to every blade of grass. They would love the earth and life irrepressibly and in the measure to which they gradually became aware of their transient and finite state, and it would be with a special love now, not as formerly. . . . They would wake up and hasten to kiss each other, hurrying to love, conscious that the days were short, and that was all they had left. 'Tomorrow may be my last day,' each of them would think, looking at the setting sun, 'but all the same, though I die, they will all remain, and their children after them'—and this thought that they would remain, loving and trembling for each other . . . would replace the thought of a meeting beyond the grave."[50]

Versilov's vision is not, however, Dostoevsky's last word on the possibility of a future without transcendence. We can juxtapose to it this later passage from "The Grand Inquisitor," as the Inquisitor speaks to Christ:

"But the flock will gather again, and again submit, and this time once and for all. Then we shall give them quiet, humble happiness, the happiness of feeble creatures, such as they were created. . . . Peacefully they will die, peacefully they will expire in your name, and beyond the grave they will find only death. But we will keep the secret, and for their own happiness we will entice them with a heavenly and eternal reward. . . . It is said and prophesied that you will come and once more be victorious, you will come with your chosen ones . . . but we will say that they saved only themselves, while we have saved everyone. It is said that the harlot who sits upon the beast and holds *mystery* in her hand will be disgraced . . . that they will tear her purple and strip bare her 'loathsome body.' [Revelation 17:15–16] But then I will stand up and point out to you the thousands of millions of happy babes who do not know sin. And we, who took their sins upon ourselves for their happiness, we will stand before you and say 'Judge us if you can and dare.' Know that I am not afraid of you."[51]

Taylor is well aware of the first passage from *The Adolescent* (to which he refers in *Sources of the Self*) and presumably also of the second. It is noteworthy that while affirming with Dostoevsky the appeal of exclusive humanism, he does not also join him in warning more forcefully about the potential darkness of that appeal, even after his own analysis clearly points to its instability, to the ugly dialectic of secular compassion and power. By the end of the long journey though *A Secular Age*, one is left with the sense that Taylor is notably sanguine about the three-cornered contemporary ideological struggle he has evoked. The outcome seems to depend entirely on which side "can respond most convincingly to commonly felt dilemmas."[52] This emphasis on an intellectual, even academic, debate going on within a stable, secure milieu into the indefinite future manifests what I would call a Taylorian dialogical optimism that seems worlds away from Dostoevsky's apocalypticism.

It might be interesting to speculate on the reasons for this difference. I will offer a few suggestions, rather baldly stated. First, a historical one: the particular circumstances of nineteenth-century Russia made it a hothouse in which Western ideas developed their fruit with extraordinary rapidity; so Dostoevsky actually watched as liberal humanism gave birth to nihilism within a generation as a political reality. It would be easy to be apocalyptic when you have someone like Stalin looming on the horizon; whereas in the liberal democracies of the West (especially in a cautious country such as Canada) such a slide would be incremental and much more concealed. Second, a strategic reason: it might be that Taylor does not believe it possible to translate apocalyptic language into philosophical language, or desirable insofar as this might close down discussion with philosophical interlocutors who would be hostile to concepts appearing so intractably theological. The third and final reason brings me back to Taylor's dialogical optimism. Here I wonder if he is too dependent on Bakhtin's early reading of Dostoevsky, which tended to overlook the darker side of Dostoevskian dialogism.

I would like to pursue this third reason at greater length, beginning with Taylor's statement, quoted earlier, that an identity that is both authentic and morally responsible is something "I negotiate through dialogue . . . with others." The use of the term *negotiate*, which unavoidably connotes relations of power, is telling. It can be the starting point of a reflection that leads to serious concerns about the limits of human dialogicality.

Dostoevsky's *Notes from Underground* has often been interpreted as one of the great modern clarion calls to authenticity because of the protagonist's uncompromising affirmation of "the chiefest and dearest thing . . . our individuality."[53] This is the work, written after Dostoevsky's Siberian exile, that Bakhtin regarded as the breakthrough to the dialogism that was to mark the subsequent great novels. It also represents the inauguration of Dostoevsky's critical engagement with Western modernity as a paradigm of human order. This was above all an engagement with Rousseau, whose thought was at the core of the intellectual westernization of Russia in the nineteenth century.[54] It is the self-exploring and self-expressing Rousseau of the *Confessions* and the *Reveries* whom Dostoevsky has in his sights in the underground-man's confession about his own quest for authentic individuality. The underground-man compares his own intention to be perfectly candid with Rousseau, who most certainly lied about himself in his confessions, and "even did so intentionally, out of vanity."[55] The charge of "vanity," which betrays the sensitive awareness of the scrutiny of other consciousnesses, is meant to render suspect Rousseau's claim to a breakthrough to self-sufficiency.

The underground-man's doubts about Rousseau are those of a disenchanted follower (as indeed was the youthful Dostoevsky, whose early literary ventures are peopled with solitary dreamers). As a young man in his twenties, the underground-man was enthralled with the solitary inward journey away from social masks to the true self; but he discovers also that after a period of solitary communing with himself, he simply must interact with other people, feeling "an irresistible need to rush into society."[56] What happens when the self, fated to be dialogic rather than monologic, encounters the others with whom he must "negotiate" his identity? The answer is not hopeful. Consider, for instance, the first of the social adventures re-counted by the underground-man, his humiliation by the husky six-foot army officer in a tavern: "I was standing by the billiard table, blocking the way unwittingly. . . . [H]e took me by the shoulders and silently—with no warning or explanation—moved me from where I stood to another place, and then passed by as if without noticing. I could even have forgiven a beating, but I simply could not forgive his . . . just not noticing me." Filled with resentment toward the officer and with self-loathing for his own cow-ardice, the underground-man retreats to his solitary corner, where he imag-ines romantically inspired scenarios of an elaborate revenge that would at the same time be a reconciliation. For instance, he imagines challenging the officer to a duel in a letter so nobly sensitive in tone that the officer would rush to his place to offer him undying friendship. He never sends the letter and, as it turns out, exacts his revenge almost by accident: while walking down the crowded Nevsky Prospekt, he sees the officer approaching him. "Suddenly, within three steps of my enemy, I unexpectedly decided, closed my eyes, and—we bumped solidly shoulder against shoulder! I did not yield an inch and passed by on a perfectly equal footing! . . . Of course, I got the worst of it; he was stronger, but that was not the point. The point was that I had achieved my purpose, preserved my dignity, yielded not a step."[57]

That unyielding collision in a bid for respect is utterly emblematic of Dostoevsky's realism (in this case, comic) about the prospects of negoti-ating one's identity in dialogue with others. Dostoevsky's literary universe is replete with characters for whom coexistence is a constant process of vigilant self-assertion in response to the self-assertion of others. While the violence of self-assertion is reduced to its crude physical dimension in the emblematic episode with the officer, everywhere in Dostoevsky we witness characters wielding the more subtle weapon of language. Take, for instance, the last defiant words of the underground-man, flung out as a challenge to his imaginary readers: "I have merely carried to an extreme in my life what you have not dared to carry even halfway, and . . . you've taken your cowardice for good sense."[58] The dialogical nature of the self revealed by Dostoevsky is therefore not nearly enough by itself to justify the hope that the quest for authentic individuality goes hand in hand with recognition of our moral ties to others. It is, in fact, very difficult to read Dostoevsky and remain sanguine about the prospects of a *peaceful* dialogic sphere. Bakhtin himself came increasingly to see the darker side of "dialogism." The opti-mistic tone of his discussion of multivoicedness-as-harmony in the book on Dostoevsky gives way in later essays (written after his experience of exile in Siberia under Stalin) to the increasing recognition that we live in a human world in which language is an expression of will to power, the word a weapon of self-assertion: "When we seek to understand a word, what matters is not the direct meaning the word gives to objects and emotions—this is the false front of the word; what matters is rather the actual and al-ways self-interested *use* to which meaning is put and the way it is expressed by the speaker." The influence of Dostoevsky in Bakhtin's later sensitivity to the contagious reality of self-interested "word-violence" is revealed in this reference to the value of silence: "The unspoken truth in Dostoevsky (Christ's [silent] kiss)."[59]

The silent Christ of "The Grand Inquisitor" is the sign that, for Dos-toevsky (as for Bakhtin), dialogicality has its limits. In the face of a word-violence that utterly rejects truth, there can only be silence. Yet while this silence acknowledges the failure of dialogue, this is not tantamount to the failure of truth, which now takes the form of decision and judgment—that is, the silence is authoritative.[60]

The dialogue with exclusive humanism in Dostoevsky finally gives way to silent judgment because the "achievement" of exclusive humanism is chimerical, founded literally on nothingness (the "spirit of self-destruction and non-being," to quote the Grand Inquisitor). The radical instability of the humanist order, marked by the slide from compassion into the vi-olence of manipulative power, is not accidental; it is the inevitable out-come of the "cut" between transcendence and immanence that marks the Western path to secularity. This cut is indeed as central as Taylor maintains it is to understanding the development of exclusive humanism. Yet, for Dostoevsky, the question of how transcendence and immanence *ought* to be related—the subject of the Trinitarian controversies—is no less important. While Taylor focuses primarily on the eclipse of transcendence brought about by the cut, Dostoevsky focuses *also* on the obverse: the eclipse of immanence. For him, there is actually no immanent "living life" without transcendence, as there is no transcendence without its immanent expression. In this, his vision is in accord with the patristic Trinitarian the-ology that was concerned with *preserving* (not reconciling, as in Hegel) the paradox of both the total transcendence and the total immanence of the divine: that God is utterly beyond all finite determination, all becoming, *and* at the same time is present in all becoming, creating, sustaining, and transforming the living world. This Trinitarian vision suffuses Dostoevsky's art, but is given its most explicit expression in these words of the Russian monk Zosima:

> The roots of our thoughts and feelings are not here but in other worlds. That is why philosophers say it is impossible on earth to conceive the essence of things. God took seeds from other worlds and sowed them on this earth, and raised up his garden, and everything that could sprout sprouted, but it lives and grows only through its sense of being in touch with other mysterious worlds; if this sense is weakened or destroyed in you, that which has grown up in you dies. Then you become indifferent to life, and even come to hate it.[61]

Zosima's words make it clear why, for Dostoevsky, the humanist attempt to attain the fullness of life through the exclusion of transcendence can only be self-defeating, and why any "achievement," any modern moral order, thus realized will be illusory or parodic, no matter how glittering the parody.

The silence of Dostoevsky's Christ before the Inquisitor is authoritative because it is pregnant with apocalyptic judgment. Having dwelled at length on the third reason given above for Taylor's reticence on the apocalyptic question, I will by way of conclusion return to the second. It might well be that biblical apocalyptic is part of the tradition that Taylor considers best left to a lost past rather than creatively reappropriated; and this perhaps because apocalypse seems such a conversation-stopper, not only because of its intractable imagery, but also because it is so closely associated with a violence and a juridical-penal concept of God that has so badly discredited Christianity. Surely, however, Dostoevsky's art demonstrates that biblical apocalyptic need not simply be an admonition to cover our heads with ashes and wait for the divine wrath; it need not be the exclusive preserve of the fundamentalists. What Dostoevsky's poetics of apocalypse shows is that the apocalyptic vision is not about divine wrath; it is a divine unveiling (*apokalypsis*) of a *human* world of violence, will to power, and lies that preclude dialogue, though they do not finally prevail—on the contrary, it is this world that is "overcome" by agapic love. Charles Taylor has made an immense contribution to showing us why and how (with the help of literary geniuses such as Dostoevsky) we must "re-invent" Christian transcendence in a "subtler language." Is it not both possible and necessary to include Christian apocalyptic in this project of reinvention?

## Notes

1. Fyodor Dostoevsky, *Demons*, trans. Richard Pevear and Larissa Volokhonsky (New York: Random House, 1995), 690. See also Dostoevsky's letter of 15 February 1854 to Natalya D. Fonvizin.

2. For a fascinating account of Nietzsche's engrossed encounter with Dostoevsky's novels, and of the way in which Nietzsche's entry into Russian intellectual life was prepared by Dostoevsky's Nietzschean characters (for instance, Kirilov in *Demons*), see Mihajlo Mihajlov, *Nietzsche in Russia* (Princeton: Princeton University Press, 1986).

3. See, for instance, Charles Taylor, *A Secular Age* (Cambridge, MA: Belknap Press, 2007), 593, 731, 745–46, 755.

4. Charles Taylor, "Dostoevsky and Terrorism," *Lonergan Review* 4 (1993–94): 131–50.

5. For instance, Charles Taylor, *Sources of the Self: The Making of the Modern Identity* (Cambridge, MA: Harvard University Press, 1989), 518; and Taylor, *Secular Age*, 731. Both of these references to Dostoevsky will be highlighted in this essay.

6. I am indebted here to a very interesting paper sent to me by a former student of Taylor, Charles Guignon, "Inarticulacy: Searching for Meaning in the Modern World," presented at the annual meeting of the American Political Science Association in 2008.

7. Taylor, *Sources of the Self*, 518.

8. *Mutation* is Taylor's favored word; see, for instance, his foreword to David Cayley, *The Rivers North of the Future: The Testament of Ivan Illich as Told to David Cayley* (Toronto: Anansi Press, 2005).

9. See John Milbank, "A Closer Walk on the Wild Side: Some Comments on Charles Taylor's *A Secular Age*," *Studies in Christian Ethics* 22, no.1 (2009): 89–104.

10. Taylor, *Secular Age*, 18.

11. See ibid., 158.

12. Fyodor Dostoevsky, *The Brothers Karamazov*, trans. Richard Pevear and Larissa Volokhonsky (New York: Random House, 1990), 256.

13. "This is a remarkable fact. I don't pretend to have an explanation for it, but I offer it as a fact. . . ." Taylor, *Secular Age*, 242.

14. Dostoevsky, *Brothers Karamazov*, 257.

15. Charlemagne (742–814), with whom the Western church allied itself closely and whom Pope Leo III crowned as emperor in 800, was a strong advocate of the *filioque*, the adoption of which he promoted throughout his empire. It is also worth noting that he convened the Council of Frankfurt in 794, which condemned the Seventh Ecumenical Council (787) that had sanctioned the practice of devotion to icons in response to the iconoclast movement.

16. Philip Sherrard, *The Greek East and the Latin West* (London: Oxford University Press, 1959), chapters 3 and 4. Sherrard's study of the Great Schism remains one of the most philosophically and theologically astute, not least because he relates it to the development of modernity.

17. Taylor, *Secular Age*, 15–16; see also 143–45.

18. See G. W. F. Hegel, *The Phenomenology of Mind*, trans. J. B. Baillie (New York: Harper & Row, 1967), 589. Taylor's own familiarity with Hegel needs no comment.

19. Taylor, *Secular Age*, 693.

20. See Richard Rorty, "The Continuity between the Enlightenment and 'Postmodernism,'" in *What's Left of Enlightenment: A Postmodern Question*, ed. Keith Michael Baker and Peter Hanns Reill (Stanford, CA: Stanford University Press, 2001).

21. Ibid., 693.

22. Dostoevsky posed the question in a letter of 11 June 1879 to Nikolai A. Lyubimov.

23. Taylor, *Secular Age*, 636–39.

24. See, for instance, Friedrich Nietzsche, *Twilight of the Idols*, trans. R. J. Hollingdale (London: Penguin, 1990), 80–81.

25. Friedrich Nietzsche, *Beyond Good and Evil*, trans. Walter Kaufmann (New York: Random House, 1966), 66.

26. Note, for instance, Jeffrey Stout's critical observation against the argument for theism made by Basil Mitchell on the basis of Nietzsche's critique of secular liberalism: "Even if we agree with Mitchell that some theology or other would lend coherence to our discourse, this doesn't tell us which theology to adopt." See Jeffrey Stout, *Ethics After Babel: The Languages of Morals and Their Discontents* (Boston: Beacon Press, 1988), 221–22.

27. Taylor, *Secular Age*, 637.

28. Ibid., 593, 755–65.

29. One of those telling strategic references to Dostoevsky I noted near the beginning of this essay is found in the last chapter of *A Secular Age*, where Taylor speaks of "the shift in moral perspective which Dostoevsky helped make, and which I drew on in much of the discussion of the previous chapters" (731).

30. Dostoevsky, *Brothers Karamazov*, 592.

31. See George Pattison and Diane Oenning Thompson, eds., *Dostoevsky and the Christian Tradition* (Cambridge: Cambridge University Press, 2001), 113.

32. Taylor, *Secular Age*, 697.

33. Dostoevsky, *Brothers Karamazov*, 245. See also *The Notebooks for the Brothers Karamazov*, trans. and ed. Edward Wasiolek (Chicago: University of Chicago Press, 1971), 75.

34.  See my extended discussion of this paradox embodied in Ivan Karamazov, with reference also to Nietzsche's critique of humanism, in P. Travis Kroeker and Bruce K. Ward, *Remembering the End: Dostoevsky as Prophet to Modernity* (Boulder, CO: Westview Press, 2000), chapter 5.

35.  Dostoevsky, *A Writer's Diary*, trans. Kenneth Lantz (Evanston, IL: Northwestern University Press, 1994), 735.

36.  Taylor, *Secular Age*, 232–33, 305–6.

37.  Taylor, *Sources of the Self*, 517.

38.  Taylor, *Secular Age*, 684, 687–88.

39.  Taylor, *Sources of the Self*, 451.

40.  Taylor, *Secular Age*, 697.

41.  Dostoevsky, *Brothers Karamazov*, 56.

42.  Taylor, *Secular Age*, 739.

43.  "Let us agree here by Ilyusha's stone, that we will never forget—first, Ilyushechka, and second, one another. And whatever may happen to us later in life . . . let us always remember how we buried the poor boy, whom we once threw stones at . . . and whom afterwards we all came to love so much. He was a nice boy, a kind and brave boy, he felt honor and his father's bitter offense made him rise up. And so, first of all, let us remember him. . . . Let us never forget one another. . . . I give you my word . . . that for my part I will never forget any one of you; each face that is looking at me now, at this moment, I will remember, be it even after thirty years. Kolya said to Kartashov just now that we supposedly 'do not care to know of his existence.' But how can I forget that Kartashov exists and . . . is looking at me with his nice, kind, happy eyes? Gentlemen, my dear gentlemen, let us all be as generous and brave as Ilyushechka, as intelligent, brave, and generous as Kolya . . . and let us be as bashful, but smart and nice as Kartashov. But why am I talking about these two? You are all dear to me . . . from now on I shall keep you all in my heart, and I ask you to keep me in your hearts, too!" Dostoevsky, *Brothers Karamazov*, 774–75.

44.  See Taylor, *The Malaise of Modernity* (Toronto: Anansi Press, 1991), 127, note 25.

45.  See Mikhail Bakhtin, *Problems of Dostoevsky's Poetics*, trans. Caryl Emerson (Minneapolis: University of Minnesota Press, 1984), 6–7, 30–31, 270.

46.  Taylor, *Malaise of Modernity*, 47.

47.  In this regard I agree with John Milbank's characterization of Taylor's voice, though I think he goes too far in claiming Taylor for Radical Orthodox theology in particular. See Milbank, "A Closer Walk on the Wild Side."

48.  See Jean Baudrillard, *The Spirit of Terrorism*, trans. Chris Turner (New York: Verso Press, 2002), 103–4; René Girard, *I See Satan Fall Like Lightning*, trans. James G. Williams (Maryknoll, NY: Orbis Books, 2001), 180–81; Cayley, *Rivers North of the Future*, 9–10, 34, 60, 61, 80.

49.  Taylor, *Secular Age*, 376.

50.  Fyodor Dostoevsky, *The Adolescent*, trans. Richard Pevear and Larissa Volokhonsky (New York: Knopf, 2003), 470–71.

51.  Dostoevsky, *Brothers Karamazov*, 259–60.

52. Taylor, *Secular Age*, 675.

53. Fyodor Dostoevsky, *Notes from Underground*, trans. Richard Pevear and Larissa Volokhonsky (New York: Random House, 1994), 28–29.

54. See Dostoevky's reference to the "Geneva idea" as the idea "underlying today's civilization" in *Adolescent*, 103, 212.

55. Dostoevsky, *Notes from Underground*, 38–40.

56. Ibid., 58.

57. Ibid., 49–55.

58. Ibid.,129–30.

59. These statements by Bakhtin are quoted in Ruth Coates, *Christianity in Bakhtin: God and the Exiled Author* (Cambridge: Cambridge University Press, 1998), 117, 121.

60. For a splendid discussion of the authority of silence in the face of the catastrophic events of the twentieth century, see George Steiner, "The Silence of the Poet," in *Language and Silence* (New Haven, CT: Yale University Press, 1998).

61. Dostoevsky, *Brothers Karamazov*, 320.

# Contributors

Ruth Abbey is Professor, Department of Political Science, at the University of Notre Dame. She researches and teaches in the areas of contemporary political theory, history of political thought, and feminist political thought. She is the author of *Nietzsche's Middle Period* (Oxford University Press, 2000); *Philosophy Now: Charles Taylor* (Acumen Press and Princeton University Press, 2000); and *The Return of Feminist Liberalism* (McGill-Queens University Press, 2011). She is the editor of *Contemporary Philosophy in Focus: Charles Taylor* (Cambridge University Press, 2004) and *Re-Reading the Canon: Feminist Interpretations of Rawls* (Penn State University Press, 2013). She has also written a number of journal articles with topics ranging from contemporary liberalism to conceptions of marriage to animal ethics.

Ian Angus is Professor, Department of Humanities, at Simon Fraser University. He is the author of *A Border Within: National Identity, Cultural Plurality, and Wilderness* (McGill-Queens University Press, 1997); *(Dis)figurations: Discourse/Critique/Ethics* (Verso, 2000); *Primal Scenes of Communication: Communication, Consumerism, Social Movements* (SUNY, 2000); and *Emergent Publics: An Essay on Social Movements and Democracy* (Arbeiter Ring, 2001). He has also recently published long essays on the viability of Socratic inquiry in a contemporary context, the relation between Athens and Jerusalem in Western civilization, the concept of modernity, and the ethic of philosophy.

Carlos D. Colorado is Assistant Professor, Department of Religion and Culture, at the University of Winnipeg. His research attends critically to the place of religious and political thought in Western secular modernity (particularly in Canada). He is currently completing two book projects. The first is a monograph entitled *The Kenotic Self: Charles Taylor's Catholic Thought,* which is an exploration of Taylor's religious ethics. The second is a coedited volume entitled *Religious Outliers in the Public Sphere,* which consists of essays focusing on religious practitioners in the peripheries of both Western and East Asian society. His publications deal with technology and sexuality, challenges to Canadian liberal multiculturalism, religion in the public sphere, and Mennonites and utopianism, and include a review essay on Taylor's *A Secular Age.*

ERIC GREGORY is Professor, Department of Religion, at Princeton University. He is the author of *Politics and the Order of Love: An Augustinian Ethic of Democratic Citizenship* (University of Chicago Press, 2008), and various articles related to his interests in religious and philosophical ethics, theology, political theory, law and religion, and the role of religion in public life. In 2007 he was awarded Princeton's President's Award for Distinguished Teaching. A graduate of Harvard College, he earned an M. Phil. and Diploma in Theology from the University of Oxford as a Rhodes Scholar and his doctorate in religious studies from Yale University. He has received fellowships from the Erasmus Institute, the University of Notre Dame, the Safra Foundation Center for Ethics, Harvard University, the Tikvah Center for Law & Jewish Civilization, the New York University School of Law, and the National Endowment for the Humanities. Among his current projects is a book tentatively titled *What Do We Owe Strangers? Globalization and the Good Samaritan,* which examines secular and religious perspectives on global justice.

JENNIFER A. HERDT is Gilbert L. Stark Professor of Christian Ethics at Yale Divinity School. She is the author of *Religion and Faction in Hume's Moral Philosophy* (Cambridge University Press, 1997) and *Putting on Virtue: The Legacy of the Splendid Vices* (University of Chicago Press, 2008). Her primary interests are in early modern and modern moral thought, classical and contemporary virtue ethics, natural law theory, and contemporary theological ethics and political theology. In 2013 she delivered the Warfield Lectures at Princeton Theological Seminary on Christian eudaimonism and divine command morality. An ongoing project on ethical formation, *Bildung*, and the Bildungsroman is supported by a research fellow-ship from the Alexander von Humboldt Foundation. She has been the re-cipient of a Carey Senior Fellowship at the Erasmus Institute (2004–2005), a postdoctoral fellowship from the Center for Philosophy of Religion (1998–1999), a Mellon Graduate Prize Fellowship from the University Center for Human Values at Princeton University (1992), and a Mellon Fel-lowship in the Humanities (1989). She has served on the board of directors of the Society of Christian Ethics and is an associate editor for the *Journal of Religious Ethics*.

LEAH HUNT-HENDRIX received her Ph.D. in Religion, Ethics, and Politics from Princeton University. Her research is in political theory and intellectual history, where she focuses on the history of social movements and revolution. Her dissertation, *The Ethics of Solidarity*, is a genealogy of the concept of solidarity and an examination of philosophical and theo-logical conceptions of political community. She is also very active in com-munity organizing and is on the board of directors of three organizations, including the New Economics Institute, which seeks to challenge assump-tions about the nature of the economy and assert alternative economic practices and structures that are more just and democratic.

PAUL D. JANZ is Professor of Philosophical Theology and Head of the Department of Theology and Religious Studies at King's College London. He is the author of *God, the Mind's Desire: Reference, Reason and Chris-tian Thinking* (Cambridge University Press, 2004) and *The Command of Grace: A New Theological Apologetics* (T&T Clark, 2009). He is coauthor of *Transformation Theology: Church in the World* (T&T Clark, 2007). Janz works at an intersection of theology and philosophy, focusing primarily on specific epistemological and ethical challenges facing contemporary theology. His current research seeks to move theological orientation and self-understanding beyond grammatical and doctrinal self-sufficiency into an attentiveness to the real world of embodied human life as the ongoing site of God's revealed reality today. Key themes in this project are divine causality, the "critical" use of reason, sensible embodiment, and moral consciousness.

Justin D. Klassen is currently Sessional Instructor, Religious Studies Department, at Trinity Western University. He was previously Visiting Assistant Professor of Theology at Bellarmine University in Louisville, Kentucky, and Visiting Assistant Professor of Religious Studies at Austin College in Sherman, Texas. He is the author of *The Paradox of Hope: Theology and the Problem of Nihilism* (Cascade Books, 2011) and of several articles. His research focuses on theological ethics, existentialism (especially Kierkegaard), and continental philosophy of religion.

Charles Mathewes is Carolyn M. Barbour Professor of Religious Studies, Department of Religious Studies, at the University of Virginia. His research and teaching are broadly in the areas of Christian ethics, comparative religious ethics, and religion and society. He is the author of *Understanding Religious Ethics* (Wiley-Blackwell Publishers, 2010); *The Republic of Grace: Augustinian Thoughts for Dark Times* (Eerdmans Publishers, 2010); *Evil and the Augustinian Tradition* (Cambridge University Press, 2001); and *A Theology of Public Life during the World* (Cambridge University Press, 2007). He served as editor of the *Journal of the American Academy of Religion* from 2006 to 2010.

William Schweiker is Edward L. Ryerson Distinguished Service Professor of Theological Ethics and Director of the Martin Marty Center in the Divinity School, University of Chicago. His scholarship and teaching engage theological and ethical questions attentive to global dynamics, comparative religious ethics, the history of ethics, and hermeneutical philosophy. Schweiker's books include *Mimetic Reflections: A Study in Hermeneutics, Theology, and Ethics* (Fordham University Press, 1990); *Responsibility and Christian Ethics* (Cambridge University Press, 1995); *Power, Value, and Conviction: Theological Ethics in the Postmodern Age* (Pilgrim Press, 1998); *Theological Ethics and Global Dynamics: In the Time of Many Worlds* (Wiley-Blackwell, 2004); *Religion and the Human Future: An Essay in Theological Humanism* (Wiley-Blackwell, 2008, with David E. Klemm); and, most recently, *Dust that Breathes: Christian Faith and the New Humanisms* (Wiley-Blackwell, 2010). Schweiker has published numerous articles and award-winning essays, and has edited and contributed to six volumes, including, most recently, *Humanity before God: Contemporary*

*Faces of Jewish, Christian, and Islamic Ethics* (Fortress Press, 2006). Professor Schweiker is also chief editor of and contributor to *The Blackwell Companion to Religious Ethics* (Wiley-Blackwell, 2004), a comprehensive and innovative work in the field of comparative religious ethics. He is working on a book, forthcoming from Wiley-Blackwell, titled *Religious Ethics: Meaning and Method.* His current research is for a book on ethics and the integrity of life. Professor Schweiker is an ordained minister in the United Methodist Church.

BRUCE K. WARD is Professor and Chair of Religious Studies at Thorneloe University College (Laurentian University). His research focuses on religion and political thought, philosophy of religion, and religion in literature. He is the author of *Redeeming the Enlightenment: Christianity and the Liberal Virtues* (Eerdmans, 2010), as well as *Dostoevsky's Critique of the West: The Quest for the Earthly Paradise* (Wilfrid Laurier University Press, 1986) and coauthor with P. Travis Kroeker of *Remembering the End: Dostoevsky as Prophet to Modernity* (Westview Press, 2000). He has also published articles on Rousseau, Kafka, Camus, George Grant, and Thomas Merton. He is currently working on a translation of the religious writings of Charles Péguy.

JOSHUA YATES is Research Assistant Professor of Sociology at the University of Virginia and Managing Director of the Institute for Advanced Studies in Culture. Professor Yates is a cultural and historical sociologist who studies the evolving normative frameworks and institutional arrangements of human thriving in the late modern world. He has written on the cultural significance of sustainability as an emerging social ethic, on the changing moral practices and understandings of economic life in American history through the prism of thrift, and on the imperatives of international humanitarian and human rights organizations as carriers of a distinctive global moral and ethical order. He is currently working on two projects. The first is a book on the moral dimensions of globalization, entitled *The Problem of the Good World: Reflections on Globalization and Moral Life.* The second is "The Thriving Cities Project," a multiyear initiative to create a new form of community assessment based on a holistic understanding of "thriving" in twenty-first-century American cities.

# Index